AMERICAN CATHOLIC

A volume in the series

RELIGION AND AMERICAN PUBLIC LIFE

Edited by R. Laurence Moore and Darryl Hart

For a list of books in the series, visit our website at cornellpress.cornell.edu

AMERICAN CATHOLIC

The Politics of Faith during the Cold War

D. G. HART

CORNELL UNIVERSITY PRESS
ITHACA AND LONDON

First published 2020 by Cornell University Press

Printed in the United States of America

Library of Congress Cataloging-in-Publication Data
Names: Hart, D. G. (Darryl G.), author.
Title: American Catholic : the politics of faith during the Cold War / D.G. Hart.
Description: Ithaca [New York] : Cornell University Press, 2020. | Series: Religion and American public life | Includes bibliographical references and index.
Identifiers: LCCN 2020016730 (print) | LCCN 2020016731 (ebook) | ISBN 9781501700576 (cloth) | ISBN 9781501751974 (epub) | ISBN 9781501751981 (pdf)
Subjects: LCSH: Catholic Church—United States—History—20th century. | Christianity and politics—United States—History—20th century. | Christianity and politics—Catholic Church—History—20th century. | Church and state—United States—History—20th century. | Conservatism—United States—History—20th century.
Classification: LCC BX1406.3 .H37 2020 (print) | LCC BX1406.3 (ebook) | DDC 261.7088/28273—dc23
LC record available at https://lccn.loc.gov/2020016730
LC ebook record available at https://lccn.loc.gov/2020016731

To Crawford Gribben

CONTENTS

Preface   ix

Introduction: How Americanism Won   1

1. Belonging to an Ancient Church in a Modern Republic   18

2. Public Duty, Private Faith   41

3. Americanism for the Global Church   65

4. Liberal Catholics, American Conservatives   88

5. The Extremities of Defending Liberty   112

6. The Limits of Americanism   136

7. Americanism Revived   160

8. Americanism Redux   184

Conclusion: Freedom and Roman Catholicism
in Postconciliar America   209

Notes 229

Bibliographic Essay 243

Index 253

PREFACE

As a general rule, confessional lines divide the study of Christianity and politics in the United States. One might think that the literature on Protestants and politics in America would be larger than that on Roman Catholics since the former had a bigger role in shaping the nation, since Protestant institutions (even in secularized forms) have dominated the study of religion, and since contemporary Protestants themselves have dominated public perceptions of major episodes in recent political history (civil rights and the religious Right). As it turns out, a quick search at OCLC's WorldCat shows that librarians have catalogued more than twice as many books on Roman Catholics and U.S. politics (385) than on Protestants (152). As inexact as that search may be (simply adding "Protestant" or "Catholic" to the subject heading of "Christianity and Politics United States"), the point remains that scholars from Protestant backgrounds generally explore Protestant-related subjects, while a similar trend characterizes the history of Roman Catholicism in the United States. Since this author has contributed to the Protestant side of the academic enterprise, a short explanation for venturing into foreign scholarly territory is in order.

This book emerges from working in conservative (political and intellectual) circles for the past fifteen years. Before this, I found employment at Protestant institutions during a time when evangelicals and the Republican Party dominated much coverage of religion in national politics and sustained a remarkable flowering of scholarship on born-again Protestants. As early as 1992, Jon Butler observed (but in a plaintive way) that for the "past two decades evangelicalism (and not merely 'religion') has emerged as the *single* most powerful explanatory device adopted by academic historians to account for the distinctive features of American society, culture, and identity."[1] My prior investigations into religion and politics featured mainline, evangelical, and fundamentalist Protestants and fit generally into the dominant narrative of Christianity and American politics,[2] which went something like this: white Protestants of a certain stripe (chiefly Calvinist—Congregationalist and Presbyterian) supported a national founding that repudiated an ecclesiastical establishment (Church of England) and yielded a society whose government freed churches to regulate themselves. Fears about deism, the French Revolution, and unbelief in general fueled revivals in the early nineteenth century that produced Protestant organizations to civilize the frontier and revitalize settled territories, and whose cooperation consolidated Anglo-American Protestants as the "mainline" churches. These churches achieved greater unity and gained additional clout after the Civil War, when progressive politics and the Social Gospel movement combined to provide Protestants with political and activist outlets for Christianizing national life. The fundamentalist controversy challenged the mainline, and in the 1940s fundamentalists' kinder, gentler siblings, evangelical Protestants, took more resources away from the largest denominations and related institutions. But until 1965 or so, white Protestants (whether conservative or liberal) enjoyed unparalleled access to the levers of political and cultural power. When during the 1960s and 1970s the challenges of race, gender, and war undermined assumptions of a homogeneous nation and made secularization plausible, evangelicals, also known as the religious Right, picked up the challenge of maintaining the older Protestant sense of responsibility for the nation and its government. Trying to explain that history and the motivations for those Protestants was part of what drew me to the topic of Christianity and politics in the United States.

When I left the world of evangelical academics and worked for institutions that are part of movement conservatism, first at the Intercollegiate Studies Institute (ISI) and now at Hillsdale College, I began to follow more closely Roman Catholic involvement in national debates than I had previously. Not only did I become aware of the rise of conservatism during the 1950s through William F. Buckley, Jr. (ISI's first president), Russell Kirk, and Whittaker Chambers and the institutions it had created, but the importance of Roman Catholicism to conservatism also became immediately apparent. Buckley himself was devout, Kirk converted, and Chambers went from communism to Quakerism. Meanwhile, many of the authors and colleagues with whom I worked had either grown up Roman Catholic or had converted from Protestant backgrounds. Since I knew something about Protestantism's inveterate anti-Catholicism and was becoming more aware of Roman Catholicism's anti-Americanism at least up until the Second Vatican Council, the idea of Roman Catholics in the United States picking up the slack of mainline Protestants' Christian nationalism became intriguing to say the least.

To be sure, post–World War II Roman Catholic political conservatives (referred to in this book as "neo-Americanists") did not follow the same script as Protestants had—opposition to alcohol, promotion of prayer and Bible reading in public schools. But by the 1950s, when many Americans believed the nation needed a Christian identity to stand up to Soviet communism, neo-Americanists were ready to defend the United States as the best embodiment of the West's religious and political achievements. Roman Catholics may have understood the Christian character of the United States differently, but they became formidable proponents of American exceptionalism that political conservatives approved and circulated.

The presence of Roman Catholicism in American political and intellectual conservatism is a subject often overlooked to many who write about church and state or religion and politics in the United States. Recent coverage of evangelical Protestants' votes for President Donald Trump is just one example. Yes, Roman Catholics are the largest communion in the United States, possess extensive institutional resources, have many fellow church members serving in state and federal offices, and make up a majority of justices on the Supreme Court of the United States. But those demographic and political realities have not merited the attention of historians and social scientists the way that Protestants have.

The story of how Roman Catholics became such prominent players in conservative circles is one aim of this book, with an implicit purpose being to understand the affinity and tension between national and Roman Catholic traditions and ideals. The long history of anti-Catholicism from Protestants in the United States should make any historian wary of suggesting that Roman Catholics fit awkwardly in American society. At the same time, any historian who considers the longer history of Christendom, the confessionalization of European states, the French Revolution, and the Vatican's responses to those developments becomes readily aware of the unlikelihood of Roman Catholic authors and public intellectuals becoming the spokesmen for a form of American patriotism that celebrates the very political ideals that Rome opposed until the 1960s. Even more striking is the way Roman Catholics filled the gap of defending the United States' founding, history, and influence at precisely the same time that mainline Protestants turned from celebrating to debunking the United States. No matter what a reader's political outlook or religious convictions, the unlikeliness of this story makes it remarkable and perhaps as exceptional as neo-Americanists believed the United States to be.

Former ISI colleagues, especially Mark Henrie, Jeremy Beer, and Jeffrey Cain, deserve credit for introducing me to the literature, authors, and networks of Roman Catholicism and intellectual conservatism. The same goes for colleagues at Hillsdale College, including Matthew Gaetano, Brad Birzer, Nathan Schlueter, Lee Cole, and Dwight Lindley. Participants in the University of Notre Dame 2014 Rome summer seminar, "American Catholicism in a World Made Small: Transnational Approaches to U.S. Catholic History," led by Kathleen Sprows Cummings, John T. McGreevy, and Matteo Sanfilippo, were of great help in clarifying many points of Roman Catholic history and the dynamics between the United States and the Vatican. A grant from Hillsdale College's Summer Program for Professional Development made those three weeks in Rome possible. Another generous grant for faculty development from the college helped offset this book's production costs. Both grants put me in further debt to Hillsdale's administrators, who have graciously supported my work for the last nine years and made teaching at the college the most pleasant chapter of my peripatetic career. This Cornell University Press series's coeditors, R. Laurence Moore and Michael McGandy, along with anonymous readers, all supplied comments and corrections that have improved this book substantially. All remaining weaknesses are mine.

The book is dedicated to a friend who teaches history in Northern Ireland and knows firsthand the challenges that come when both Protestants and Roman Catholics venture into politics. His intellectual and fraternal exchanges during the past eight years have been an unexpected blessing.

D. G. Hart
Hillsdale, Michigan
February 21, 2020

AMERICAN CATHOLIC

INTRODUCTION

How Americanism Won

When John F. Kennedy won the November 8, 1960, election for president of the United States—a close election not called by NBC News until seven the next morning—Roman Catholicism entered the mainstream of national life. Although the comments that the *New York Times* editors aggregated from newspapers around the country for their November 11 coverage said much more about the Cold War and deficit spending than religion, some journalists knew Kennedy's victory was a milestone. An editorial for the *Boston Sun* concluded that the election brought "an end to the religious test for the Presidency." The *New York Mirror* echoed the Boston opinion by declaring that the election had "confounded" the nation's "bigots" and "purveyors of hate." Adam Clayton Powell, Jr., an African American pastor in Harlem and U.S. congressman, interpreted the election as a major victory for Roman Catholics and a stepping stone for other minorities. Americans, he said, had shown "spiritual maturity" in voting for Kennedy and should now address "the issue of Jews and Negroes." Meanwhile, observers within the Vatican saw Kennedy's election as grounds for appreciating "the high democratic principles of freedom that guide American public life" and assure access to the highest office "regardless of social class, race, or religion."[1]

Historians of the United States have been equally clear, especially with the advantage of hindsight, about the meaning of Kennedy's presidency. Mark S. Massa, a historian at Boston College, observed that the election signaled the end to what Arthur Schlesinger, Jr., had termed "America's oldest prejudice." In his spirited and comprehensive survey of U.S. Roman Catholicism, Charles R. Morris conceded that despite a "razor-thin victory," Kennedy had proved that a "Catholic [could climb] the greasy pole" and lay to rest forever the question "of whether Catholics could be full participants in American society." Martin E. Marty, later the dean of American religious historians, interpreted Kennedy as the symbolic end to "Protestant America." Jay P. Dolan, an important historian for grafting Roman Catholicism onto the trunk of the nation's religious history, argued that Kennedy was an inspiration to Roman Catholics who could "stand a little taller" and, in the words of one Roman Catholic, were now "comfortably integrated in to American society." Meanwhile, Daniel Boorstin, the historian who oversaw the Library of Congress after teaching at the University of Chicago, in 1969 introduced John Tracy Ellis's volume on Roman Catholicism for the Chicago History of American Civilization series with this pronouncement: "The election of John Fitzgerald Kennedy to the Presidency in 1960 signaled a new era in American history." Prior to that decisive moment, Roman Catholics had been a "minority." But Kennedy's victory marked "the full assimilation of these millions of Americans into the mainstream of our political life." In sum, the 1960s were the time when Roman Catholicism became American.[2]

The problem with these interpretations is that Kennedy's candidacy depended on reassuring American voters that he would not be Roman Catholic in office. As Boston College's Massa observed, those closest to the president did not consider him to be very devout. Jackie Kennedy, for instance, told a journalist that the controversy over her husband's faith was a mystery because "Jack is such a poor Catholic." Kennedy himself knew that reporters had picked up on his apparent religious indifference, and such coverage frustrated him. At the same time, close aides said that Kennedy "cared not a whit for theology," and when he quoted the Bible out of convention, the English translation he used was not the

Douay version (the one for English-speaking Roman Catholics) but the standard Protestant text. The president's speechwriter, Ted Sorensen, also later recalled that for as long as he knew Kennedy (eleven years), "I never heard him pray aloud . . . or despite all our discussions of church/state affairs, ever disclose his personal views on man's relation to God."[3] In other words, the man responsible for overcoming barriers of religious prejudice had done so by abandoning the standards of his faith. Kennedy's Roman Catholicism was the kind that Americans and the press found acceptable.

For this reason, the better indicator of Roman Catholicism's entrance into the cultural mainstream was *Time* magazine's decision to feature John Courtney Murray on its cover for the December 12, 1960, issue, under the headline, "U.S. Catholics and the State." Only a month after the election, the anonymous reporter for *Time* understood that Kennedy's performance was more of a capitulation to the United States than a vindication of Roman Catholicism: "Some critics in his own faith have occasionally held him to be more American than Catholic." Not so in the case of Murray, who rather than trimming the faith to fit national norms, was asking whether America itself was "safe for Catholicism." In fact, Murray's basis for supporting the separation of church and state was not to regard the American founding as a "new order for the ages." Instead, the distinction between the temporal (political) and spiritual (ecclesiastical) realms was at least as old as the ancient church, when popes such as Gelasius I instructed Roman emperors such as Anastasius I in 494 about a separation of powers. That older understanding of church and state left the church a "limit [on] the power of government" and brought the "moral consensus of the people to bear upon the King." The American founding was not pro-church, but its opposition to absolutist monarchy put the new nation on the side of a church that had perpetually struggled with secular rulers for its own rights and authority. According to *Time*, Murray's praise for the American revolution was unmixed: "For the first time in centuries, the Catholic Church was free to work and witness as it saw fit, without special privileges but also without requiring a whole chain of consent from secular government." That freedom had allowed the church to flourish, both numerically and intellectually. The result was that Roman Catholics participated in what Murray called "building the city," that is, "contributing both to the civic machinery and the need for consensus beneath it."[4] Only a decade or so into the Cold War, such approval of the United States created lots of space for Roman Catholics to support the nation in its defense of liberty and fight against tyranny.

Time's story on Murray did not neglect the opposition he had endured at the very same time that John F. Kennedy was campaigning for the presidency. In *We Hold These Truths* (1960), Murray had drawn denunciations from church officials for arguing that "the Vatican should give its formal blessing to the U.S. pluralist system as a new, permanent and viable kind of relationship between religion and government." The response from Jesuit and Vatican authorities was to have Murray "clear all his writings on this particular subject with Jesuit headquarters in Rome" before publication. In fact, the article ended on an ambivalent note, not in the reporter's regard for Murray but about how church officials would dispose of the Jesuit theologian's ideas. "If anyone can help U.S. Catholics and their nonCatholic countrymen toward the disagreement that precedes understanding—John Courtney Murray can."⁵Unlike Kennedy, whose electoral victory was an example of religious indifference, Murray represented a potential breakthrough for Roman Catholicism by harmonizing church teaching with national ideals. His success would depend on winning the bishops' approval, many of whom still deferred to church teaching on politics about the dangers of freedom to faith. One example of that outlook was Pope Leo XIII's 1899 condemnation of Americanism—or adjusting the church to freedom, democracy, and popular sovereignty—as a heresy. As late as the 1950s, Roman Catholics were still laboring under papal opposition to modernity.

After almost sixty years, the Vatican's fears about Murray's views seem antiquated, since religious freedom is a cheer led by popes and bishops as much as presidents and legislators, and practically no one wonders if Roman Catholicism is compatible with the United States. In 1960, however, the church's relationship to liberal politics was still formally hostile. For instance, John T. Noonan, Jr., a celebrated federal judge and law professor at University of California, Berkeley, who authored important books about the church's evolving moral theology, recalled in his memoir, *The Lustre of Our Country* (1998), what it was like growing up in Boston before Vatican II. The archbishop of Noonan's youth was William Cardinal O'Connell, a figure who dominated local politics, especially on matters such as abortion and the lottery. Such episcopal authority aligned with the dominant theory of church-state relations, which even for Monsignor John A. Ryan, arguably the leading Roman Catholic advocate of the New Deal, was far removed from liberalism when it came to religious freedom.[6] In a 1941 paper that Noonan read during his undergraduate education, Ryan argued that the duty of the state was the "protection and promotion of the [one true religion], and the legal prohibition of all direct assaults upon it."[7] In Noonan's words, all the theologians that he knew were on the side of state support for Roman Catholicism and suppression of heresy. The lone exception was John Courtney Murray, who in 1948 had delivered a paper in Chicago that argued the state should not prohibit false religion even when it was possible. That was a position that could and did put the author at risk from his Jesuit superior and Vatican officials. Freedom of conscience involved liberty for false beliefs and so contradicted the church's opposition to modern political arrangements that gave legitimacy to error. Deep down in the church's reflection was even the Augustinian argument that recommended the coercion of heretics under unusual circumstances.

The rest of Noonan's book showed how he and the church evolved. From his time at Harvard when he thought Murray's views were diametrically at odds with the church's teaching, to 1962 with the convening of the Second Vatican Council, Noonan traced the intellectual path that made possible the church's embrace of James Madison's views on religious freedom. Whether the American political tradition was as decisive on the international body of bishops in Rome as he alleged, Noonan did capture the drama of Murray's defense of the nation's founding and its fundamental incompatibility with church dogma. Prior to Vatican II, Americanism was still a heresy, and most church officials still regarded defenses of modern political liberalism as antithetical to papal teaching and the proper ordering of society.

Such opposition to liberalism, both formal and imagined, was one source for anti-Catholicism among mid-century mainline Protestants and secular liberals. Paul Blanshard's best seller, *American Freedom and Catholic Power* (which more people may have purchased than read, as John T. McGreevy wryly observed), was not "a cautious" book, but it tapped the prevailing sense that Roman Catholics were outsiders looking in at liberal society. Blanshard dabbled in unalloyed bigotry, such as blaming Roman Catholicism for producing "the bulk of white criminals," or describing parochial schools as "the most important divisive" institution for American children.[8] He also wondered, as Protestants going back to Ben Franklin had, about church power in relation to citizens within a constitutional republic.

More evenhanded than Blanshard were the objections that ran in the liberal Protestant weekly *Christian Century* five years earlier. In an eight-part series under the heading "Can Catholicism Win America?," Harold E. Fey, former director of a pacifist organization, Fellowship of Reconciliation, and field editor for the magazine, expressed typical worries about Roman Catholics. The introductory piece elaborated a theme that recurred in Fey's articles, namely, Roman Catholic authoritarianism. This was obviously a fraught term to use at a time when the United States was fighting a two-front war against totalitarianism. Fey was still adamant even as he tried to be gracious: Rome's "authoritarian conceptions" were at odds with the Protestant faith, "which once molded the pattern of American national life."[9] He produced evidence he believed revealed Rome's ambitions to dominate national life, whether in small towns, among workers and soldiers, or especially in politics. Fey's survey of Roman Catholic institutions suggested the outline of a program that, if successful, would "include other faiths in American culture only on Catholic terms." Indeed, Roman Catholicism represented a profound challenge to basic liberties, even a "radical modification" of "all other freedoms in American democracy."[10]

Thanks to Murray's influence, the determinations of Vatican II, and the evolution of the church, most contemporary observers of the church, including Roman Catholics themselves, have almost no awareness or recollection of the hierarchy's previous, long, and pronounced antipathy to political liberalism or of Leo XIII's condemnation of Americanism. In fact, since 2012 the U.S. bishops have conducted an annual "Fortnight for Freedom" to encourage church members to support and pray for religious liberty. Even Pope Francis, during his 2015 visit to the United States, spoke warmly of the American founding and the value of liberty and equality to Roman Catholics and all people around the world. Such support for modern political norms has also prompted a reaction among some Roman Catholic intellectuals who have serious reservations about both the blessings of modern liberty and its compatibility with church tradition. Many of these critiques have blamed Murray for introducing an alien outlook into Roman Catholic political theology.

Even so, for the bulk of Roman Catholics in the United States, Americanism is the default setting for thinking about church-state relations. As University of Notre Dame historian R. Scott Appleby wrote in 1995,

American Roman Catholicism was experiencing an "unprecedented situation" in which politically liberal and conservative church members and clergy "share a basic orientation and set of assumptions about the United States and its worthiness as a model" for the church. Mark S. Massa concurred. During the post–World War II era, "American Catholicism became the culture's loudest and most uncritical cheerleader." For Garry Wills (featured in the pages that follow), "with amazing rapidity" the remnants of "the 'integral' church-state monarchy, which had been constructed over centuries," vanished after Vatican II. Likewise, "Americanism had gone from silenced heresy to orthodox belief."[11]

This book explores this transformation in American Roman Catholicism. Other historians, notably Patrick Allitt (*Catholic Intellectuals and Conservative Politics in America, 1950–1985*) and George H. Nash (*The Conservative Intellectual Movement in America since 1945*) view changes among American Roman Catholic intellectuals through the lens of faith and conservative ideas—that is, how Roman Catholicism buttressed a set of arguments on the Right about American society and world affairs. This book takes a different approach by exploring how politically conservative Roman Catholics, primarily in the world of opinion journalism and magazines, made Americanism safe for the church. It tells the story of Roman Catholic political conservatives, first associated with William F. Buckley, Jr., at the *National Review* and later the colleagues with Richard John Neuhaus at *First Things*, who retrieved and revised national political ideals in ways that made Americanism acceptable for Roman Catholicism and political conservatism (especially the Republican Party) plausible to Roman Catholics. Their arguments accomplished for a vibrant sector of the Roman Catholic Church what Protestants had previously done by casting the United States in a role as redeemer nation, or as a "city on a hill," a divine gift to liberate the world from tyranny.

The American Experience as Americanism

One reason for ignorance of Rome's opposition to Americanism prior to 1960 is that most American Roman Catholics experienced practically no tension between church and nation. Phyllis Schlafly, for instance, a force in Republican politics during the 1960s and a prominent spokesperson for various conservative causes, experienced no ecclesiastical restrictions on her efforts to return the nation to its political ideals and embrace its duties as the leader of the free world. Although a devoted Roman Catholic, Schlafly was so thoroughly at home that Protestants in the Republican Party never doubted her political bona fides. A housewife in suburban Saint Louis, who juggled child-rearing and political activism, Schlafly emerged in the 1950s as a force in local politics. She ran unsuccessfully for Congress in 1952, but she soon joined the ranks of conservatives who objected to the GOP's East Coast establishment's timid moderation in domestic and foreign affairs. These conservatives' discontent found an outlet in Barry Goldwater, a Republican senator from Arizona and presidential nominee. While John Courtney Murray was at Vatican II, Schlafly's book, *A Choice Not an Echo* (1964) became a best seller in the run-up to the 1964 election, thanks in part to her objection to the Republican Party's feckless compromise with New Deal programs and diplomacy with the Soviets. She went on to achieve national fame for spearheading opposition to feminism and the Equal Rights Amendment through her activist organization, Eagle Forum.[12]

William F. Buckley, Jr., was another devout lay Roman Catholic who led the conservative movement by calling the country to its founding principles and instructing Americans about their significance in world affairs. While Schlafly was running for Congress, Buckley was finishing a book-length lecture to Yale University's white, Anglo-Saxon Protestant leadership. His subject was the faculty's failure to support the United States' blend of faith and patriotism. A precocious offering from a man whom the university had recently graduated, the manuscript appeared in 1951 as *God and Man at Yale* and exposed the Protestant establishment's equivocation about the nation's history and purpose. On the one hand, Yale shattered "the average student's respect for Christianity." On the other, Yale's Economics Department was "thoroughly collectivist" and delinquent in teaching the dangers of communism. The net effect, Buckley lamented, was to unsettle the very convictions that had taken him to Yale as a freshman—"a firm belief in Christianity and a profound respect for American institutions and traditions." As a result, Yale was no longer performing what as recently as 1937 Yale's former president, Charles Seymour, said was its service to the nation: to recognize "the tremendous validity and power of the teachings of Christ in our life-and-death struggle against the forces of selfish materialism." By 1951 Buckley was as worried as Seymour had been that by losing its bearings in the larger struggle between Americanism and communism, Yale would let "scholarship and religion" disappear.[13]

Buckley's was a stunning intellectual performance for two reasons beyond his youth and chutzpah. The author of God and Man at Yale was a self-professed and (at least liturgically) conservative Roman Catholic who was writing at a time when Yale still owned prime real estate in the institutional district known as America's Protestant establishment. The difference between Roman Catholicism and white Protestantism in the United States still mattered significantly in 1951, the year of Buckley's book's publication, as Blanshard's American Freedom and Catholic Power indicated. For Buckley, an outsider to WASP circles no matter how privileged his background, to challenge Yale's Protestants for abdicating their historic mission of civilizing and Christianizing both the nation and the world was truly audacious.

What was happening at mid-century was the curious phenomenon of Roman Catholics, such as Schlafly and Buckley, starting to take over positions of political advocacy that Protestants had minted and monopolized since the middle decades of the nineteenth century. Even more curious, they were doing this while Murray was under suspicion for erroneous views about the American political system. Politically conservative Roman Catholics pumped fresh air into the sort of nationalism that rendered the United States, in messianic terms, as a redeemer nation. For instance, in one of the brochures Schlafly produced to recruit fellow Roman Catholics to the grassroots anticommunist movement, she wrote, "As Catholic Americans, we are proud of our heritage and believe that our Republic offers the greatest opportunity for individual freedom and the pursuit of happiness." She added that her aim was to "insure for ourselves and future generations the God-given rights proclaimed by the Declaration of Independence and guaranteed by the United States Constitution." As Schlafly's biographer, Donald Critchlow, observes, she was "not defensive about [her] Catholicism" because faith and Americanism went hand in hand.[14] For Roman Catholics such as Schlafly, the church was not a higher loyalty, above the nation, but the greatest aid to the United States and its political institutions. When it came to supporting Goldwater, her arguments were pragmatic and showed little awareness of political theories about the merits of republicanism, federalism, or the theological debates that surrounded the late eighteenth-century rebellions against divine-right monarchy in North America and France. Indeed, Christians (Protestant or Roman Catholic) who celebrated the United States' founding showed little awareness that the American and French Revolutions had dramatically upended the very political order that popes invariably defended as the most stable and orderly, and the most Christian.[15] For Roman Catholics living in the United States, the Old World contests between emperors and popes were safely behind them. In contrast, in the context of the Cold War, America's political traditions demanded the loyalty and defense of all citizens, Roman Catholic or not.

Aside from the irony of lay Roman Catholics ignoring virtually the side their bishops had taken in political debates for the better part of four centuries, these same Christians oddly adopted a conception of the United States that had looked to the rise of Protestantism as the inspiration for the American founding. Ever since the 1820s, Protestants of British descent—the so-called mainline churches (Episcopal, Presbyterian, Congregational, Methodist, Baptist)—had forged a national identity that was synonymous with being Protestant. As Sam Haselby argues in *The Origins of Religious Nationalism*, the voluntary societies (Bible, tract, Sunday school, missions) that Anglo-American Protestants built and sustained to support the Second Great Awakening were not only among the first national organizations in the United States but also constructed a national identity, precisely when the nation was expanding and establishing its borders, that rejected deism and infidelity for generic (or ecumenical) Protestantism. As two missionaries from New England, Samuel J. Mills and Daniel Smith, reported on their survey of the western frontier, the entire country "from Lake Erie to the Gulf of Mexico" remained in a "deplorable state." Only a "Christian America" could remedy the new nation's defects. That understanding of America drew heavily on the Connecticut Wits, a group of writers and poets that included Timothy Dwight, president of Yale College. For these New Englanders, the redemption of the world was bound up with American independence and national purpose. It would become an "empire" to which "splendors shall flow" and "earth's little kingdoms . . . shall bow." Not only did mainline Protestants draw inspiration from poets such as Yale's President Dwight, but the college itself became "an imperial force of American tertiary education and

missions."[16] Its graduates went out to teach, evangelize, preach, and organize across the nation and so ensure the advance of Christian civilization
across the continent (and around the world).

The Christian nationalism that nineteenth-century Protestants planted
and watered was sufficiently vigorous to accommodate Christian ideals
and national purpose during civil war, world wars, social reform, and
modernization. Through it all, the Protestant mainline remained a chief
source of collective identity for Americans down to the post–World War II
era. In fact, white Christian America, as the historian and demographer
Robert P. Jones calls it, did not decline seriously until the 1960s, when the
most influential churches looked increasingly hollow to people advocating civil rights for blacks and women, and opposing the nation's foreign
policy.[17] Buckley had tried to remind Yale's WASP leadership in 1951 that
the university had a duty to uphold the nation's religious and political heritage. So too, Schlafly (as well as Buckley) rebuked the Republican Party's
East Coast establishment for abandoning national prerogatives that came
with being the leader of the free world and the Christian West. Mainline
Protestants may have lost their vigor, but Roman Catholics were rallying
to fill the void.

More Than Assimilation

On one level, a chronicle of Roman Catholics in the United States after
World War II, no matter what the political outlook, is part of a larger
story about assimilation. As challenging as adapting to America has been
for any number of religious groups, Roman Catholics possessed their own
set of burdens. With the small exception of English church members who
enjoyed political power in colonial Maryland, the American church after
the 1840s became an institution marked by ethnic immigrants. Bishops
and priests throughout most of American history provided ways to absorb these newcomers by providing services not yet available through governmental agencies. The result was a polyglot communion with diversity
as its hallmark, despite the uniformity that the hierarchy was supposed to
provide. Roman Catholics left their mark in urban politics and culture,
but they did not overcome the reputation of the ethnic ghetto or political
bosses until the post–World War II economic boom when they moved to

the suburbs and sent children to college. After 1950, the effects of afflu-ence and individualism were as much a threat to Roman Catholic identity as excessive patriotism.

Adding to the burden of American Roman Catholics was the Vatican's disregard for the United States. For much of American history, Vatican of-ficials could plausibly look at America as either dominated by British Prot-estants or as another version of France's secular republicanism. Until the world wars of the twentieth century when Europeans began to look to the United States for support and even leadership, church officials had no com-pelling reason to take the American situation seriously. Combine the United States' ambivalence about Roman Catholics and the American church's immigrant character and you have the ingredients for a religious identity in which American church members were marginal ecclesiastically and na-tionally. These obstacles did not prevent Roman Catholics from establish-ing a presence in American life through culturally thick institutions, both churchly and urban, that characterized parish life from 1850 to 1950. Only in the 1950s and 1960s, when the United States became a global power and defender of the West, which coincided with the election of the nation's first Roman Catholic president, did the old relationship between the Vatican and America change. In fact, with the Second Vatican Council's determination to adapt to the modern world, American Roman Catholics felt a measure of vindication—that their experience in a modern political order would prove instructive to the church worldwide. Seemingly overnight, Roman Catholics had the opportunity to instruct their nation about the Christian basis for freedom and the global church about accommodating modernity.

What is remarkable about the Roman Catholic political conservatives first associated with Buckley at the *National Review* and later with Neu-haus at *First Things* is the outsized influence they had on both American politics and church life. First in order of significance was their ability to domesticate Americanism, a low-level heresy that had hung over Ameri-can bishops and priests since the 1890s. With American audiences this was a relatively easy feat because Roman Catholics in the United States had long since come to terms with liberalism. Roman Catholic political conservatives took the initiative of popularizing a vocabulary that com-bined devotion and patriotism without ambivalence.

Second, the flip side of these arguments was equally decisive, namely, to bring Roman Catholics into discussions of national identity that had previously been the monopoly of Protestants. In effect, thanks to these writers and intellectuals, the task of joining the national conversation about national identity and purpose became easier while also making more acceptable Roman Catholic affirmations of modern politics. As historian Tom Sugrue observed about Roman Catholicism and the 1960s in America, no "sensible" historian or cultural observer from the 1920s or 1940s could have predicted that Roman Catholics and Protestants would cooperate politically, "whether in the pages of the *National Review*, in the corridors of the American Enterprise Institute, or in the plethora of lobbying groups dedicated to restoring the patriarchal family, thwarting sexual liberation, and restoring a now-common system of 'Judeo-Christian values.'" The people responsible for this surprising turn, also featured in this book, were L. Brent Bozell, Michael Novak, and George Weigel. They in turn forged a "Catholic Americanism" that shaped the church's participation in national politics, which, according to Sugrue, is "one of the most important and understudied themes in the history of postwar America."[18]

A third important consideration for explaining the prominence of these thinkers is the Cold War setting. The Roman Catholic Church had historically condemned communism, going back to Pius IX, who also opposed liberalism and, for good measure, all things modern. Even so, Rome had taught that communism ran contrary to the social good of private property. By the time of the Russian Revolution (1919), communism's atheism and anticlericalism also provided grounds for fear and opposition. For politically conservative Roman Catholics in the 1950s, the reasons for opposing communism gained urgency owing to the global contest between the United States and the Soviet Union. The Cold War opened opportunities for a variety of anticommunist intellectuals such as neoconservative Jewish American writers Daniel Bell, Nathan Glazer, and Irving Kristol. Just as those analysts, through journals, think tanks, and university appointments, overcame an outsider status and found opportunities at a time when the United States needed forceful arguments against the Soviets, so anticommunism proved to be a gateway for politically conservative Roman Catholic thinkers. Buckley, Novak, Bozell, Weigel, and Neuhaus each gained a standing in mainstream policy debates thanks in part to the nation's important place in world affairs.

A fourth and last factor in the rise of politically conservative Roman Catholic public intellectuals is the phenomenon that James Chappel describes in *Catholic Modern*, a book about European Roman Catholic intellectuals in the same era. His study is an answer to the question of what drove lay Roman Catholic thinkers in France, Germany, and Austria "to abandon their opposition to modernity" and what strategies replaced antimodernism. Chappel argues that in the 1930s, Roman Catholic writers exchanged an "anti-modern" stance for an "anti-totalitarian" one.[19] In the process, their arguments worked up through the hierarchy and prevailed at the Second Vatican Council, where the bishops dropped the antimodernism that had defined the church's outlook, at least since 1789. *American Catholic* explores a parallel route to modernity for American Roman Catholic intellectuals. Here the story is not how specific persons flipped from antimodern to liberal (political) views as much as it is the way that Americanism, though unacceptable until Vatican II, became the legitimate way for the laity and bishops to be Roman Catholic in the United States. Whereas for European thinkers, communism inspired an antitotalitarianism that facilitated acceptance of modernity, in the United States opposition to the Soviet Union's tyrannical ways only underscored the genius of American politics and the importance of its mission to protect the free world.

Roman Catholics' emergence as prominent spokespeople for the nation's political ideals and Christian origins unfolds in the pages that follow in three stages. The first section (chapters 1 through 3) explores the setting in which post–World War II Roman Catholics found themselves and the ways they chose to reconcile duties of church and nation. The bookends are Governor Al Smith's 1928 run for the presidency of the United States and the Second Vatican Council (1962–65). This was a period when Americanism was officially a heresy (though almost never prosecuted) even as American Roman Catholics exhibited remarkable degrees of nationalism. Yet even as Roman Catholics in the United States participated seamlessly in most arenas and praised the nation in almost jingoistic cadences, anti-Catholicism persisted. In the minds of many Protestants (fundamentalist and mainline) as well as American liberals, Roman Catholicism represented a stage of historical development that was inherently premodern and illiberal. In this context, public figures such as Al Smith and, later, John F. Kennedy needed to distinguish between their civic duties and personal devotion to the church. That distinction implicitly recognized, no matter how clichéd, the tension between the United States as modern and Roman Catholicism as antiliberal.

In this setting, John Courtney Murray endeavored to explain that the American founding actually drew on older Western political and legal traditions (i.e., natural law). In so doing, he argued that anti-Catholics were misguided and that Roman Catholicism was fully compatible with national life properly understood. That effort received opposition from the Vatican, and for a time during the 1950s church officials censured Murray's views. But between 1959 and 1965 a new day dawned for American Roman Catholics. Pope John XXIII sounded positive notes about modernity and called for a council of bishops (the first in almost a century); John F. Kennedy became the first (and only) Roman Catholic president of the United States; and Murray himself was instrumental in the Second Vatican Council's approval of religious and civil liberties in a manner that made Americanism acceptable.

The second part of the book (chapters 4 through 6) follows one of the chief sources of Christian nationalism among Roman Catholics. Even before the Second Vatican Council cleared the way for positive estimates of Americanism, political (or movement) conservatives were arguing for America as an exceptional nation, owing both to its unique founding and its leadership in combating communism. For these writers, the contest between the free world and communism warranted ascribing to the United States a commanding position in world history. Conservatives' estimate of the United States also drew deeply on the Constitution's provisions for limited government, which became a vehicle for opposing the growth of the federal government under the New Deal, which in turn upset the status quo of the Republican Party and landed Barry Goldwater as the 1964 presidential nominee. Murray's own formulation of a semireligious foundation for the American founding was particularly useful for countering the idea that the nation was not Christian but secular in character. Buckley's Americanism launched a minor skirmish with other American Roman Catholics who believed conservatives were adhering more to American political realities than to church teaching. The Second Vatican Council ended that contest for the most part. Yet even with the bishops' and cardinals' apparent blessing of modernity, the challenge of reconciling Roman Catholicism and national ideals remained. Members of Buckley's inner circle, Brent L. Bozell and Garry Wills, could not sustain the balance between faith and politics and consequently left the conservative movement either for Roman Catholic traditionalism or the ebb and flow of liberal politics.

The final section chronicles Roman Catholic arguments for American superiority during the Reagan era. Here neo-Americanists such as Richard John Neuhaus, Michael Novak, and George Weigel affirmed a somewhat different brand of patriotism. Whereas Buckley's movement conservatives had needed to work without the church's blessing, neoconservatives not only encountered little resistance from the hierarchy (Weigel even wrote a biography of John Paul II) but also raised the stakes by arguing that Roman Catholicism itself would restore the United States to its rightful place in world affairs as a Christian and liberal society. This was more than what Murray had argued when claiming that the American founding drew on natural law. His was an important starting place for neo-Americanists who went on to assert that of all Christian groups in the United States, Roman Catholics were in the best position (thanks to tradition and authority) to prevent the secularization of national life and restore Christianity to prominence. The influence of Neuhaus and others in turn prompted debate among American Roman Catholics about faith and politics that once again raised the specter of Rome's historic ambivalence about modern society. To put the disagreement simply, were the American Founders better guides to modern political arrangements than popes and theologians?

Despite the widespread appeal among political conservatives of Roman Catholic neo-Americanism, since 1990 or so Roman Catholic intellectuals and pundits have debated Americanism in ways much more extensive than those that took place between the Vatican and American church officials in the late nineteenth century. Blanshard's anti-Catholicism has largely disappeared only to be replaced by Roman Catholic traditionalists who argue that their faith and liberal politics are inherently at odds. For this vocal minority of theologians and intellectuals, the United States has become a source of instability and even undermines church teaching about human dignity, economics, sex, human nature, and political authority. These criticisms of the United States are primarily the work of lay Roman Catholics and find little support among the U.S. bishops or even Pope Francis himself, who speaks often, even if vaguely, about liberal political ideals of freedom, equality, and popular sovereignty. These recent critiques of Americanism, even without episcopal support, reflect a history much older than the Cold War era or even the period of the American founding, when the Vatican's outlook on politics and society had little regard for a secular republic that ensured the rights of heretics, schismatics, and unbelievers.

1

BELONGING TO AN ANCIENT CHURCH
IN A MODERN REPUBLIC

At the time that Al Smith became the first Roman Catholic to gain the nomination for president of the United States by a major party, in this case the Democrats, American Roman Catholics were hardly new to New World politics, even if their church hierarchy bore all the marks of Europe's premodern society. In 1816 Jacques Villeré, a Roman Catholic, became the second governor of Louisiana. That heavily Roman Catholic state also in 1891 sent Edward Douglass White, an Irish American member of the church, to the U.S. Senate by way of its state legislature (before progressives through the Seventeenth Amendment opened the Senate to direct elections by the states' voters). Roger B. Taney, the U.S. Supreme Court justice who penned the verdict in *Dred Scott v. Sandford* (1857), was another Roman Catholic to hold federal office. Meanwhile, New York City's first Roman Catholic mayor was a Democrat who ran on an anti–Tammany Hall ticket and was in office to receive France's gift of the Statue of Liberty.

These names suggest that Americans were generally comfortable with Roman Catholics holding public office. But the presidency was different.

Although every politician at the state and local levels swore an oath to uphold the Constitution of the United States, a vow that some thought was in tension with submission to the papacy, not every federal or state official functioned as the figurehead of the nation. America's growing presence in international affairs gave the president substantial power as commander in chief. The modern presidency—even more so since the 1930s—has assumed monarchical proportions as those who work out of the Oval Office speak for the American people, console them in times of crisis, remind citizens of responsibilities, and officiate at national occasions. To contemplate a Roman Catholic carrying out those functions for a nation that for its first 150 years of existence stood for a political order at odds with the one preferred if not required by the Vatican was a challenge if not oxymoronic.

The man who decided to remind Americans of the incompatibility between Roman Catholicism and American politics was Charles C. Marshall, a New York attorney and member of the Episcopal Church. His standing within the informal Anglo-American Protestant establishment made *Atlantic Monthly* a welcome platform for Marshall to question Al Smith's American bona fides. The Columbia University graduate began by complimenting Smith on his rags-to-riches biography, and for conducting his work as a public servant with moral integrity. Even so, Marshall opined that Americans wanted Smith to answer questions about how the Democrat, "as a loyal and conscientious Roman Catholic," was reconcilable "with that Constitution which as President you must support and defend, and with the principles of civil and religious liberty on which American institutions are based." From there Marshall piled up a series of quotations and examples, some cut and pasted from the *Catholic Encyclopedia*, others from papal encyclicals that highlighted the antagonism between Rome's outlook on political authority and the nation's liberal political structures. For instance:

Pope Leo XIII says: "It is not lawful for the State, any more than for the individual, either to disregard all religious duties or to hold in equal favor different kinds of religion." But the Constitution of the United States declares otherwise: "Congress shall make no law respecting an establishment of religion or prohibiting the free exercise thereof."

Thus the Constitution declares the United States shall hold in equal favor different kinds of religion or no religion and the Pope declares it is not lawful to hold them in equal favor. Is there not here a quandary for that man who is at once a loyal churchman and a loyal citizen?

Pope Leo says that the Roman Catholic Church "deems it unlawful to place the various forms of divine worship on the same footing as 'the true religion.'" But the Supreme Court of the United States says that our "law knows no heresy and is committed to the support of no dogma, the establishment of no sect." . . .

Americans indulge themselves in the felicitation that they have achieved an ideal religious situation in the United States. But Pope Leo, in his encyclical letter on Catholicity in the United States, asserts: "It would be very erroneous to draw the conclusion that in America is to be sought the type of the most desirable status of the Church."[1]

Marshall was just getting warmed up. He went on to point out the conflict between Roman Catholic canon law on marriage and the secular laws governing the institution in Protestant countries such as the United States and England, and he even threw in some less-than-flattering material on Mexican politics and the Vatican's policies south of the Texas border. These instances were the hors d'oeuvres for Marshall's 1928 main course, *The Roman Catholic Church in the Modern State*, a book whose research and author's correspondence are part of the Library of Congress's holdings. He concluded by trying to reassure Smith that he meant no harm. Marshall respected both Smith and his church. But the historical and contemporary record raised any number of instances that deserved Smith's answers.

Of course, Smith's response was not good enough to change voters' minds. To be sure, not many voters in the South were avid readers of *Atlantic Monthly*. But the traditional loyalty of southerners to the Democrats and the South's suspicion of the party of Lincoln were the only reason for Smith's positive results in the Electoral College—87 out of 531 votes. Massachusetts and Rhode Island were the only states outside the South to vote for Smith. Even parts of the South, such as North Carolina, Tennessee, and Virginia, supported the Republican, Hoover.

Aside from what election returns revealed about the Democratic Party's patchwork coalition, Smith's candidacy revealed even more about Roman Catholicism in the United States. Contrary to an average Protestant's perceptions, Smith himself reflected an American church that was overwhelmingly comfortable with the nation's politics. In his response published in

Atlantic Monthly, the New York governor outlined the Americanist Roman Catholic position, which included freedom of conscience, the separation of church and state (which affirmed the First Amendment), support for public schools, noninterventionism in foreign policy, and goodwill among all religions. Smith's religious profession was certainly different from that of Vatican officials, and it was not the way many American Protestants perceived the Roman Catholic Church in the United States. Even so, Smith embodied a Roman Catholicism that, no matter how much associated with immigrants or the ghettos where they lived, was proudly American.

A Forbidden Way of Life

If Charles Marshall viewed Roman Catholicism simply from the perspective of the papacy after the French Revolution, his worries about Smith had merit. Even before 1789 the papacy had emerged as the authoritative center of church life and a political force in European politics with capacities to bestow spiritual blessings that were useful to monarchs and princes. After the Reformation, the papacy generally reacted negatively to new ideas in religion and science. The French Revolution was another matter, however, with decisive implications for the papacy's initial perceptions of republicanism and popular sovereignty, and the way that the magisterium would defend its long-standing contention that the church, as a divinely appointed institution, should oversee the state. (The other eighteenth-century revolution, America's War of Independence, made little impression on the Vatican officials if only because it was a problem for a Protestant empire in a remote part of the world.) French revolutionaries not only toppled the church's holdings and authority in France, but their ideology also implicated the Vatican's position within Europe's fragile political order. Under Napoleon the papacy lost some of its own territories in the Papal States but also became synonymous with the tyranny from which republicans hoped to liberate humankind. After the French Revolution nineteenth-century popes clung to their older authority (both spiritual and temporal) and opposed the emergence of liberalism in Europe.

Pius IX, who became pope in 1846, gave some Vatican watchers hope that the papacy might loosen its opposition to most aspects of modern society. Indeed, his election owed to the desire of many cardinals to liberalize the Vatican's institutions. Initially, Pius IX fulfilled those hopes by instituting a constitutional framework for the papacy's temporal rule and freeing many of the Vatican's political prisoners. But the democratic revolutions that broke out across Europe in 1848, and violent opposition to the papacy among Italians who wanted a unified nation, which forced Piux IX to flee Rome, put an end to the pope's reforms. Evidence of his conservatism came in two dramatic episodes during the longest papacy in Roman Catholic history. The first was Pius IX's 1864 publication of *The Syllabus of Errors*, a document that condemned eighty different aspects of the modern world, such as the separation of church and state and religious toleration. The last of the list of modern heresies was a condemnation of the idea that "the Roman Pontiff can, and ought to, reconcile himself, and come to terms with progress, liberalism and modern civilization."[2] That was an assertion that critics could easily ridicule, but it also signaled how deeply the papacy saw modern developments as hostile to the faith.

The second instance of Pius IX's conservatism was the declaration in 1870 of papal infallibility at what became the First Vatican Council. Aside from assigning dogmatic authority to a truth that had long been part of the popes' self-understanding, infallibility was also one way for Pius IX to assert his supremacy even while he was losing his temporal authority on the Italian peninsula. For at the very same time that the cardinals assembled in Rome, Italian rulers were orchestrating a plan to unite the newly minted nation of Italy. As absolute as papal infallibility sounded, bishops in France and the United States were sufficiently clever to avoid the force of such statements. Bishop of Orléans Félix Dupanloup argued that Pius IX was condemning an idea, the threat of radicalism in Europe, not liberal politics per se. In the United States, Archbishop Martin John Spalding invoked Dupanloup in a pastoral letter that explained the pope was castigating "radicals and infidels" but left untouched the American system of government, which promised "not to interfere with religious matters."[3]

The tumultuous conditions of nineteenth-century Europe gave popes every reason to ignore whatever difficulties the republic of the United States might mean for the faith of Roman Catholics. To be sure, Pius IX oversaw the American bishops who created the administrative structures that facilitated the arrival of large numbers of Irish and German immigrants during the mid-nineteenth century. Still, the papacy's antimodern position reflected European conditions, not the American republic's rejection of British rule. In fact, in 1899, when Pope Leo XIII finally spoke of "Americanism" as a heresy, the reasons behind this condemnation owed as much to European church politics as they did to conditions in the United States. For instance, in 1883 the wealthy German church member and politician Peter Paul Cahensly visited the United States and came away convinced that the church in America was not providing adequate spiritual care for her immigrant members. His 1891 report to Leo XIII, the Lucerne Memorial, alerted the Vatican to the need for a different kind of ecclesiastical leadership in the United States. Another instance of European fears about American developments was the case of Isaac Hecker, a priest in New York and founder of the Paulists. He emerged as a model for some French priests and bishops who wanted the church to adapt to new political realities. Hecker for them was an example for reconciling Roman Catholicism with the dynamics of modern society, which included the proposition that the American form of government was not antithetical to the church. For the French proponents of a modern version of Roman Catholicism, one that was open to modern politics and ideas, a biography of Hecker translated into French and published in 1897 became the incident that finally provoked the papacy to render a verdict on Hecker and what he signified within Europe, namely, Americanism. Although debates among European clergy about the church's relation to the state had been long and detailed since the First Vatican Council, the pope's rejection of modernity functioned as the lens through which to view church-state relations in the New World.[4]

Leo XIII, the pope credited with launching the modern church's tradition of social teaching in the 1891 encyclical *Rerum novarum* (prolabor but antisocialist), became the pontiff responsible for rendering a verdict on the situation of Roman Catholics in the United States. He inherited Pius IX's conservatism but explained it in intellectual tropes that were (and still are) less jarring to moderns. This capacity was evident in *Testem benevolentiae* (1899), the encyclical that condemned Americanism as a heresy. The language of condemnation and heresy is technically accurate, but Leo himself couched his judgment in ways designed more to calm French conservatives than to produce fear among America's faithful. Indeed, Leo's earlier encyclical, *Longinqua* (1895), in which he explained the appointment of an apostolic see in the United States and recommended support for the church's universities, reflected the pope's congenial attitude to the relatively young republic. The nation, Leo observed, was "progressing and developing by giant strides," and such improvement was good for the church. "We are animated with hope and filled with joy," he wrote, at rates of ordinations, the formation of confraternities and parochial schools, the use of Sunday schools for "imparting Christian doctrine," and the creation of mutual aid societies "for the relief of the indigent." Roman Catholicism in the United States seemed, from the pope's perspective, to be thriving.[5]

Soon after that generous estimate, however, Americanism emerged as a problem. Its chief challenge was the liberty granted to persons "to act more freely in pursuance of his own natural bent and capacity."[6] In other words, the church, through her bishops under the papacy's prerogatives, was still responsible for determining truth and cultivating genuine devotion. Father Hecker's notion, sometimes only implicit, that the Holy Spirit was providentially at work through modern societies such as the United States betrayed tradition. At the same time, Leo was quick to distinguish between religious and political Americanism, a distinction that gave the bishops in the United States a longer leash than ultraconservatives thought permissible. If Americanism referred simply to "the condition of your commonwealths, or the laws and customs which prevail in them," then Leo had no reason to "discard" them.[7] But if it meant that American politics set the standard for understanding authority or that the United States was a model for the rest of the world, then Americanism was a direct challenge to the church's ideal of Christendom with the pope as the ultimate arbiter of personal and social life. Gerald Fogarty, the historian whose comprehensive account of the Americanist controversy is without peer, argues that *Testem benevolentiae* may have identified Americanism as a heresy, but it was actually an expression of episcopal compromise. A recognition of legitimate forms of Americanism was a victory for bishops in the United States who had been arguing for the better part of two decades that Roman Catholicism and the nation's political system were entirely compatible. Yet European bishops who feared a unique version of Roman Catholicism leavened by the American experience took comfort from Leo's reassertion of Rome's supremacy.

What *Testem benevolentiae* did not address, however, was the tension that most Americans sensed (both Protestant and Roman Catholic) between the papacy's political ideals and the legitimacy of their national government. For almost a millennium the bishops of Rome had insisted that between the temporal and spiritual powers ordained by God, the church was the one with greater authority because it represented Christ on earth. Add to this the pope's universal jurisdiction, an authority not bound by national borders, and heads of state, not to mention their subjects, could well wonder if the Roman Catholic hierarchy might insinuate itself into a nation's affairs. Conservative European Roman Catholics throughout the nineteenth century had continued to conceive of church-state relations this way, especially after the French Revolution, which shared egalitarian and liberal sensibilities with the newly minted federated republic in North America. What added to the tension for Roman Catholics in the United States was the papacy's own temporal power. Because the pope served as the sovereign ruler over the Papal States until 1870, Roman Catholics in the United States needed to explain to nativist Protestants how those under papal oversight could also affirm independence as a personal and national ideal.

Because the United States, in fact, had no religious tests for holding office and promised freedom of religion to all citizens, conflicts between loyalty to the Constitution and religious devotion were always possible. Mormons themselves at different periods in their history had to explain the apparent tension between church authority and national sovereignty. Some could but almost never thought to question how Protestants could reconcile the authority of scripture with the Constitution's provisions for the U.S. government. What made Roman Catholics stand out among America's many believers was the papacy and its recorded hostility to the modern world. Even when some church members sided with the papacy in debates about Italy's secular politics after the Vatican lost its temporal powers, Roman Catholics in the United States practiced a vigorous patriotism and preferred church-state relations in America compared to Europe's confessional states or France's anticlericalism.[8] The papacy, in other words, made little difference for the way ordinary Roman Catholics living in the United States thought about their nation's secular government.

If Not Americanist, at Least American

The issues that drove the Americanist controversy on the American side of the Atlantic had less to do with institutional order and ecclesiastical hierarchy than with the struggles that confronted a church of immigrants. The

first was a conflict very much germane to the urbanization and industri-
alization of the United States after 1870 that attracted Europeans to hope
that the words underwriting the Statue of Liberty—"Give me your tired,
your poor, / Your huddled masses yearning to breathe free"—were true.
The Knights of Labor was a popular national labor union that alarmed
some Roman Catholics because it had all the marks of a secret society (forbidden by the church), like the Masons. Although condemned in 1884 by
the bishop of Quebec (a judgment ratified by the papacy), American bishops rejected a resolution to follow suit, and a few, such as James Gibbons
of Baltimore and John J. Keane of Richmond, defended the Knights of
Labor. Another topic of debate was schooling. The Third Plenary Council of Baltimore in 1884 mandated the establishment of Roman Catholic
grammar schools in every parish within the United States. John Ireland,
another Americanist bishop, admired the nation's public schools, however, and proposed ways for Roman Catholics to supplement public education. Leo XIII determined to bypass the conflict over parochial schools
by letting the American bishops sort it out among themselves. Adding
to frictions in the United States were antagonisms between Irish American and German American bishops, with the former favoring assimilation
while the latter tended toward European norms.

The lesson learned from the Americanist controversy was hardly one
that parochial schoolteachers could use to marshal greater obedience to
the hierarchy from their pupils. *Testem benevolentiae* did little to change
daily routines in dioceses and parishes. In fact, after Leo XIII's 1902 encyclical, *In amplimissimo*, Roman Catholics in the United States could
well have imagined the fine points of the Americanist heresy were akin to
arcane debates among theologians. Only three years after mildly condemning Americanism, Leo wrote, "And Our daily experience obliges Us to
confess that We have found your people, through your influence, endowed
with perfect docility of mind and alacrity of disposition. Therefore, while
the changes and tendencies of nearly all the nations which were Catholic
for many centuries give cause for sorrow, the state of your churches, in
their flourishing youthfulness, cheers Our heart and fills it with delight."[9]
Leo cautioned that American law gave Roman Catholic institutions "no
special favor," but he also recognized that the nation's civil polity did
nothing to restrain the church in its "just liberty." Favorable conditions
in the United States were as much an opportunity for "spreading . . . the

light of the truth" as they were an obstacle to faith. A bigger problem for the church arguably was the independence of mind that such conditions nurtured, which in turn potentially undermined episcopal authority.

James Cardinal Gibbons, archbishop of Baltimore and then the only American cardinal (compared to nine in 2015), must have been encouraged by *In amplimissimo*. As one of the leading Americanists, Gibbons believed that *Testem benevolentiae* failed to understand the American experience. Leo's condemnation of Americanism went directly to Gibbons, who turned around and used his authority as cardinal to delay distribution. He also wrote a letter to the pope and explained that the matters described in the encyclical did not exist in the United States. Gerald Fogarty, the historian, agreed with Gibbons. "The condemnation of Americanism arose," Fogarty wrote, "from the impossibility of translating American ideas into a nineteenth-century European setting."[10] Part of what was likely impossible for Europeans to understand was the United States' strange alchemy of secularity and religion, which later acquired characteristics of a civil religion or Christian nationalism. The creation of Protestants who blended postmillennial hopes for the kingdom of God with patriotic beliefs in a secular republic, such civil religion rendered the formal separation of church and state as simply the price of creating a Christian nation. Though used often to express anti-Catholicism, American civil religion was one of the moves from the Americanist bishops' playbook. As Gibbons explained in a homily before the 1912 presidential election, the United States had not removed "god" from public discourse the way the French had in establishing their republic. All presidents invoked God's aid and set aside a day of national thanks every November; Congress opened with prayer; and public functions invariably invoked God's blessing and presence. Instead of being separated, "church and state move in parallel lines." In the United States, the state protects the church without "interfering" in matters of conscience, and the church aids the state through adding "moral sanctions" to civil law.[11] Indeed, a belief in divine providence upholding the United States was Gibbons's explanation for the republic's success and its hope for the future.

The nation's founders and Protestant supporters may have patented such a blend of patriotism and piety, but it was characteristic not just of Americanist bishops but of Roman Catholics in the United States more generally. The reasons for Americanism's appeal to bishops resembled those that informed the narrative of American exceptionalism. To unite a nation of diverse immigrant groups, Protestants and politicians needed a pious patriotism that resolved differences through a national mission underwritten by divine blessing. The same was true for the Roman Catholic Church in the United States, the one Christian communion that had to absorb the nation's ethnic diversity in ways that Protestants did relatively easily through separate denominations. Charles Morris's description of the nationalistic antagonisms of the early twentieth-century church may be overdone, but it still captures the demographic crisis that the United States and Roman Catholics confronted together even as Protestants of British descent looked on with disdain: "Italian priests refused to baptize Lithuanians, Poles detested Czechs, Germans contended with Irish. Immigrant Irish priests attacked the laxity of Irish-American priests. Ethnic pastors shamelessly competed with one another for parishioners, and territorial pastors protested bitterly when ethnic parishes siphoned off their revenues. . . . Immigrant Italians found American clergy, particularly Irish Americans, cold and puritanical and preferred native Italians, even when they were obviously charlatans."[12] If the ideal of Christendom could not prevent the fractious nature of ethnic and language differences among Roman Catholics in Europe, why would papal supremacy work its wonders in the New World? If bishops needed to adjust to the political realities of a federated constitutional republic that guaranteed religious freedom, adapting to the demographic diversity that the nation encouraged was all the more reason to embrace some form of Americanism to assimilate and unify Roman Catholics in the United States.

Whether bishops' attitudes were at all responsible for Roman Catholics serving in the U.S. military, William Henry O'Connell's assessment during the Spanish-American War that God was passing "the banner to the hands of America, to bear it, in the cause of humanity" was indicative of church members support for their nation. After having fought on both sides in the Civil War and against Spain in the Spanish-American War, a contest that could have alienated Roman Catholics inclined to choose religion over national identity, the people whom Protestants suspected of disloyalty proved to be just as patriotic as their neighbors. World War I again raised questions of divided loyalties for Roman Catholics in the United States. Irish Americans who were generally hostile to British and German Americans, depending on their time of arrival in the United States, may have had reasons to sympathize with the kaiser. Despite the prominence of Irish and German ancestry among bishops in the United States, as a body they pledged support during the war "to the end that the great and holy cause of liberty may triumph, and that our beloved country may emerge from this hour of test stronger and nobler than ever." Cardinal Gibbons put an exclamation point on that assertion by declaring that "both Houses of Congress are the instruments of God in guiding us in our civic duty."[13] Lay Roman Catholics outdid their bishops by fighting against the German kaiser in remarkable numbers. Roughly a million Roman Catholics fought for the United States out of the total 4.7 million serving in the armed forces, a higher proportion than the percentage of Roman Catholics living in the country. On the other side, conscientious objectors with Roman Catholic convictions were tiny. Of the almost four thousand Americans who refused to fight on the basis of conscience, only four Roman Catholics avoided service on religious grounds.

World War I was even indirectly responsible for Americanizing the institutions of the church. In 1917 under Cardinal Gibbons's leadership, American bishops formed the National Catholic War Council. Its functions were to coordinate Roman Catholic activities in connection with the war effort—from chaplains to religious literature for the troops. After the war, this council blossomed into the National Catholic Welfare Council, an agency that continued to oversee Roman Catholic efforts in response to the hardships caused by war. The idea of a regular meeting of bishops in a "council" was technically a violation of canon law. The late medieval history of bishops' councils (conciliarism) trying to rein in the papacy still loomed in the imagination of Pope Benedict XV, who worked to suppress institutions that might cultivate separate national identities and undermine the catholicity of the Roman communion. Through much behind-the-scenes lobbying, among the bishops both in the United States and inside the Vatican, Pius XI, who succeeded Benedict in 1922, approved the new American association of bishops. To comply with canon law, the organization needed to abandon the word "council" in favor of "conference," thus making it the National Catholic Welfare Conference. It turned out to be a useful organization for the papacy both in its relations with the U.S. government and in stabilizing the church in Mexico. But the NCWC was another instance of the way that bishops in the United States were establishing an American version of Roman Catholicism.

Ghetto Americanism

When Al Smith asked, "What the hell is an encyclical?" he was not simply expressing the ignorance of a layperson but also reflected the independence of mind that had characterized Roman Catholicism in the United States for much of the nation's history. He had grown up in New York City's Fourth Ward, a working-class neighborhood on Manhattan's Lower East Side that was home to a melting pot of Americans. His education came from the nuns and priest at Saint James School, where he distinguished himself less for his grades and more for his public speaking. Smith finished first in competitions during high school, which explained the school's decision to choose an average student from the class of 1886 for its commencement exercises. Part of the curriculum at Saint James was Christian doctrine. But observers knew that Smith learned little from the class. According to Frances Perkins, Smith "never knew" Roman Catholic theology and did not "care much about it." What he knew was religion, which was something that for many immigrants gave dignity to their difficult circumstances and hope for escape from a life of poverty. Smith never missed Mass. His grandson recalled that Smith was not a "philosopher" about his faith and never "flaunted" it. At the opposite end of the family, Smith's grandfather recalled that the governor "didn't talk about his religion, but lived it."[14] As part of the warp and woof of his life, even as a career politician in New York City and New York State, Roman Catholicism was unexceptional to Smith. For him to emerge during the 1928 campaign as a bellwether of the church hierarchy's teachings about government and church-state relations was as baffling as it was surprising. Smith's first reaction to the *Atlantic* article was, "I have been a Catholic all my life and I never heard of these encyclicals and papal bulls." His first inclination was not "to answer the damn thing."[15]

   If Smith, not exactly the most knowledgeable of church teaching, were to respond credibly to the charges that Marshall laid out in the *Atlantic*, he would need help. That assistance came from another figure who provided yet more evidence of how assimilated Roman Catholics were in the United States. Francis P. Duffy was the priest to whom Smith turned, the one who met his condition for a cleric "with a record of Americanism and patriotism that no person in the world can possibly question."[16] He was arguably the most popular priest in New York City thanks in part to his service in World War I as chaplain for the Sixty-Ninth New York Regiment. For his service, Duffy received decorations from both the U.S. and French governments. The highest flattery may have come from Hollywood, who hired Pat O'Brien to play Duffy in *The Fighting Sixty-Ninth* (1940). Underneath his patriotic exterior was a Roman Catholic scholar. Before the war Duffy had taught at Saint Joseph's Seminary, the training site for priests in the diocese of New York. In addition to teaching he helped found and edit the *New York Review*, considered at the time one of the most important theological journals. Its reputation derived in part from the editors' willingness to engage modern scholarship, which after Pope Pius X's 1907 condemnation of theological modernism was also responsible for the hierarchy's doubts about Duffy. In 1909, when Archbishop John Murphy Farley dismissed James Driscoll from Saint Joseph's faculty, he also considered firing Duffy.

Thanks to his popularity in the classroom, Duffy survived at the seminary for another three years before Farley moved him to a new parish in the Bronx. Even so, Farley continued to suspect that despite his intelligence, Duffy showed "a strong leaning toward the liberal tendency of the time called modernism." Such openness to innovation may explain why once Duffy went off to war, non-Catholics in the Sixth-Ninth considered the priest the most valuable source of spiritual advice. Another way of describing Duffy's approach was cooperative. And back in the United States after the war, Duffy advocated for Roman Catholics fitting in. In 1923 he wrote, "If we can go along serving our Church and our country as a sincere, patriotic body, then all the forces of anti-Catholic bigotry will go to pieces."[17]

Before going into print, Duffy's response to Marshall on behalf of Smith had to go through layers of review, first the candidate himself but also the archbishop, Cardinal Hayes. The latter gave two thumbs up: "good Catholicism and good Americanism." The *Atlantic Monthly* ran a similar title in its May 1927 issue: "Catholic and Patriot: Governor Smith Replies." Smith acknowledged that he had received help and highlighted that assistance came from a priest who had received war honors from both the United States and France. The governor also pointed to his own public service and noted that he had taken oaths to the uphold the U.S. Constitution nineteen times and had never seen any conflict between politics and faith. Smith was fuzzy on the status of encyclicals, as he had not followed them, and then he informed Marshall and magazine readers that papal statements such as *The Syllabus of Errors* had no binding force as church dogma. He conceded that the union of church and state was the Roman Catholic ideal. At the same time, it was the model only for Roman Catholic societies of the past. The real authority for Smith, as it was for any Roman Catholic, was individual conscience, "the supreme law which under no circumstances can we ever lawfully disobey." Under those rare circumstances when the pope might interfere with civil government, Smith had a ready response, one that came from the Americanist bishop John Ireland: "Back to your own sphere of rights and duties, back to the things of God." Smith even replied to Marshall's insinuation that parochial schools were subversive of American ideals. The governor himself was a graduate of such schooling and had "never heard of any such stuff being taught or anybody who claimed that it was."[18]

Smith's response concluded with a creed that the Americanist bishops in the United States could well have affirmed and that foreshadowed John F. Kennedy, Jr.'s later response to anti-Catholic arguments:

I believe in the worship of God according to the faith and practice of the Roman Catholic Church.

I recognize no power in the institutions of my Church to interfere with the operations of the Constitution of the United States or the enforcement of the law of the land.

I believe in absolute freedom of conscience for all men and in equality of all churches, all sects, and all beliefs before the law as a matter of right and not as a matter of favor.

I believe in the absolute separation of Church and State and in the strict enforcement of the provisions of the Constitution that Congress shall make no law respecting an establishment of religion or prohibiting the free exercise thereof.

I believe that no tribunal of any church has any power to make any decree of any force in the law of the land, other than to establish the status of its own communicants within its own church.

I believe in the support of the public school as one of the cornerstones of American liberty.

I believe in the right of every parent to choose whether his child shall be educated in the public school or in a religious school supported by those of his own faith.

I believe in the principled noninterference by this country in the internal affairs of other nations and that we should stand steadfastly against any such interference by whomsoever it may be urged.

And I believe in the common brotherhood of man under the common fatherhood of God.[19]

It did not have the elegance or depth of the Nicene or Chalcedonian creeds, but Smith's statement of faith was an apt summary of the faith of the vast number of Roman Catholics living in the United States, from laity to cardinals.

No Satisfying the Real Patriots

Nevertheless, Smith lost the 1928 presidential election thanks to Protestant fears of a Roman Catholic president. The New York governor did manage to take South Carolina, Georgia, Alabama, Mississippi, Louisiana, Arkansas, Massachusetts, and Rhode Island to account for his eighty-seven electoral votes. His 41 percent of the vote was actually a better showing than the two previous Democratic nominees. In 1920 James Cox had attracted 34 percent of the electorate, and Democratic voters in 1924 slumped with John Davis as their nominee—he received only 28 percent of the vote in a contest where the Progressive Party was still a strong option. Smith's showing as the first Roman Catholic candidate for president was, all things considered, not as bad as many feared it might have been. Even so, as Allan J. Lichtman concludes in his study of the 1928 election, "Reaction against Smith's religion . . . mirrored the heritage of immigrant groups, Protestant religious training, and doubts about the autonomy of a Catholic president."[20] Uncertain also was the mission of priests and bishops since the "official" position of the church, as explained by John A. Ryan and Morehouse Millar in *The State and the Church* (1922), was that in theory the state should support the true church (Rome). The United States posed a different situation from the theory, but Ryan and Millar left open the possibility that if Protestants lost their strength, "a political proscription of religion" by the American government followed from the logic of church teaching.[21]

A factor in the New York governor's relative success was the identification of Roman Catholics with American ways of life. That trajectory continued after the 1928 election through the Depression and World War II. To be sure, voices such as those of Dorothy Day, whose newspaper, the *Catholic Worker*, labeled capitalism as un-Christian, or Father Charles Coughlin, whose national radio broadcasts attracted millions of middle-class listeners to suspect big business, labor unions, and the New Deal of ruining the nation, sounded a chorus of dissent. But Franklin Delano Roosevelt's policies echoed Roman Catholic social teaching on a just wage for workers and the need for healthy families, which in turn encouraged some church leaders to back parts of the New Deal. In addition, Roosevelt wooed the church on a number of fronts. For instance, of the 196 federal judges that the president appointed, 51 were Roman Catholic (compared to only 8 out of 214 in the previous three administrations). Roosevelt also in 1939 appointed Myron C. Taylor as a presidential representative to Pope Pius XII. This was by no means a full-blown diplomatic recognition of the Vatican as critics interpreted it. The move primarily reflected a pragmatic response to open channels of communication with Europe at the beginning of World War II. But it was one more indication of the increasing assimilation of Roman Catholics as part of the fabric of American life.

The Second World War provided yet another chance for Roman Catholics in the United States, both laity and clergy, to display their patriotism. Even though some worried about a coalition between the United States and Soviet communists, the National Catholic Welfare Conference, through its administrative secretary, Edward Mooney, archbishop of Detroit, pledged its support to FDR in entering the war. The historic position of the U.S. bishops yielded "a tradition of devoted attachment to the ideals and institutions of government we are now called upon to defend."[22] Mooney's communication received support from the Vatican, which threatened any bishop who publicly dissented from the NCWC's promise of loyalty. In the armed forces again Roman Catholics served in significant numbers. They made up 25 percent of the soldiers. More than three thousand priests served as chaplains. Of the close to twelve thousand registered conscientious objectors, only 135 Roman Catholics joined the dissent. After the war, the G.I. Bill's provisions for veterans did even more than anyone might have imagined to integrate further Roman Catholics and American society. Roman Catholic veterans attended college and university in record numbers after the war and joined the ever-expanding middle class in the march of upward mobility, which left its mark on the nation's landscape with the proliferation of suburban developments and institutions (parishes, schools) to sustain them. The influx of students at Roman Catholic colleges and universities also transformed the church's higher education. Out went the older seminary-styled forms of campus discipline and in came an ethos geared more for a laity that had left behind the ghetto and shared ambitions with other non-Catholics in the pursuit of an American way of life.

These trends make the outbreak of anti-Catholicism after the war look bizarre.[23] Despite most Roman Catholics living in the United States functioning for all intents and purposes as "red-blooded" Americans, even to the point of backing the separation of church and state as Smith had, Paul Blanshard was unimpressed. His 1949 book, *American Freedom and Catholic Power*, voiced a liberal and progressive version of anti-Catholicism that turned out to be the last gasp of respectable Protestant fear of Roman Catholicism. Blanshard had studied at Union Seminary in New York City to be a Congregationalist minister but lost his faith while opposing the U.S. entry into World War I and went on to be a writer and editor (primarily at the *Nation*). His background was far from the worlds of evangelical and fundamentalist Protestantism where suspicions of Roman Catholicism also ran deep. Blanshard's book was a best seller—it sold forty thousand copies in its first three months. It did so because it tapped the mood of American intellectuals. Even before Blanshard wrote his book, John Dewey had complained that Roman Catholicism represented a "reactionary world organization." Reinhold Niebuhr had also recognized the antagonism between "the presuppositions of a free society and the inflexible authoritarianism of the Catholic religion." Blanshard's own contribution to these perceptions received positive estimates. George Boas, who taught philosophy at Johns Hopkins University, recommended Blanshard's book to readers for understanding a "bitter opponent of the liberal tradition."[24]

That the American intelligentsia would rally around Blanshard's depiction of church power as a threat to American freedom was odd given how little authority the papacy actually possessed in the postwar world. After the unification of Italy in 1870, the papacy lost its temporal authority over those territories on the Italian peninsula that had made up the Papal States. The Lateran Treaty of 1929 between Italy's fascist government and the Vatican had finally settled the decades-long Italian dispute between church and state—the so-called Roman Question—and defined the autonomy of Vatican City within Italian society.

Nevertheless, negotiating with authoritarian governments was precisely what troubled progressive Americans such as Blanshard. The church may have lost its temporal authority, but the political instincts it nurtured— U.S. Roman Catholics notwithstanding—ran against the liberal assumptions about freedom. Blanshard's litany was long: the Vatican negotiated with Italian fascists, opposed the Republicans in the Spanish Civil War, and refused to condemn German National Socialism. Did this constitute evidence of a "clerical-fascist International"? Blanshard could not answer definitively. His safe conclusion was that the church had "never spoken out against fascist dictatorship with one-tenth of the ferocity of its attack on Communist dictatorship." Meanwhile, it had "aligned itself with the most reactionary forces in Europe and Latin America." Rome's foreign policy, however, was not nearly as troubling as its domestic strategy, and here domestic was synonymous with the Roman Catholic family. If Roman Catholics had achieved "success in outbreeding Protestant Canada," imagine what church members south of that border might accomplish. In fact, if Americans looked at their national neighbors they might worry, since Roman Catholics were gaining ascendancy in Canada (according to Blanshard) and controlled Mexico. Some bishops were boasting that Roman Catholics were procreating at a faster rate than the rest of the U.S. citizens. Aside from sheer demographics, a faster birth rate spelled the doom of the nation's public schools, the institution on which "the outcome of the struggle between American democracy and the Catholic hierarchy" depended.[25]

The rivalry between public and parochial schools revealed the other aspect of Roman Catholicism that progressive thinkers such as Blanshard could not abide, namely, the split loyalty that the hierarchy demanded from its members. Never mind that in a liberal society like the United States, with a welter of voluntary associations and a vibrant civil society where citizens negotiated a diversity of identities all the time— church, local school board, state government, Kiwanis Club, major league baseball—the institutional life of Roman Catholics in the United States ran against the grain of assumed national identity. Everywhere Blanshard looked, he saw a set of institutions that set Roman Catholics apart and prevented assimilation. They had their own schools, their own hospitals, their own training for doctors, their own political affinities, their own (inferior) scholars, their own marriage laws, their own narrative of the West, and of course their own clergy who were part of a hierarchy that was at odds with democracy and equality.

Blanshard's coverage was encyclopedic. He even called attention to the "Seton Series in Arithmetic, widely used in Catholic schools, [which] forms 'the Catholic mind' by inserting fifteen pictures of saints, priests, altars, and angels in first-grade arithmetic in teaching children how to count."[26] Rather than regarding this proliferation of associational life as a testament to the healthy civil society and the freedoms afforded to all citizens, Blanshard only saw a separate Roman Catholic identity as a threat. It was, in fact, the reverse of the Vatican's view of the United States. For both anti-Catholics such as Blanshard and hard-line bishops (conceivably), personal identity was a zero-sum game with either the United States or Rome demanding total allegiance. Of course, most Roman Catholics in the United States, whether clergy or lay, would not have recognized themselves in Blanshard's portrait—certainly not Al Smith (if he had been alive to read the book—he died in 1944). Even so, Blanshard continued to regard the church the way nineteenth-century liberal nationalists in Europe had—as a threat to the nation-state's control of society's workings and personal identity.

The other aspect of Roman Catholicism that fueled criticisms such as Blanshard's was the teaching of the church itself on church-state relations. Whether Roman Catholics in the United States believed it and whether the papacy could enforce it, popes and theologians for the better part of a millennium had insisted that the church was superior to the state by virtue of its divinely instituted authority and holy mission. The assertions of papal supremacy, again not very well known among the laity, were easy to find, and Americans suspicious of Roman Catholics, such as Charles Marshall and Blanshard, could readily produce examples, as the former did in his article addressed to Al Smith:

> We quote Pope Leo in his encyclical letter on The Christian Constitution of States: "Over the mighty multitude of mankind, God has set rulers with power to govern, and He has willed that, one of them (the Pope) should be the head of all." We quote Pope Leo in his encyclical letter on The Reunion

of Christendom: "We who hold upon this earth the place of God Almighty."
It follows naturally on all this that there is a conflict between authoritative
Roman Catholic claims on the one side and our constitutional law and prin-
ciples on the other.[27]

The question facing Roman Catholics in the United States, especially
those who had purchased Blanshard's book or worried about neighbors
who had, was how to resolve the apparent tension between Roman Catholicism and Americanism.

The man to the rescue was John Courtney Murray, a middle-aged Jesuit (born in 1904) who taught for the bulk of his career at the Jesuit seminary in Woodstock, Maryland. As John McGreevy shows, Murray was
the American member of a group of Roman Catholic thinkers (all clergy)
who took up the charge that authoritarianism was endemic within their
church and instead looked for ways to affirm in a Roman Catholic idiom
the modern ideals of religious freedom, democracy, and human rights.
Murray stood out in this group if only because *Time* magazine put him
on its December 10, 1960, cover, a tribute to his intellectual powers and
standing within the American church. The editor of *Theological Studies*
and the religion editor for the Jesuit magazine *America*, Murray moni-
tored and offered opinions on any number of issues—from race and ecumenism to church-state relations—that animated mid-twentieth-century
Roman Catholic intellectual life. In order to defend religious freedom
specifically, Murray needed to explain papal directives, such as those of
Leo XIII, that affirmed the value of the unity of church and state, or the
idea that the state should promote true religion and weed out error. Murray's rationale was the historicist one that allowed readers to regard Leo's
stance as plausible and true for its own time but not necessarily a universal
and timeless understanding of church-state relations. It also involved a
close reading of the pope who had condemned Americanism. This was not
a repeat of Father Duffy's prepared defense for Al Smith and the conformity of Roman Catholics to American political traditions. Murray's was
an effort to harmonize papal teaching with liberal politics.

In contrast to what Murray called a "sectarian liberalism" that dominated nineteenth-century Europe and that haunted the papacies of Pius IX
and Leo XIII was an Anglo-American liberalism that was fundamentally
constitutional. As such, constitutional liberalism placed restraints on civil
authorities, which in turn created legal space for the church. Murray also

contended that papal teaching was thoroughly compatible with the Anglo-American tradition. On the one hand, a separation of church and state was beneficial when government recognized that religion was the responsibility of the church and government guaranteed freedoms that allowed the church to fulfill its task. "The role of government is to see to it, by appropriate measures both positive and negative, that the Church is free to go about her creative mission," Murray explained. It was "likewise to see to it that such conditions of order obtain in society as will facilitate the fulfillment of the Church's high spiritual task." On the other hand, he found in Leo XIII's teaching a recognition of institutional pluriformity that again resonated with constitutional liberalism. Murray conceded that at times Leo sounded authoritarian when calling for a kind of "police action" in religious and cultural spheres. But the Jesuit chalked this up to historical context and argued that the fundamental principle in Leo's encyclicals was "as much freedom as possible, as much government as necessary." For support, Murray quoted one German scholar who concluded, "Thus Leo was the first Pope who relinquished in every form all residue of medieval ecclesiastical supremacy; he positively proclaimed the full qualifications and the relative autonomy or sovereignty of the politico-social power." The reason Leo had condemned Americanism was not based on a fundamental antagonism between Roman Catholic views about the state and American conceptions of government. The issue had been certain European clerics who wanted to use the American system of government as a universally valid arrangement. They failed to understand the contingency of all political forms as Leo himself had recognized: "Leo XIII willingly admitted that American constitutional law is good law. What he will not admit is that the goodness of American legal experience can be made the basis for theoretical conclusions. What is good law is not therefore true dogma."[28]

Murray's views were confined to theological journals and Roman Catholic audiences but received much closer inspection than Al Smith's affirmation of an Americanist faith that circulated among the nation's magazine readers. Joseph Fenton and Francis Connell, both of whom taught at Catholic University of America, opposed Murray as a departure from received teachings on church and state. Conservatives in the United States sent notice about Murray's ideas to Vatican officials who indicated displeasure to such an extent that his Jesuit superiors compelled him to abandon the subject. John McGreevy includes in his history of Roman Catholicism in the United States an account of a vivid image of Murray sorting through the books on his shelves: ones "on church-state issues would go back to the seminary library; only books on other topics could remain."[29] Obviously, interpreting papal statements was a much weightier activity than formulating the personal convictions of presidential candidates.

Even so, the clash between Blanshard's suspicions of Roman Catholic antimodernism and Murray's appropriation of Enlightenment politics did little to slow down the assimilation of Roman Catholics in the United States. Part of what contributed to the "normalization" of Roman Catholicism was the support various church leaders gave to the civil rights movement. John A. Ryan, a prominent voice since the 1920s on welfare and the economy, lent his moral authority to early efforts to dismantle racial segregation. Roman Catholics also turned out in force after World War II in opposition to communism, which in the context of the Cold War made the Roman Church look much less authoritarian than it had to those inclined to agree with Blanshard-style anti-Catholicism. A final aspect in the Americanization of the church in the United States was the possibility of articulating arguments like those of Murray. Although he was by no means confrontational, Murray's willingness to express ideas that were critical of the church's inveterate opposition to modernity signaled an intellectual climate that reflected an American church increasingly independent from the hierarchy. Whether the ideas were the chicken or suburbanization was the egg, 1950s Roman Catholicism in the United States was entering a phase in which the moorings of ethnicity, ghetto parishes, and forceful priests and bishops were no longer secure. Charles Morris described it this way:

> Emancipated Catholics chuckled at, were embarrassed by, or openly ridiculed the largely Irish Catholic folkways that still permeated their Church. Parallel Catholic professional organizations, like Catholic medical societies and teachers' guilds, began to be abandoned by their members, or to play down their Catholic affiliation. The *American Catholic Sociological Review* changed its name to *Sociological Analysis.* Upwardly mobile parents did not scruple to choose a public school for their kids if it seemed educationally superior. Bright college-bound Catholics could figure out that Fordham or Boston College did not open the same doors as Harvard.[30]

Paul Blanshard had little to worry about.

2

PUBLIC DUTY, PRIVATE FAITH

As much as Paul Blanshard considered Roman Catholics in the United States a threat, church officials had real reasons to be concerned about Blanshard and the anti-Catholic nerve he apparently hit. The writer for the *Nation* followed up *American Freedom and Catholic Power* with *Communism, Democracy, and Catholic Power* (1951), a book that played on Cold War fears in its comparisons of the Vatican's tools of authoritarianism to the Kremlin's. Chapter by chapter, Blanshard covered the Vatican's and the Kremlin's "structure of power," "thought control," and "management of truth."[1] Blanshard tapped American fears that flared in movies such as *Invasion of the Body Snatchers* (1956) even as he prepared the way for Dan Brown of *Da Vinci Code* fame. At the same time, Blanshard was the object of the Vatican's attention. Already in 1950 Bishop Martin J. O'Connor, rector of the North American College in Rome, requested a meeting with Pope Pius XII to discuss Blanshard's attacks. Meanwhile, the apostolic delegate to the United States, Cardinal Amleto Cicognani, discussed with the general secretary of the National Catholic Welfare

Conference (in effect, the deliberative body of the U.S. bishops) the possibility of forming a committee to respond to the recent spate of anti-Catholicism. The idea was to assemble a political scientist, a theologian, and a philosopher to answer the charges of anti-Americanism. John Courtney Murray's name surfaced as a potential contributor. One of Cardinal Cicognani's advisers mentioned specific doubts about Murray's judgment. "He may be a good scholar but needs watching."[2]

So alarming was Blanshard's case that even Roman Catholics on different sides of the Americanist controversy lined up against him. Murray himself objected to Blanshard if only because he thought possible a harmonization of papal teaching and Anglo-American constitutionalism, a position that Blanshard never considered. But one of Murray's fiercest critics from inside the church, Francis J. Connell, also took exception to Blanshard. His objections had less to do with defending either modern politics or church authority than with accuracy. Connell thought that Blanshard had baited and switched readers. Instead of objecting to Roman Catholic teaching on church and state, Blanshard had opposed Roman Catholicism for claiming to possess the one true religion. The American liberal had also shown bias against the church's ethical teaching, from contraception to divorce. In Murray's case, the Jesuit's opposition to Blanshard could not make up for fundamental defects that placed the Jesuit theologian outside the good graces of Vatican and Jesuit officials. According to Connell, "It has always been taught by the Catholic Church that civil rulers in their official capacity, as well as private individuals, are subject to the authority of Jesus Christ, and have been commanded by Him to recognize His one true Church." As a result, all governments should defer to the church and, according to Pope Leo XIII, "show special favor to the Catholic Church." Instead of twisting himself in knots trying to harmonize Rome's views with political liberalism, Connell recommended that figures such as Murray devote his energies to expounding on church teaching. "If all priests fulfilled their duty . . . there would be three times as many converts in the United States." But if Murray persisted in defending the American form of government, he "should be admonished to be silent, at least until the Holy See has given a decision."[3]

That determination came indirectly when in 1958 Pope Pius XII died and Murray became an adviser to another Roman Catholic presidential candidate. A harmonic convergence of historic proportions occurred during the summer and fall of that consequential year. First, Murray tried to explain a Roman Catholic reading of the U.S. Constitution's First Amendment as a positive historical development for *Civiltà Cattolica*, the premier journal of the Jesuits. Second, his explanation was part of a reply to Sen. John F. Kennedy's request for assistance on church-state questions as he prepared to run for the 1960 Democratic nomination for the presidency. Third, the bishops in the United States were hoping to reach a consensus on the relationship between church and state both to resolve questions surrounding Murray and in response to Blanshard's anti-Catholicism. Finally, on October 8, 1958, Pius XII died and the College of Cardinals elected Cardinal Angelo Roncalli, John XXIII. The change in the papacy set a different tone for the church worldwide. Bishops who had formerly been close to the papacy no longer had easy access. Furthermore, within months of his inauguration as pope, John XXIII called for a council of bishops whose responsibility would be to update the Roman Catholic Church in relation to the modern world.

This was the immediate backdrop for Kennedy's campaign for the presidency. Not only were bishops and cardinals debating the nature of America's political system. Once again a Roman Catholic layman was having to explain how he understood his faith in relation to his duties as a public servant. With these developments Americanism began to lose its stigma as a heresy even while setting into motion questions about Roman Catholic identity. What would an ancient faith and set of institutions such as Roman Catholicism look like once adapted to modern society and politics?

The Making of a Roman Catholic President

John F. Kennedy's experience of Roman Catholicism was about as different from Al Smith's as church life in the United States made possible. Unlike Smith, who grew up in an Irish American working-class family in gritty urban conditions and attended parochial schools, Kennedy was the son of wealthy Irish Americans who moved from Boston to suburban New York (while maintaining a New England presence on Cape Cod) and sent their son to an elite WASP prep school. Indeed, while Smith never finished high school, Kennedy, though an average student, graduated from the Choate School in prosperous Wallingford, Connecticut, on his way to Harvard University. If Al Smith's parents could not imagine—let alone dream of—circumstances of privilege that would allow an Irish American access to the Yankee's elite institutions, Kennedy's parents, Joe and Rose, had little empathy with the ethnic solidarity and religious devotion that informed New York City's Lower East Side. In fact, Joe Kennedy's decision to relocate the family from Brookline to Riverdale, New York, owed precisely to a desire to shield his children from the prejudices that informed typical ethnic parishes.

Rose Kennedy, the future president's mother, was the devout member of the marriage. A graduate of Boston's Convent of the Sacred Heart, Rose experienced a relatively sheltered life before she was married to Joe, whom she had met in 1906 (when they were teenagers) and married eight years later. Although Joe's womanizing was an obvious departure from church teaching, Rose and her husband differed in more ways than marital fidelity. Her piety was conventional, while Joe defied most constraints. One observer of the family remembered that Rose "organized and supervised the large family with the institutional efficiency she had learned from the Ursuline nuns of the Sacred Heart Academy." She demanded from her children "strict adherence to domestic routines and an idealistic dedication to the doctrines of the Roman Catholic Church."[4] Without reinforcement from Joe, the Kennedy children did not always conform to Rose's wishes. Jack (John F.) followed his father's path of sexual exploits. The combination of Rose's devotion and Joe's conduct left the sons (if not all the children) with an existential conflict seemingly impossible to resolve. Attending Mass weekly was part of the family routine. Joe required the boys to "go through all the motions of proper Roman Catholics." At the same time, by his example Joe taught his sons that "real men were profane, aggressive, and ruthless." As Thomas Reeves observes, this set an example of outward religious conformity and private rule breaking: "Lechery . . . would be a way of life for the Kennedy males. And in politics they would do what it took to win."[5]

Aside from whatever piety Kennedy absorbed at home, he did attend a private church school for the seventh grade. Canterbury School in New Milford, Connecticut, had all the marks of a WASP institution because its graduates—roughly nine per teacher—typically went on to an Ivy League college. Kennedy's speechwriter, Theodore C. Sorensen, popularized the story of one episode at Canterbury where Jack heard a missionary at daily Mass talk about evangelism in India, "one of the most interesting" Kennedy had ever heard. For Sorensen, Kennedy's reaction was indicative of a "desire to improve" the world. The speechwriter was also aware of his boss's desire to enjoy the world. On the one hand, one of Kennedy's Choate roommates remembered Jack saying his "prayers on his knees every night before going to bed." On the other hand, Kennedy was loath to resist temptations of the flesh. In one Cambridge letter to a friend he wrote, "We are having one hell of a fine time." Kennedy added, "I am now known as a 'Play-boy.'" His classmate, John Kenneth Galbraith, confirmed that impression. He remembered Kennedy as "handsome . . . gregarious, given to various amusements, much devoted to social life and affectionately and diversely to women."[6]

Biographers also record incidents from Kennedy's life when questions of faith surfaced in his self-understanding. For instance, in 1939, while his father was the U.S. ambassador to the United Kingdom, the younger Kennedy gained some awareness of the emerging European conflict and also traveled to the Middle East. After his return to the United States, Kennedy asked a priest for help in trying to make sense of the world's religions: "I saw the rock where our Lord ascended into Heaven in a cloud, and [in] the same area, I saw the place where Mohammed was carried up to Heaven on a white horse, and Mohammed has a big following and Christ has a big following, and why do you think we should believe Christ any more than Mohammed?"[7] The priest, according to Robert Dallek, responded that Kennedy needed to receive instruction in the faith as soon as possible lest he become an atheist.

Despite such doubts, Kennedy was outwardly and conventionally pious. While an undergraduate at Harvard and making plans to attend Mass on one of the church's holy days, a peer asked Kennedy why he continued to observe the faith when his social antics suggested a lack of religious seriousness. Kennedy explained, "This is one of the things I do for my father. The rest I do for myself." The conflict between familial obligations and personal interests flared again soon after Kennedy entered the military and struck up a relationship with Inga Arvad, a Danish columnist suspected of espionage for the Nazis. For a brief time during this affair some feared the couple might wed, especially if the Kennedy clan could secure an annulment of Inga's two previous marriages. Of course, that was not what Joe or Rose wanted. In fact, Joe likely arranged both for the young Kennedy's transfer from Washington, D.C., to Charleston and for Inga to end the romance. But Jack contemplated revenge by threatening to teach a Bible class in South Carolina, an activity that would look "un-Catholic." In Kennedy's correspondence with Rose about faith, he wondered if "good works [don't] come under our obligations to the Catholic Church." "We're not a completely ritualistic, formalistic, hierarchical structure," he added, "in which the Word, the truth, must only come down from the very top—a structure that allows for no individual interpretation." Or, he asked, "are we?"[8]

However Kennedy reconciled his doubts, observers and colleagues saw little evidence of such spiritual struggle. Sorenson remembered that Kennedy did not "care a whit for theology" even while refusing to "downgrade" his "Catholic faith" or conceal his church attendance. Clergy, who had their own incentives for assessing Kennedy, told a different story. A priest from Middleburg, Virginia, claimed that Kennedy "displayed a remarkable awareness of the finer points of Catholic dogma." Cardinal Richard Cushing, archbishop of Boston, saw in Kennedy a "grace of style," "boundless courage," "patient suffering," "self-assurance," and personal warmth indicative of a faith "firmly rooted in God." Even a Southern Baptist congressman from Arkansas, Brooks Hays, described Kennedy as a "devout Christian whose dedication to the work of Our Lord is beyond challenge."[9]

Once Kennedy found a footing in American politics and took aim at the White House, his bona fides as a Roman Catholic would receive their most demanding test. His calculations had started as early as 1956 when advisers and staff of Kennedy, then a U.S. senator from Massachusetts, assessed the value of Roman Catholic candidates for the Democratic Party. Sorenson had produced a memo, released through Democratic Party officials, that showed how powerful the Roman Catholic vote was despite being split between the major parties. It was concentrated in fourteen states that accounted for 261 electoral votes. Sorenson's strategy was to unseat the Republican president, Dwight Eisenhower, but his ulterior motive was to help Adlai Stevenson recognize the value of selecting Kennedy as his vice-presidential candidate.[10] That plan failed once Stevenson let the delegates to the 1956 Democratic Convention determine his running mate. The selection turned out to be Estes Kefauver, a U.S. senator and Southern Baptist from Tennessee.

Kennedy's awareness of the religious question was responsible in part for his efforts three years later, before announcing his candidacy for the presidency, to meet with Protestants and hear objections to a Roman Catholic occupying the White House. The standard fears among Protestants about Roman Catholics in America were funding for parochial schools, the church's authority over the laity (especially politicians), segregating children into parochial instead of public schools, refusing to use birth control, and establishing diplomatic relations between the United States and the Vatican. On April 15, 1959, thanks to back channels opened up by meetings with G. Bromley Oxnam, a prominent bishop in the Methodist Episcopal Church, Kennedy met with fifty-one bishops of the largest Protestant denomination in the United States. *Life* and *Time* magazines covered the gathering. The former's headline indicated that the Methodists had given Kennedy a "fair grade." *Time* described the event as Daniel entering the lions' den and included comments both hostile and favorable from the Methodist clergy. The potential candidate emphasized his support for a strict separation of church and state. This included opposition to funding for parochial schools and to the creation of a U.S. embassy to the Vatican. In an interview with *Look* magazine that appeared in the spring, Kennedy insisted, "I believe as Senator that the separation of church and state is fundamental to our American concept and heritage and should remain so." In the same piece, he also stated in language intended to reassure Protestants, federal funds for parochial and private schools was "unconstitutional." Kennedy's outreach to non-Catholics also included a meeting with the president of the Church of Jesus Christ of Latter-day Saints and two talks in Salt Lake City during that visit. The senator praised Mormons for their "edifying" work and "devotion to principle," which constituted "a firm bulwark against . . . the godless enemies of western and Christian civilizations."[11] Kennedy's courting of Protestants and Mormons created some discomfort for Roman Catholics. *America* magazine, an organ of the Jesuits, faulted Kennedy for trying to appease bigots and reminded readers that religious obligations took precedence over public office. Cardinal Richard Cushing, Kennedy's archbishop in Boston, came to the rescue by reassuring Roman Catholics that

Kennedy had a proven track record of maintaining his faith and serving the public. The question of reconciling conscience and political loyalty was not an issue.

Overcoming believers' worries was one thing, but securing the Democratic nomination required an entirely different set of calculations. The first challenge for the senator from Massachusetts was whether to enter the Wisconsin primary and run against Hubert Humphrey, the senator from Minnesota, or to try to secure the nomination at the national convention, a process that still depended heavily on securing the favor of party bosses. Although the nominating convention would still be the forum for choosing the final ticket, entering and winning state primaries could indicate electability. For Kennedy, who was young (forty-three) and could not be pigeonholed on a variety of issues, proving his ability to attract voters was important. Especially pressing was his religious identity. The candidacy of Al Smith was not so distant that leading Democrats could afford to ignore anti-Catholicism. What party leaders likely did not consider—especially Humphrey's advisers—was Kennedy's wealth. If having a strong organization for state primaries was important for success, money was the grease that made the political machine hum. In 1959, for instance, Joe Kennedy arranged for the purchase of a campaign plane for $385,000, a mode of transportation much faster than a bus or car, and easier on the candidate's bad back. Despite such resources and organizational heft in key states, Kennedy failed to attract endorsements. Some on Capitol Hill regarded him as a wealthy ladies' man. By the spring of 1960 he had endorsements from only two U.S. senators—Henry Jackson and Edmund Muskie.

The first Democratic primary in Wisconsin revealed the strengths of Kennedy's organization. On the one hand, his team outmaneuvered Humphrey's at practically every stop. For instance, while Kennedy had campaign offices in eight of the state's ten congressional districts, Humphrey had an inefficient headquarters in Milwaukee and a volunteer-run office in Madison, with staff from his home state organizing support in those parts of Wisconsin closest to the Minnesota border. On the other hand, Kennedy's team understood the importance of the press and made access to the candidate along with publicity of his policies a top priority. Humphrey became frustrated by journalists' fawning over the young senator and complained, "We're not in American politics to select a lead star for

Hollywood drama." The Minnesotan also sounded envious of Kennedy's wealth when he let loose with, "Mink never wore so well."[12]

The next primary was West Virginia where the question of Kennedy's religion emerged explicitly. But rather than hurting Kennedy's candidacy or being a topic that Humphrey interjected to damage his opponent, the Kennedy campaign used the issue to its advantage and secured a relatively easy victory. Advance work by the Kennedy campaign revealed that Al Smith had won the 1928 primary in West Virginia and that anti-Catholicism was much less pronounced because a majority of the state's residents had no religion. Advisers also calculated that Roman Catholic voters might be more inclined to vote in the primary—and for Kennedy—if the contest generated the sort of intensity associated with personal beliefs. As such, by insisting that he was not *the* Catholic candidate for president, Kennedy identified indirectly with the faith of Roman Catholics while affirming American ideals of religious tolerance. In effect, he raised the specter of anti-Catholic bigotry to appeal to the better angels of non-Catholic voters while also reminding his coreligionists of the prejudice the church had faced.

Humphrey understood precisely what Kennedy was doing. He told one reporter, "Apparently it is perfectly okay for every person of the Catholic faith to vote for Kennedy, but if a Protestant votes for me then he is a bigot."[13] Even so, Kennedy kept using Roman Catholicism to his advantage. In a television interview, a paid broadcast two nights before the vote in West Virginia, Kennedy responded to questions orchestrated by his staff and addressed to him by Franklin D. Roosevelt, Jr. According to the journalist, Theodore H. White, it was "the finest TV broadcast . . . any politician [made]." To one of Roosevelt's questions, the candidate replied: "When any man stands on the steps of the Capitol and takes the oath of office of President, he is swearing to support the separation of church and state; he puts one hand on the Bible and raises the other hand to God as he takes the oath. And if he breaks his oath, he is not only committing a crime against the Constitution, for which the Congress can impeach him—and should impeach him—but he is committing a sin against God." At that point, Kennedy raised his hand from an imaginary Bible to stress the stakes of this oath: "A sin against God, for he has sworn on the Bible." White concluded that Humphrey was "powerless" against this logic and recalled that the Kennedy campaign "savagely" increased the pressure on the religious question.[14] The journalist apparently saw no inconsistency in using an icon of Protestant devotion to swear allegiance to the laws of a secular state.

As it turned out, Kennedy hardly needed to invoke God to defeat Humphrey in West Virginia. Again, the Kennedy campaign showed a superior operation and deluged the state with advertising, publicity, and staff, all the product of a better organization and more money. Several of Humphrey's backers stopped contributing, and at one point he was forced to write a personal check for a $750 television advertisement. Estimates vary over what Kennedy spent for the West Virginia primary—from $300,000 to $4 million. Humphrey could muster only $30,000. But to ensure his victory, Kennedy also used Franklin Delano Roosevelt, Jr.—despite the latter's reluctance—to deliver the false charge that Humphrey had dodged the draft during World War II. Kennedy himself later disavowed the accusation, but it raised questions in voters' minds about Humphrey's patriotism. It also gave Humphrey a grudge against the Kennedys that he nursed the rest of his career. In the end, Kennedy defeated Humphrey 236,510 to 152,187 and eliminated his chief rival from the race. Two more opponents, Lyndon Baines Johnson and Adlai Stevenson, surfaced in weeks before the Democratic national convention, which met in Los Angeles and still allowed the delegates to choose their own candidate. Despite stiff opposition from a "stop Kennedy" movement in Los Angeles that had more to do with power in the Democratic Party than the Massachusetts senator's ties to the Roman Catholic Church, Kennedy secured the nomination on the first ballot with 52 percent of the vote.

The Roman Catholic to Overcome Anti-Catholicism

During the fall race against Richard M. Nixon, the Republican nominee for president, religion surfaced not through party or campaign operatives but from grassroots efforts within the electorate. Billy Graham was a highly publicized and popular revivalist who in 1960 was still making his way onto the world stage. In the summer of 1960 he had finished preaching in Europe and led a gathering of Protestant clergy who convened in Montreux, Switzerland, to strategize about the presidential campaign. The group leaned heavily evangelical Protestant since that was Graham's background, but it included as well such notable mainline pastors as Norman Vincent Peale, a Manhattan preacher and best-selling author, and Daniel Poling, an associate of Peale's at Marble Collegiate Church. Poling was the father of Clark Poling, one of the famous Four Chaplains who died in 1943 during an extraordinary act of heroism that involved giving up their own life jackets to soldiers on the army transport ship the SS *Dorchester* (about one-quarter of the ship's nine hundred passengers survived). Graham's closest allies at the meeting may have been ambivalent about the mainline Protestant churches, but politically the two wings of Anglo-American Protestantism had always had much in common, from support for public schools to Prohibition and worries about Roman Catholic power. A firm supporter of Nixon, Graham intuited that Kennedy would receive 100 percent of the Roman Catholic vote. Polls he read indicated that 76 percent of Protestant pastors in the United States favored Nixon. The reason for the meeting by Lake Geneva was to increase Protestant support for the Republican nominee. In a letter to Nixon after the meeting, Graham wrote, "I have just written a letter to my mailing list of two million American families, urging them to organize their Sunday school classes and churches to get out the vote."[15]

Peale may have led some to think that the emerging opposition to Kennedy went deep in mainline Protestant circles, but the anti-Catholic plot that surfaced during the summer of 1960 had born-again Protestant fingerprints all over it. Peale did allow for evangelicals to coordinate their activities with the Protestant and Other Americans United for Separation of Church and State, an organization formed in 1947 by prominent figures in mainline Protestant institutions. Its chief aim was to organize opposition to public funding for parochial schools. Still, the most vocal critics of a Roman Catholic president were evangelicals. Earlier that year, the National Association of Evangelicals had adopted a set of resolutions on "Roman Catholicism and the President of the United States" that stressed the imperative for all candidates to affirm the separation of church and state. This was especially true for Roman Catholic candidates because "the real source of unrest in respect to church-state separation is the total lack of any convincing commitment of the Roman Catholic Church to the principle of church-state separation, which could only come from the highest authority of that organization and could only be evidenced by the realignment of Catholic policy in those countries where Catholicism is now the established religion." The resolutions included the doubt that any Roman Catholic president "could resist fully the pressures of the ecclesiastical hierarchy."[16]

Evangelical Protestants kept the pressure on Kennedy at the September 7, 1960, meeting in Washington, D.C., sponsored by the National Conference of Citizens for Religious Freedom. Prominent among the speakers was Harold J. Ockenga, a national spokesman thanks to his status as pastor of Park Street Church in Boston and president of Fuller Theological Seminary in California. His text was Matthew 22:21, where Jesus tells the Pharisees to "render unto Caesar the things that are Caesar's and to God the things that are God's," a classic text for asserting church-state separation. Though a mile apart in doctrine from the Unitarian anti-Catholic Paul Blanshard, Ockenga also regarded Roman Catholicism as a threat to the nation. As some perceived it, the church was a monolith with well-defined teaching about politics from which neither clergy nor lay members could dissent. Like Blanshard, Ockenga also played on fears that Roman Catholics, by virtue of their teaching on reproduction, would become the majority group in the United States. The possibility of a Roman Catholic president raised a specter that had haunted American Protestants going all the way back to Lyman Beecher, another pastor at Park Street Church, 125 years before Ockenga: "Are we moving into an era of Roman Catholic domination in America? . . . If and when this becomes a fact, will the principle of Roman Catholic political theory be applied? Will there be a denial of rights, freedom and privileges for non-Roman Catholics? If so, should we aid and abet this situation by electing a president who has more power to advance such a goal than any other person?"[17] Ockenga's round of questions was not rhetorical.

Kennedy's campaign, of course, needed to address Protestant worries, but the electoral college allowed the candidate to identify regions of the country where evangelical anti-Catholicism could do the most damage. Because his running mate, Johnson, was from Texas and that state itself was a Democratic stronghold with a large number of electoral votes, Kennedy was particularly sensitive to the tactics of Texan Protestants. Texas had voted for Democrats consistently except in 1928, when Al Smith was on the ballot, and more recently the state had voted for Dwight Eisenhower, a reason for putting Johnson on the ticket. As early as July 21, 1960, the Kennedy campaign received a memo that indicated the emergence of concerted opposition by Dallas Protestant ministers. W. A. Criswell, pastor of Dallas's First Baptist Church, a congregation with twelve thousand members, had denounced Kennedy publicly, and rumors suggested members would be active in efforts to prevent Kennedy's election. In Tennessee journalists reported on similar opposition to the Democrat from Protestant ministers. As was the case for Smith, the South, a Democratic stronghold, was going to be pivotal for Kennedy. That meant Kennedy needed to address religion directly. According to one memo from a staffer, "The sooner Kennedy's religion is brought out into the open, the better, and it should be in Texas before the State Convention."[18] One proposal was a press conference. Another was a televised speech.

The campaign wound up with both, a speech and a question-and-answer session after it, in Houston on September 12, 1960, only a few days after Protestants had gathered in Washington, D.C. Speaker of the House Sam Rayburn warned Kennedy that the group was not a body of "ministers" but "politicians." He added, "They hate your guts and they're going to tear you to pieces."[19] Sorensen, a Unitarian, was responsible for assembling a draft of the candidate's talk. He relied on previous speeches and answers to the press in published interviews. Sorensen also consulted John Courtney Murray, a man who was ambivalent about Kennedy, had voted twice for Eisenhower, and had little sympathy for the Democrats. But Murray was at least willing to hear Sorensen read one paragraph from Kennedy's speech and comment. The reason had as much to do with Murray's distaste for the anti-Catholic bigotry of Protestants as it did with fellow feeling for Kennedy. His advice for Sorensen was to distinguish between faith and morals on the one side and public policy on the other. The church's bishops had legitimate authority to instruct on the former, but the Vatican had no say on the latter.

Kennedy's speech to the Greater Houston Ministerial Association was, though about a third of the length, remarkably similar to Al Smith's 1927 article for the *Atlantic Monthly*. The issues that had dogged Smith were still the ones the 1960 nominee felt compelled to address. Consequently, Kennedy reaffirmed statements he had been making for at least two years. Only a minute or so into the speech he asserted, "I believe in an America where the separation of church and state is absolute." "Absolute" was a strong word that conjured up older usages such as royal absolutism. But for Kennedy, liberalism was now absolute and involved no Roman

Catholic prelate telling the president how to act, or Protestant ministers telling church members how to vote. It also meant that "no church or church school is granted any public funds or political preference; and . . . no man is denied public office merely because his religion differs from the president who might appoint him or the people who might elect him."[20] The only issue that Kennedy failed to mention was the appointment of a U.S. ambassador to the Vatican.

The general tenor of Kennedy's remarks, however, departed from Smith, who had primarily argued that serving as a public official and belonging to the Roman Catholic Church were not at odds (and had never dawned on him or most Progressive-era Roman Catholics). For Kennedy, his faith was a private matter and would not inform his judgments as president. He insisted that he was not a Roman Catholic running for office but the Democratic Party's nominee: "I do not speak for my church on public matters, and the church does not speak for me." The same separation of religion and public policy would guide his deliberations in the White House: "Whatever issue may come before me as president—on birth control, divorce, censorship, gambling or any other subject—I will make my decision in accordance with these views, in accordance with what my conscience tells me to be the national interest, and without regard to outside religious pressures or dictates." Kennedy's own posture as religiously neutral was also his hope for the United States. Indeed, his Houston speech articulated one of the first explicitly secular visions of American identity— that it came from a Roman Catholic was telling: "I believe in an America that is officially neither Catholic, Protestant nor Jewish; where no public official either requests or accepts instructions on public policy from the Pope, the National Council of Churches or any other ecclesiastical source; where no religious body seeks to impose its will directly or indirectly upon the general populace or the public acts of its officials; and where religious liberty is so indivisible that an act against one church is treated as an act against all." That outlook was likely a reason for Murray's wariness of Kennedy and some of the muttering among bishops about the nominee's failure to represent the church's views fairly.

At the same time, Kennedy's appeal to history suggested an understanding of personal identity that shared much with the civil rights movement. Just as Martin Luther King, Jr., would inspire a national audience during the summer of 1963 with his "I Have a Dream" speech, so Kennedy foreshadowed King's appeal to a color-blind and creed-ignorant United States. Not only did King close with the hope that "black men and white men, Jews and Gentiles, Protestants and Catholics," all as "God's children," could sing together, "Free, at last," but he also had a dream that one day black children would belong to a "nation where they will not be judged by the color of their skin but by the content of their character."[21] So Kennedy appealed to a national identity that looked beyond church membership to participation in the life of the country. The nation for which Americans like himself had fought, from the United States' earliest days to its recent involvement in World War II, stood for the ideals affirmed in "the Constitution, the Bill of Rights and the Virginia Statute of Religious Freedom," the latter capturing a struggle that had included colonial Baptists on the front lines.

Kennedy also appealed to locals as he circled the history of religious freedom by mentioning the Alamo. This was a place where Bowies and Crocketts had fought side by side with Baileys and Careys. In that contest for Texan independence, no one knew whether the Americans were "Catholic or not, for there was no religious test at the Alamo." The same was true for Roman Catholics serving in World War II, in which the candidate had served in the South Pacific and his brother "had died in Europe." "No one suggested then that we may have had a 'divided loyalty,'" Kennedy asserted, "that we did 'not believe in liberty,' or that we belonged to a disloyal group that threatened the 'freedoms for which our forefathers died.'" Actually, Kennedy knew that Americans such as Paul Blanshard had questioned Roman Catholic patriotism even after the display of national service from church members during the war. But the Democratic nominee also understood that his record of military service would appeal to American Protestants.

In the question-and-answer session that followed Kennedy's eleven-minute speech, the candidate fielded queries designed to catch him in the gap between his own freedom and the authority of the church's hierarchy. When asked if he would submit his ideas about church and state to Cardinal Cushing in hopes of having the Boston archbishop forward them to the Vatican, Kennedy replied that no ecclesiastical authority had the power to instruct him "in the sphere of my public responsibility as an elected official." He added that he believed he spoke on this point for "American Catholics from one end of the country to the other." Another question included a detailed set of statements, similar to Paul Blanshard's, on the authority of the magisterium to guide lay Roman Catholics and about the unity of church and state. Kennedy's answer conceded that a priest or bishop was responsible to guide a Roman Catholic in matters of faith and morals, just as "any Baptist minister or Congregationalist minister has the right and duty to guide his flock." But in public matters, Kennedy believed, his bishops had no power over him. One last question came from a Presbyterian pastor who pressed Kennedy on whether as president he would resign over a matter that compromised his conscience. The specific dilemmas the pastor posed were the separation of church and state, religious toleration, and freedom of conscience, all topics condemned in Pope Pius IX's *Syllabus of Errors*. The question might have been poignant had the Presbyterian framed it in the context of using nuclear weapons or segregationist public policy. But because these were subjects the candidate had already addressed, all he could do was affirm his commitment to church-state separation, freedom for all religious groups in the United States, and the importance of protecting a person's conscience.[22] After explaining again that his understanding of Roman Catholicism's claim on him as a public official was common among the rank and file of Roman Catholic politicians in the United States, he departed Houston's Rice Hotel for another stop on his campaign.

The event in Houston was the high point for Roman Catholicism in the Kennedy-Nixon contest, even though the subject did not go away entirely. In the four televised debates that took place between September 26 and October 21, the issue of anti-Catholicism came up only once in connection with a question to Kennedy about the Ku Klux Klan and how the candidate "felt" about such bigotry. Kennedy insisted that he had never sensed or suggested that Nixon had any sympathy with the Klan or its methods. Nixon concurred and outdid Kennedy in asserting that religion should have no role in the selection of a president. "We can't settle for anything but the best," Nixon explained, and "that means that we can't have any test of religion." Having said that, the Republican candidate could not help himself when in the final debate he did bring up the nation's religious identity: "And so I say in conclusion, keep America's faith strong. See that the young people of America, particularly, have faith in the ideals of freedom and faith in God, which distinguishes us from the atheistic materialists who oppose us."[23] Of course, in the anxiety-rife Cold

War days where America's civil religion was a balm against the Soviet Union's godlessness, many Americans likely regarded the nation's faith in generically Protestant terms. But Nixon's invocation of the nation's religion here was boilerplate political rhetoric that Kennedy himself could also employ (and would as president). As the candidates went into the final weeks of the campaign, Kennedy had according to the polls as much as an eight-point lead, which Nixon was diminishing despite not appearing as telegenic as his competitor.

The Kennedy Presidency

After election commissions tallied the results and pollsters refined their data, the close contest between Nixon and Kennedy—the closest popular-vote margin of the twentieth century—turned on the religious question. Protestants who attended church regularly and black Protestants provided tepid support at best. Fifty percent of black Protestants voted for Kennedy, the lowest figure for a Democratic candidate in elections between 1948 and 1984. But on the whole, Kennedy received 34 percent of the white Protestant vote, virtually the same level of support that Adlai Stevenson had received in the 1956 election. The difference for Kennedy was the Roman Catholic vote. He received 83 percent of Roman Catholic votes compared to Stevenson's 45 percent in 1956. In the electoral college the consequences were decisive. Not only did Kennedy manage to hold on to the seven states (all southern except for Missouri) that Stevenson had won in 1956, but he added fourteen others with significant Roman Catholic populations—including New York, Pennsylvania, Massachusetts, Rhode Island, and Louisiana. Kennedy even won in Texas. Although Roman Catholics had begun after World War II to identify with the Republican Party, as the victories of Dwight Eisenhower indicated, the hint of anti-Catholic bigotry that surrounded Kennedy's campaign, both in the primaries and then in the national contest, was an important factor in rallying Roman Catholic voters to help elect the first Roman Catholic president. The solidarity that came with the immigrant experience, as well as the ethnic parish and neighborhood, was hard to shake even as Roman Catholics were assimilating by the American middle-class means of suburban homes and college education.

As president, Kennedy did more to nurture the assimilation of Roman Catholics to partisan politics than he did to buttress religious solidarity. In fact, debates over domestic and foreign policy heightened during the Kennedy administration would draw the lines that fragmented American Christians for the next forty years and provided the rationale for Roman Catholics to self-identify as political conservatives. The first issue was civil rights for African Americans, a question that placed moral idealism side by side with constitutional realities. On the one hand, Kennedy took steps to advance blacks in federal positions and employed the Justice Department to prosecute violations of voting rights—more than any previous president. On the other hand, critics faulted the Kennedy administration for not moving more quickly on civil rights, a reluctance that owed to the Democratic Party's electoral strength in the South and the president's narrow victory over Nixon.

The second divisive matter was the Cold War–inspired arms race with the Soviet Union. Kennedy's inaugural and first years of diplomacy took a hard line with the Soviets to the point of supporting the 1961 Bay of Pigs invasion in Cuba and staring down Nikita Khrushchev in 1962 during the Cuban Missile Crisis. The president received support in his opposition to communism in 1961 even from Pope John XXIII, whose encyclical, *Mater et magistra*, tapped Roman Catholicism's historic and deep anticommunism. At the same time, opposition to the arms race surfaced among Roman Catholics in the United States, which tempered the church's anticommunist predilections. After the sobering events of 1961 and 1962, Kennedy pressed for a treaty with the Soviets on testing nuclear weapons, signed in the summer of 1963, which also seemed to coincide with John XXIII's January 1963 encyclical, *Pacem in terris*, which questioned the nuclear arms race (see chapter 3).

The last major item of debate during the Kennedy years that divided Christians was contraception. Initially, the president had followed the Eisenhower administration in forbidding population control assistance to other countries. But Kennedy's administration changed course, first surreptitiously and then publicly by 1963, when it cooperated with the United Nations in support for a birth control assistance program. Here the president received practically no church support. Even so, the debates surrounding civil rights, anticommunism, and sexual reproduction that hounded Kennedy's time in office wound up defining in uncanny ways the culture wars that would divide Democrats and Republicans for the rest of the century.

President Kennedy also contributed to later partisanship with his own construction of American exceptionalism, a theme that Republicans would later exploit to attract Roman Catholic voters. The president's inaugural address itself, delivered on January 20, 1961, rendered the American founding in planetary proportions: "The same revolutionary beliefs for which our forebears fought are still at issue around the globe." The beliefs that "rights of man come not from the generosity of the state but from the hand of God" still undergirded the nation's mission "at home and around the world." That commitment contained a threat, one that came in one of the speech's most familiar refrains, namely, an announcement to "every nation" that Americans would "pay any price, bear any burden, meet any hardship, support any friend, oppose any foe to assure the survival and success of liberty." Less familiar perhaps was Kennedy's conclusion, which expressed the nation's civil religion with as much gusto as any of his Protestant predecessors in the White House: "With a good conscience our only sure reward, with history the final judge of our deeds, let us go forth to lead the land we love, asking His blessing and His help, but knowing that here on earth God's work must truly be our own."[24] That may have been standard fare for other presidents, but for a Roman Catholic who had signaled he would keep his beliefs private, Kennedy was also indicating he would not dissent from the American civil religion that had informed the nation's foreign policy at least since the Spanish-American War.

Another revealing line in that inaugural address was Kennedy's conception of the United States as the light of the world, a biblical image that would have consoled the president's Puritan forebears from Massachusetts. The nation's commitment to defending freedom was one to which Kennedy himself was devoted. In fact, "the energy, the faith, the devotion which we bring to this endeavor will light our country and all who serve it—and the glow from that fire can truly light the world." Those words sounded a lot like the language of "a city upon a hill," the phrase from Christ's so-called Sermon on the Mount that John Winthrop, the first governor of Massachusetts Bay Colony, had invoked to inspire the first Puritan colonists. The similarities were not coincidental because only eleven days earlier, in his farewell speech to the General Court of Massachusetts, also known as "City upon a Hill," Kennedy had connected the dots from Jesus and Winthrop to modern America. The path that led him to the Puritans was an acknowledgment of the nation's debt to Massachusetts's founders. "No man about to enter high office in this country can ever be unmindful of the contribution this state has made to our national greatness," Kennedy asserted. Massachusetts's "leaders have shaped our destiny long before the great republic was born," its principles "have guided our footsteps," its "democratic institutions—including this historic body—have served as beacon lights for other nations as well as our sister states." But Kennedy's tie to the Puritans, as uncanny as that might be for a Bostonian of Irish Roman Catholic descent, went even deeper. The president-elect explained that Winthrop had supplied him with inspiration as he prepared for the "voyage" of his administration. Kennedy then invoked Winthrop, who in turn had appropriated the Sermon on the Mount—"we shall be as a city upon a hill—the eyes of all people are upon us"—to explain his own calling. "Today the eyes of all people are truly upon us—and our governments, in every branch, at every level, national, state and local, must be as a city upon a hill—constructed and inhabited by men aware of their great trust and their great responsibilities." Kennedy felt as if he were "setting out upon a voyage in 1961 no less hazardous than that undertaken by the Arabella in 1630," "committing ourselves to tasks of statecraft no less awesome than that of governing the Massachusetts Bay Colony, beset as it was then by terror without and disorder within."[25]

Kennedy may have been responsible for divorcing religion from politics as he explained his own personal convictions to Protestant ministers in Houston four months earlier, but he was equally adept at using the Protestant-infused civil religion that informed the nation's self-understanding in foreign affairs. As Richard M. Gamble has carefully demonstrated, the Roman Catholic, at times secularist-sounding President Kennedy deserves credit for launching "the biblical, Puritan metaphor" of the "city upon a hill" into "contemporary American politics and culture." "This powerful symbol, now so closely identified with the populist Right," Gamble explains, "entered modern American politics as an emblem of the internationalist Left." Sorensen, the president's speechwriter, "a half-Jewish, Scandinavian Unitarian from Nebraska, took a full-blooded Irish Catholic from Boston and grafted him into the stock planted and tended for more than 300 years by the Puritan Brahmins."[26] From that moment on, when

U.S. politicians spoke of the nation as a city upon a hill, they invoked Jesus first through John Winthrop and then the first Massachusetts governor through Kennedy. This was an amazing feat, all the more impressive when performed by the United States' first Roman Catholic president.

Americanism Resurrected

The tragic death of President Kennedy in Dallas did not conclude but instead reinvigorated U.S. Roman Catholics' appropriation of national ideals—the very phenomenon that Pope Leo XIII had condemned as the Americanist heresy. The simple and immediate need to dispose of the deceased president's remains provided an occasion for merging national and ecclesiastical ceremonies in ways that firmly identified Kennedy as a Roman Catholic. This was the first nationally televised U.S. state funeral for a deceased president. It was also likely the first time that a majority of the nation's citizens had seen inside a Roman Catholic cathedral or observed a Mass.

Preparations for the service were difficult not simply because family had little time for complex consultations with government and church officials. Because Kennedy was a Roman Catholic, the events on Monday, November 25, 1963, beginning with a public viewing of the casket by foreign dignitaries in the Capitol Rotunda and ending with burial in Arlington National Cemetery, included a Mass at Saint Matthew's Cathedral in Washington, D.C. Those closest to the family, especially Sorensen, had little knowledge of what a funeral Mass involved or the difference between a high and low service. Consultations with Richard Cardinal Cushing, archbishop of Boston and friend of the Kennedy family, and Phillip Hannan, auxiliary bishop of Washington, broke down several times because Sorensen was completely "ignorant" of Roman Catholic liturgy. The speechwriter informed the bishops that the family wanted officials to read the deceased's favorite scripture passages and a few excerpts from presidential speeches. But Cushing had little room to negotiate according to the liturgical rules that then prevailed—this was still before the liturgical revisions that the Second Vatican Council would introduce. To a request for the five absolutions (prayers for pardon at the end of the funeral Mass) to which bishops, cardinals, or Roman Catholic heads of state were entitled

62   *Chapter 2*

(ordinary believers qualified for one absolution), Cushing objected that they would take longer than the Low Mass itself. To a request for secular music in a cathedral, the rules governing Roman Catholic services were also clear—it was impermissible. Meanwhile, Cushing's insistence that he follow the words from "the book on the altar" meant that much of the funeral service would transpire in a language that likely only a few Roman Catholics and Latin instructors understood. Cushing finally relented to the family's request for a reading of Kennedy's favorite biblical texts and quotations from his speeches. He also consoled Sorensen that the family's request for a simple service would be honored. He would not "stretch it out with a long pontifical High Mass" but would bury Kennedy "like a Jesuit," by which he meant in a pine box and with a Low Mass.[27]

Had the casket been constructed of pine, the pallbearers may not have struggled as mightily as they did while carrying the ornate casket up the stairs of Saint Matthew's Cathedral. To add to their challenge, Cardinal Cushing forced the pallbearers to stop while he sprinkled the casket with water and prayed a prayer that the soldier on the back end of the coffin thought would never end. That part of the liturgy came just after the cardinal had welcomed Jacqueline Kennedy to the cathedral, and she, with the cameras following, genuflected to kiss Cushing's hand. This was a gesture that Paul Blanshard had singled out in his book, *American Freedom and Catholic Power*, as inherently anti-American. William Manchester reported that Cushing himself was uncomfortable with such deference because of his own convictions about the separation of church and state but under the circumstances was not about to challenge the grieving widow. The service itself, a formal liturgy in Latin, was no more familiar than Jackie Kennedy's gesture. Arthur Schlesinger later observed that the rituals were "incomprehensible," McGeorge Bundy called Cushing's voice "the most grating" in Christendom, and Lady Bird Johnson called the service "just ceremonial."[28] After the Mass, Bishop Hannan uttered a modified eulogy that more or less complied with liturgical restrictions on such personal reflections. It was basically an antiphonal reading of Kennedy's favorite biblical passages and the president's own affirmations of national ideals—first a reading from the prophet Joel followed by his address to the United Nations, then selections from Joshua and Isaiah he had used in his inaugural address, then an excerpt from the speech he was going to deliver in Dallas before a reading from Ecclesiastes: "The righteousness of our cause must always underlie our strength, for as was written long ago, except the Lord guard the city, the guard watches in vain."[29] The longest section in Hannan's text was the last twelve paragraphs from Kennedy's inaugural address. There, at the end of a Christian service unrecognizable to most American Protestants, came words that had reassured them at the beginning of their first Roman Catholic president's term in office, that their nation was still blessed, special, and under God.

Displays of patriotism and piety such as this one, even a Roman Catholic Mass for the slain president of a predominantly Protestant population, led Robert Bellah to take the first steps in defining civil religion. In an essay that launched academic discussions of the subject, Bellah used Kennedy's inaugural address to assert that alongside the forms of Christian devotion practiced in churches existed "an elaborate and well-institutionalized civil religion in America." Indeed, Kennedy was simply doing what presidents and the nation's officials had done many times before him, although in the voice of a Roman Catholic, that civic faith took on an added poignancy. Bellah explained that Kennedy's inaugural tapped "a theme that lies very deep in the American tradition, namely the obligation, both collective and individual, to carry out God's will on earth." For example, the subtext of the speech was that the United States must be committed to "God's work." Kennedy's was a "very activist and noncontemplative conception of the fundamental religious obligation," one that Protestants had so often voiced before 1960. That it was "enunciated so clearly in the first major statement of the first Catholic president seems to underline how deeply established it is in the American outlook."[30]

The standard objection to civil religion is that it abuses faith, or that it appeals to high ideals for partisan or nationalist ends. One of the initial interpreters of Kennedy, Lawrence H. Fuchs, professor of American civilization at Brandeis University, conceded that the first Roman Catholic president was not a model of his church's piety, or as Cardinal Cushing put it, Kennedy "wore his religion, 'lightly.'" Fuchs also underscored the president's religious detachment by quoting one of his glib retorts to a hostile interlocutor about Roman Catholic teaching on church and state: "There is an old saying in Boston, that we get our religion from Rome and our politics at home, and that is the way most Catholics feel about it."[31] With so little a sense of obligation to integrate his faith and public service, a student of Bellah could well argue that Kennedy was ripe for appropriating the nation's civil religion. Another way of explaining Kennedy's embrace of American civil religion is to argue, as Mark S. Massa has, that Kennedy had to make his faith private in order to win election to the White House. As such, Kennedy functioned for Massa as the first stage of the bold secularization of American politics that would usher in what he called the "naked public square." In fact, Kennedy's speech in Houston "adumbrated a 'wall of separation' between religion and public service that went considerably beyond what might be termed the allaying of bigoted fears." So private did religion become for Kennedy that it possessed "remarkable a-theistic implications for public life and discourse."[32]

Such a conclusion might follow from older social teaching of the Roman Catholic magisterium but could just as easily make sense of at least a century of Americanism deep in the bones of lay Roman Catholics living in the United States. Rather than signaling the privatization of faith or the meanderings of a nominal believer, Kennedy's insistence on Protestant pieties such as church-state separation and American exceptionalism launched a new phase in the American Roman Catholic experience. Americanists had always affirmed the separation of church and state and religious liberty. But lauding the United States for its role in divine plans was a theme that Protestants had used to show that Roman Catholics were less than patriotic; because the church, not the state, was at the center of salvation history, a Roman Catholic church member would be loath to attribute to the United States a mission reserved for the church. But with a Roman Catholic as president endorsing the United States' redemptive mission in the world, Kennedy was crafting and promoting an Americanism that even popes had not considered. In addition to having the church adjust to modern social structures, Kennedy was attributing to America a divine mission once the exclusive possession of the church. No one knew how or if the bishops making plans for the Second Vatican Council in Rome would respond to the latest iteration of Americanism.

3

AMERICANISM FOR
THE GLOBAL CHURCH

The day after John F. Kennedy's assassination, Pope Paul VI issued a statement about "so dastardly a crime." On November 23, 1963, he allowed a television crew into the papal apartments to record his prepared statement, broadcast by ABC. "We are deeply shocked by the sad and tragic news of the killing of the president of the United States of America . . . by the mourning which afflicts a great and civilized country in its head, by the suffering which strikes at Mrs. Kennedy, her children and the family," the pope declared. Paul also expressed concern for the American republic, that the death "of this great statesman may . . . reinforce its moral and civil sentiments, and strengthen its feelings of nobility and concord." He prayed as well that God would use "the sacrifice of John Kennedy . . . to favor the cause he promoted and to help defend the freedom of peoples and peace in the world." On a personal note, the pope recalled his pleasure in receiving the president during a visit to Rome and "having discerned in him great wisdom and high resolution for the good of humanity."[1]

Such words of consolation and approval were hardly surprising given the circumstances, but the synergy between the papacy and the White House during Kennedy's tenure was evident well before the president's tragic death. Kennedy had actually met the man who became Pope Paul, Giovanni Battista Enrico Antonio Maria Montini, while attending with his parents the 1939 coronation of Pius XII. Montini was then one of the officials in the Vatican's secretary of state. But the president's chief interactions with the papacy involved Pope Paul's predecessor, John XXIII, who reigned from 1958 until his death in 1963 and was responsible for calling the Second Vatican Council (1962–65). During the Cuban missile crisis of October 1962, Pope John prevailed on Kennedy and Nikita Khrushchev to accept a compromise that involved the United States lifting its blockade and the Soviets promising to send no more warships to Cuba. Through back channels the Soviets accepted the plan, but Kennedy refused because it left missiles in Cuba.

Events like this nuclear confrontation were partly responsible for John's 1963 encyclical, *Pacem in terris* ("Peace on Earth"), which included a laundry list of causes that people of goodwill should support, among them halting the nuclear arms race. The encyclical spoke for many when it observed that "people live in constant fear lest the storm that every moment threatens should break upon them with dreadful violence." Any sort of "unexpected and unpremeditated act" could set off a conflagration that would result in "appalling destruction and sorrow," not to mention the fallout from nuclear tests that "seriously jeopardize various kinds of life on earth." For that reason, John, on the basis of "justice," "right reason," and consideration for "human dignity," demanded that the arms race "cease." "The stockpiles which exist in various countries should be reduced equally and simultaneously by the parties concerned," he insisted, "nuclear weapons should be banned," and all parties should "come to an agreement on a fitting program of disarmament." As positive as the response to *Pacem in terris* was in the communist press in cities such as Moscow, Budapest, Warsaw, and Havana, the Kennedy administration also gave the pope high marks. Lincoln White, spokesperson for the State Department, announced that the pope's ideas should inform the "aspirations of all governments." The president himself, while at a conference at Boston College, said that Pope John had produced "penetrating analysis of today's great problems of social welfare and human rights, of disarmament and international order and peace." Kennedy even went as far as to say that "as a Catholic" he was "proud" of the encyclical and as an American he had "learned from it."[2]

A trip to Italy in June 1963 would have given Kennedy the opportunity to meet John XXIII, thus making the president only the third occupant of the White House to be received by a pope. But John died in the middle of May. Some historians have read Kennedy's commencement speech at American University that month as a kind of eulogy for Pope John, since the president announced the suspension of nuclear weapons tests and the resumption of negotiations with the Soviets. When Kennedy visited Italy the next month, he met with Paul VI. The president did not kneel to kiss the pope's ring, but that did not prevent Paul from giving to the president the gift that John had intended to present, one of the three signed copies of *Pacem in terris*.

The convergence of papal pronouncements about international relations and a Roman Catholic U.S. president was only a small part of the larger historical alchemy that was blending church teaching and American ideals. Pope John had announced his intentions for an ecumenical council of bishops as early as 1959. The execution of those hopes took three years of planning. The Second Vatican Council convened more than two thousand bishops from all over the world for four sessions between 1962 and 1965. Pope John's reason for calling the council was to update the church's teaching and practice in the light of modern developments. In his opening address to the council on October 11, 1962, the pope acknowledged that some "prophets of gloom" saw only "prevarication and ruin" in modern society. John struck a note of optimism instead. He believed "Divine Providence [was] leading us to a new order of human relations which, by men's own efforts and even beyond their very expectations, are directed toward the fulfillment of God's superior and inscrutable designs."[3]

That sense of optimism was indicative of a new attitude toward modern society and to the political arrangements embodied in the United States. For almost a half millennium—from the Reformation to World War II—the papacy had opposed challenges to its authority and the society that had nurtured them. But John wanted to change the church's stance from one of resistance to encouragement. The political order of the United States and the related configuration of church-state relations was not the only item on the Second Vatican Council's agenda, but the gathering of bishops did afford the church a chance to revisit the very questions that had earlier led to condemnations of Americanism. And just as Pope John himself sensed a change in the relations between church and modern society, so observers within the church could not help notice more than a coincidence between the pope's hospitable attitude and the election of a Roman Catholic as president of the United States. As Richard Cardinal Cushing observed in his sermon on the first anniversary of John F. Kennedy's death, despite his "faults and failings," the president was "a precursor of another John, the loveable and loving Pope John XXIII, who during his brief Pontificate became the great Bridge Builder between the people of all faiths."[4] The question was how a church that had opposed most modern politics could approve the very liberties that had once seemed so antithetical to Christendom's social order and the papacy's central place in it.

Human Rights, Human Dignity

Angelo Giuseppe Roncalli (1881–1963) was an odd choice to succeed Pius XII. The oldest son (of twelve siblings) of a farmer in Lombardy (in contrast to his predecessor, who hailed from a prominent Roman family), Roncalli attended seminary before receiving a doctorate in theology. He served as a priest and chaplain during World War I. After the war, he held posts in Rome, became acquainted with the curia, and rose through the ranks of the episcopate. In 1934 Pope Pius XI appointed Roncalli as apostolic delegate to Turkey and Greece and bishop of Bulgaria. A decade later, a different pope, Pius XII, selected him to be apostolic nuncio to liberated France. In 1952 he became a cardinal and the patriarch of Venice. When Pius XII died in 1958 and Roncalli purchased his train ticket to Rome to attend the ceremonies, he bought a return trip. He had no idea that the College of Cardinals might elect him. Church officials needed eleven ballots to arrive at Roncalli. Historians and observers interpreted that as a sign that the cardinals chose a safe, "stopgap" person, someone advanced in years, with a reputation for maintaining church protocol. One early indication that the cardinals may have misread Roncalli was his name choice. John had not been used for more than five hundred years. The last pope to use it was in fact an antipope.[5] But by selecting

John XXIII, Roncalli both revived the name, one "sweet to us because it is the name of our father, dear to me because it is the name of the humble parish church where I was baptized," and settled once and for all that the original John XXIII (1410–15) was indeed illegitimate.[6]

Another indication that John XXIII was not going to play to form was his decision in 1960 to alter the Good Friday liturgy, which contained a prayer for the conversion of the Jews. During World War II Roncalli, as apostolic nuncio to France, had engaged in a number of efforts to save (primarily Jewish) refugees from the Nazis. Those efforts may explain his removal of the word "perfidious" from the Good Friday prayer. That was also a sign of the pope's attitude to other religions, which had implications both for ecumenism—namely, relations among religious groups and institutions—and for politics, as in securing legal protections for people to practice their own religious convictions.

Of John XXIII's six encyclicals, the two that stand out for setting the Second Vatican Council's agenda are *Mater et magistra* (1961) and *Pacem in terris* (1963), both of which may have counted as the longest encyclicals (25,000 and 15,000 words, respectively) by one of the shortest papal tenures. The former marked the seventieth anniversary of Pope Leo XIII's encyclical, *Rerum novarum*, even as it sought to apply Roman Catholic social teaching to the postwar situation. If some detected in John a softening of the church's hard-line anticommunist stance, they were justified. Although he still condemned socialism, even a moderate form of it, because it "takes no account of any objective other than that of material well-being," the pope was also critical of the injustice and inequality that so often attended economic systems devoted to wage labor and private property. The solution was a via media that subordinated "individual and group interests to the interest of the common good." For the pope, the common good demanded a set of goals that had eluded most politicians and economists:

> employment of the greatest possible number of workers; care lest privileged classes arise, even among the workers; maintenance of equilibrium between wages and prices; the need to make goods and services accessible to the greatest number; elimination, or at least the restriction, of inequalities . . . between agriculture, industry and services; creation of a proper balance between economic expansion and the development of social services,

especially through the activity of public authorities; the best possible adjustment of the means of production to the progress of science and technology;
seeing to it that the benefits which make possible a more human way of life
will be available not merely to the present generation but to the coming generations as well.[7]

Perhaps reflecting his own background in a farming community, John
identified the inequity between agricultural and industrial systems as "the
fundamental problem." Ironically enough, his solution was to bring the
city to the farm: "roads; transportation; means of communication; drink-
ing water; housing; health services; elementary, technical and professional
education; religious and recreational facilities; and the supply of modern
installations and furnishings for the farm residence."[8] The combination
of idealistic aspiration and moral posturing from the pope was responsible for William F. Buckley, Jr., the Roman Catholic editor of the politically
conservative magazine *National Review*, quipping that the holy father
had little to teach in the way of economic and foreign policy: "mater si,
magistra no" (mother yes, teacher no), a line that the political conservative heard his junior colleague, Garry Wills, use after pondering the pope's
reflections.

Mater et magistra foreshadowed the concerns of the Second Vatican
Council less than *Pacem in terris* if only because popes at least since
Leo XIII had tried to outline a position on economics somewhere between
socialism and capitalism. The subject of John's second lengthy encyclical
was political rights, the relations between rulers and citizens, the balance
of power among sovereign states, and the role of church officials and laity
in efforts to secure rights for all people. Pope John began with an explanation of rights that was as broad as it was modern. "Man has the right to
live . . . to bodily integrity and to the means necessary for the proper development of life, particularly food, clothing, shelter, medical care, rest, and,
finally, the necessary social services," and to be "looked after in the event
of ill health; disability stemming from his work; widowhood; old age;
enforced unemployment."[9] Persons also had rights to education and to
pursue the truth, and gifted members of societies had rights to advanced
forms of education. The list of rights included the kind of life someone
might choose, economic rights, access to political processes, and rights of
association. The right that more or less came out of the blue was freedom

of conscience: "Also among man's rights is that of being able to worship God in accordance with the right dictates of his own conscience, and to profess his religion both in private and in public" (14). That was a right that wound up bedeviling the bishops who participated in the Second Vatican Council, not to mention that it called into question papal resolve against political liberalism that had justified interpreting Americanism as a heresy. For John, though, this enumeration of rights made sense because he conceived of society as essentially a "spiritual reality" (36). Indeed, the sort of freedoms he championed would contribute to justice and the common good because persons, endowed with such rights, would "feel the needs of others as their own, and induce them to share their goods with others, and to strive in the world to make all men alike heirs to the noblest of intellectual and spiritual values" (35). Perhaps John was not reflecting on the U.S. Bill of Rights, after all.

The Vatican's embrace of modern conceptions of rights seemed to involve, as John articulated it, a partnership between the church and the wider world. For instance, *Pacem in terris* recognized the value of the United Nations and singled out for praise its Universal Declaration of Human Rights (1948). Although some criticisms of the document were legitimate, John endorsed the declaration for recognizing "the personal dignity of every human being" and asserting "everyone's right to be free to seek out the truth, to follow moral principles, discharge the duties imposed by justice, and lead a fully human life" (144). The pope also lauded freedom of conscience and insisted that modern governments had no power to coerce a citizen contrary to his or her religious convictions. "Since all men are equal in natural dignity, no man has the capacity to force internal compliance on another," the pope insisted. "Only God can do that, for He alone scrutinizes and judges the secret counsels of the heart." Yet the way that *Pacem in terris* framed the common good allowed room for governments, perhaps, to regard some personal expressions as beyond the pale. Rulers could not bind consciences of subjects "unless their own authority is tied to God's authority, and is a participation in it" (49). Since all authority came from God, the rule of governments was in some sense connected to divinity whether it constituted a "participation" or not. Even so, John wanted to make sure that this was not a brief for monarchy. He understood his teaching to be "consonant with any genuinely democratic form of government" (52). And with a democratic society in mind, he closed the encyclical by giving Roman Catholics permission to work with those outside the church for the common good. The pope judged that the principles he elaborated "even" involved "cooperation of Catholics with men who may not be Christians but who nevertheless are reasonable men, and men of natural moral integrity." Just because a person was in error about the truth did not mean he or she "cease[d] to be a man." People never forfeited their "personal dignity" (157, 158). As progressive as the pope sounded, his concluding reflections echoed the fortress mentality that had informed papal verdicts of the modern world.

At the same time, John's teaching was a significant detour from the earlier posture of the church, one captured in the phrase "error has no rights." The fruits of *Pacem in terris* became evident at the Second Vatican Council, where bishops modernized church teachings. Indeed, John's linkage of rights to human dignity set the agenda for the ecumenical council and beyond. According to John Langan, an ethicist at Georgetown University, *Pacem in terris* paved the road for Roman Catholicism to change from "an ally and ward of traditionalist regimes to a critic of repression by both reactionary and revolutionary" politics. Drew Christiansen, former editor of the Jesuit magazine *America*, credited Pope John, "however naive [his] encyclical might seem," with unleashing a revolution that took shape in church-based human rights commissions in locales as diverse as South Africa, Poland, and the Philippines. To realists such as Reinhold Niebuhr, that optimism was "a little too easy."[10] Some critics even faulted the pope for sounding utopian. But it was a refreshing turn for a church that had only seen social and political developments in the West as a glass almost empty.

Aggiornamento

John's arguments may have seemed a long way from John Courtney Murray's, but they were likely the product—how direct is hard to tell—of debates on church politics in the United States, of which the American Jesuit had been at the center. For the better part of almost two decades, the American John had attempted to supply a theological justification for the political order enshrined in the American founding and its constitutional republic. From an ultramontanist perspective, Murray's effort may have looked like just one more iteration of the Americanist error. Since

Murray's reflections on American freedoms gained visibility during the surge of anti-Catholicism that Paul Blanshard had provoked, the Jesuit's arguments derived much of their publicity from historical accidents rather than reflections on timeless theological truths. But Murray was no shill for the U.S. bishops, nor was he a rabble-rouser. He was a sober thinker who, like many twentieth-century Roman Catholic intellectuals, believed his tradition needed to reconsider its conservative—even reactionary—position on modernity. Unlike Pope John, who seemed to exist in the realm of utopian hopes, Murray did not propose an ideal society. He was serious about trying to reconcile papal teaching about political authority with lessons learned in the give and take of debates such as those that informed the creation of the United States.

Murray's approach to reconceiving Roman Catholic political theology was to challenge the dominant (though only two generations old) conception. The thesis-hypothesis understanding of church-state relations, first developed in the 1880s by the French bishop Félix Dupanloup, held that in the ideal situation (thesis) a state would embody and support the true (Roman Catholic) faith. But the modern world had introduced circumstances where the ideal was not possible (hypothesis). In these contexts, Dupanloup argued, Roman Catholics could legitimately make accommodations. This understanding presumed, according to the Jesuit theologian Fiorello Cavalli, that in societies where Roman Catholics were the majority or the rulers themselves were church members, "legal existence [must] be denied to error."[11] It was also the logic behind Pope Leo XIII's concession that even though Roman Catholicism had prospered in the United States, "it would be very erroneous to draw the conclusion that [this was] the most desirable status of the Church" or that church and state should be separated.[12]

Murray questioned this argument on two levels. The first was the historical reality that in modern society, church and state were not coextensive institutions but in fact differentiated along lines of social specialization and competency. The second was to remove church teaching on the state from the status of dogma. Because papal pronouncements came from historical eras where the state determined social relations, they were "time-conditioned."[13] Murray's aim was not to show that Roman Catholics were good American patriots (though later readers might use him that way) but to update theology in the light of modern social developments.

Murray's views received careful public scrutiny in theological journals, but the real test of their legitimacy came behind the scenes in correspondence between church officials in the United States and the Vatican. Francis Connell, professor of dogma at the Catholic University of America (a pontifical institution), not only challenged Murray in print (see chapter 2 above) but also appealed through back channels to church authorities about Murray's revisionist ideas. Some of these communications went as high as Giovanni Battista Montini, the Vatican's secretary of state and eventual pope (Paul VI). In 1952 Murray prepared a paper for Montini in which he explained his views on church and state. Comments Montini received were not favorable, but the church hierarchy had still not reached a verdict before Alfredo Cardinal Ottaviani entered the fray. A priest in the diocese of Rome since 1916, in 1953 he became pro-secretary of the Holy Office (later the Congregation for the Doctrine of the Faith), the Vatican agency responsible for theological assessment. Ottaviani had already begun to restrain theological novelties in France (authorities in 1950 removed Henri du Lubac from teaching at the seminary in Lyon), and he was not bashful about holding Murray to dogmatic standards.

In 1953, the same year he started to run the Holy Office, Ottaviani gave a talk about church and state that indicated Murray was on the Vatican's radar. Ottaviani identified as "enemies" those who denied the church's "divine prerogatives and powers." In fact, scholars who questioned traditional teaching on church-state relations were like "*delicatus miles,*" effeminate soldiers who were afraid to fight. He went on to insist as "incontestable truth" that societies composed of and governed by Roman Catholics should have laws that reflected church teaching. For the state to "conduct itself as though God did not exist" was a crime; to act as if good and evil, truth and error had the same rights was wrong. "Only those who obey God's mandates and possess his truth and justice have true rights." In the rest of his remarks, Ottaviani summarized as novel ideas about church and state that resembled Murray's. Evidence suggests that the cardinal was relying more on Murray's American critics than the Jesuit's own writings. The U.S. bishops wanted to see translations of Ottaviani's talk for their own deliberations. Meanwhile, Murray's American critics had the cardinal's remarks published in the *American Ecclesiastical Review*, the oldest of American theological journals for Roman Catholics. Murray also scurried to discover through church networks the status of

Ottaviani's talk. Was it an official verdict from the Vatican or a personal response? Murray's contacts indicated—and one source was Montini, the future pope—that Ottaviani's comments were "purely private."[14]

The status of Murray's own arguments became even more complicated when, nine months later, Pope Pius XII addressed the subject of the church and international relations before the Union of Catholic Jurists. In response to questions surrounding the creation of the United Nations, its "supranational juridical community," and the church's own standing among the world's nations, Pius reflected on the legitimacy of the church cooperating with political bodies that tolerated or even promoted erroneous beliefs. The important section of his address foreshadowed John XXIII's later appeal to a higher good, one bound by what Roman Catholics shared with those outside the church. "God has not given even to human authority such an absolute and universal command in matters of faith and morality," Pius explained. The "duty of repressing moral and religious error" could not be an "ultimate norm of action." The responsibility to promote the good and restrain error needed to be "subordinate to *higher and more general* norms, which in *some circumstances* permit, and perhaps even seem to indicate as the better policy, toleration of error in order to promote *a greater good*."[15]

Murray understood the pope's remarks as a vindication of his own views, though his opponents interpreted Pius XII's argument as a victory for themselves. The American Jesuit felt so confident that in a talk he gave at the Catholic University of America in the spring of 1954, he interpreted the pope's address as setting "the record straight" on debates about the church's relation to the modern state. Because the pope's remarks reflected, according to Murray, "doctrinal progress," the Jesuit was claiming a shift within the Vatican to a position closer to his. He even argued that those with views closer to Ottaviani now needed to revise their arguments. Historical circumstances provided the greatest instruction here. "All development of doctrine in this field [is] occasioned by history."[16]

Murray's confidence of victory did not last long. His talk at the Catholic University of America was incautious if only because his chief antagonists were members of the institution's faculty. Their opposition to Murray's views soon circulated through church channels and reached Ottaviani. Within a year, Murray could no longer publish in the principal organs of Roman Catholic theology or the Jesuits. One of his superiors among the

Jesuits advised that perhaps Murray could "write poetry."[17] For the next three years, until 1958, Murray contented himself with teaching about faith and public morality and refraining from writing for publication.

The year 1958 turned out to be significant for Murray and his fellow Roman Catholics because Pope Pius XII died, John XXIII succeeded him, and John F. Kennedy determined to run for the presidency. Private papers indicated that Pius was much more sympathetic to Murray than to Ottaviani. But that did not help Murray, who remained quiet until 1960, when Sheed and Ward published his book, *We Hold These Truths: Catholic Reflections on the American Proposition*. The book consisted of previously published articles—from before Murray's ban—revised for the book. The argument, much more complicated than what follows, was that Roman Catholicism was the great custodian of natural law reflection and that the American founding built on a natural law tradition and so owed a great debt to Christendom. As Barry Hudock explains, Murray argued that the Roman Catholic tradition had "made America great from the start and would preserve America's greatness" when "cultural currents of secularism threatened its future."[18] The appearance of the book at the time of Kennedy's candidacy was responsible, at least in part, for attracting a wider reading public to peruse Roman Catholic theology. The book's success and Kennedy's victory were also likely important factors in *Time* magazine's editors' decision to feature Murray on the cover of the December 12, 1960, edition. The cover story could not help but notice the contrast between pre- and post-Kennedy Roman Catholicism: "[It] was largely a church of immigrants, whose concern was to protect and build their minority religion in a Protestant land while showing their fellow Americans what all-out patriots they were. Today, an increasing number of well-educated and theologically sophisticated young Catholics are beginning to take part in what Father Murray calls 'building the city'—contributing both to the civic machinery and the need for consensus beneath it."[19]

Thanks to a Roman Catholic in the White House, Murray may have become a minor celebrity to U.S. magazine readers, but he was still on the margins of the church's hierarchy, and the validity of his views was still in question. As officials planned for the council, they decided which topics to address and which theologians to invite. Among the *periti*, the technical word for theological advisers to the bishops, were such notable twentieth-century theologians as Henri du Lubac, Yves Congar, Karl Rahner, and Joseph Ratzinger (who became Pope Benedict XVI). Whether Murray would attend the council, even though several U.S. bishops lobbied for his presence, was doubtful. The historical record itself is spotty. Murray's own memory, though not supported by archival evidence, was that he had been invited to the council and then disinvited. Whether the texts support that sequence of events, the council did open with Murray living in Woodstock, Maryland, and forbidden to publish on the subject of church-state relations. His chief theological opponent, Joseph Fenton from Catholic University, did receive an invitation to Vatican II as *peritus*. Only after the close of the council's first session (December 1962) did New York archbishop Francis Cardinal Spellman prevail on Vatican officials to include Murray at the second session of the council. Even so, although Murray was welcome in Rome, authorities at the Catholic University of America revoked an invitation for him to lecture at the Graduate Student Council.

Also uncertain during the years of preparation for the council and its early phases was the willingness of the Vatican and assembly of bishops to address religious liberty. The biggest question was which branch of the council would address the subject, and that meant sorting out the committee assignments for bishops and curia. With the help of advisers, the pope appointed ten commissions to prepare materials for the council. One of those was the Central Preparatory Commission, which Pope John oversaw and which coordinated the work of the other commissions. Possibly because assemblies of bishops were so infrequent—one of the consequences of the fifteenth-century papacy's reaction to conciliarism—the Vatican overreacted in allowing almost four years of planning how the council should conduct its business. In addition to the theological commissions, the Vatican appointed three secretariats to facilitate the work of the commissions.

The early dispute among these committees and their respective agendas was which theological commission should address the subject of religious freedom (and whether the relationship between church and state was part of that topic). Originally, the one commission tasked with theological matters, the Theological Commission (TC), headed up by Cardinal Ottaviani, received the task of adjudicating religious freedom since his body was responsible for deliberating questions about church and state. Council organizers believed religious freedom was one aspect of the ways that

temporal and spiritual powers related to each other. Communicating the
discussions and findings of the council to Protestants, Eastern Christians,
Muslims, and Jews, however, would not come directly from Ottaviani's
TC but from the Secretariat for Christian Unity (SCU), headed by Augustin Cardinal Bea, a German Jesuit who taught biblical studies and archae-
ology at the Gregorian Pontifical University in Rome.

Bea's SCU was chiefly an instrument of communication, not a body
with the authority or task of a commission, but this secretariat soon
entered the debates over religious freedom and thereby opened a window into the labyrinth of the curia. Bea believed Ottaviani and TC were
not properly addressing the ecumenical aspects of the relations between
church and state. Here Bea both reflected John XIII's background in relating to Jews and Eastern Christians while apostolic delegate to Turkey and
Greece and was sensitive to a common perception that Roman Catholic
teaching about the church above the state or the unity of church and state
was a chief stumbling block to other Christian groups. For instance, the
American Protestant theologian Robert McAfee Brown, who was an ecumenical observer to the Second Vatican Council, wrote in 1964 that a
statement from the Vatican on religious freedom was important because
"(to put it bluntly for the sake of time and not pause over ecumenical nice-
ties) the Catholic Church is not to be trusted on this point."[20]

Although the function of committee assignments was to facilitate
smooth interactions among the entire body of delegates, the ecumenical
duties of Bea's SCU and the dogmatic agenda of Ottaviani's TC came into
conflict during both the planning for the council and the bishops' meetings
in Rome. As early as the fall of 1960, SCU began a set of discussions that
led to a draft document on religious freedom. Ottaviani objected to a secretariat actually having the prerogative to prepare material for the council. But Pope John encouraged Bea to continue SCU's work when he too
understood that Ottaviani would likely reinforce traditional Roman Catholic views such as "error has no rights." In fact, when SCU finally finished
its document on religious freedom in June 1962, Pope John instructed Bea
to submit its findings to the Conciliar Preparatory Committee, the body
responsible for organizing all the commissions and secretariats.

Even so, Ottaviani's body, aside from objections to SCU's meddling,
produced its own rubric. In contrast to SCU's Schema on Ecumenism,
which affirmed toleration and cooperation with non-Catholics, as well

as the right of all persons to their own beliefs, TC's document persisted in affirming the church's unwillingness to recognize the value of religions outside the church. It claimed that the state had a duty to "perform religious obligations" and to recognize Roman Catholicism as "the one way which God wishes to be served and worshipped." It also asserted that citizens from other religions *do not have the right not to be prevented from professing their religions*; however, for the sake of common good the State may tolerate their profession."[21] Murray, who received copies of the documents, judged Ottaviani's position to be the weaker one because it rested almost entirely on "the power of the Holy Office to shut up anyone who presumes to question it." He also feared that a "heaven-sent opportunity" to "effect a genuine development of doctrine" might be missed.[22] Pope John recognized the conflict and appointed an ad hoc committee to reconcile the two opposing outlooks. Cardinal Bea presented a compromise statement by the end of the summer, but TC rejected it. Going into the first session of the Second Vatican Council, the bishops had two conflicting statements on religious freedom and the state's religious obligations.

At the opening of the council in October 1962, with almost twenty-five hundred bishops attending, Ottaviani won the opening round if only because Murray was absent and the first session was primarily about approving an agenda rather than adopting formal policies. Bishops from the United States objected behind closed doors to the exclusion of the man who made the best case for reconciling Roman Catholicism and America's political order. The most decisive aspect of the first session, however, was the pope's opening remarks about the council. His optimism about the direction of world history—"Divine Providence is leading us to a new order of human relations which, by men's own efforts and even beyond their very expectations, are directed toward the fulfilment of God's superior and inscrutable designs"—was an omen for the old guard suspicious of reform of the church. Joseph Fenton, one of Murray's most vigorous opponents, lamented after hearing the pope that "real trouble is on the way." In his journal he added, "We should, I believe, face the facts. Since the death of St. Pius X the Church has been directed by weak and liberal popes, who have flooded the hierarchy with unworthy and stupid men." Where Pope John saw signs of circumstances working for the good of the Church, Fenton observed what seemed to be "the Lord Christ . . . abandoning his church."[23]

During the second session of the council, which ran from September 29 to December 4, 1963, now with Murray working as a *periti*, the members of the hierarchy he identified as "the Good Guys" experienced a "glorious victory." To outsiders it must have seemed minor since it only involved moving the SCU document on religious liberty from committee to the main body of bishops and cardinals. But considering what Murray had been through for the preceding decade, to have a statement that recognized the value of modern political arrangements was a significant breakthrough. No doubt, this development was also encouraging given the uncertainty after Pope John's death in June 1963. Not to be missed was the coincidence of John F. Kennedy's assassination during the second session of the council, an event that did prompt a funeral Mass led by American bishops at the Basilica of Saint John Lateran. If American bishops and churchmen sensed an urgency to prevail on the council, it was surely during the fall of 1963. Indeed, a four-page memo that Murray prepared for the U.S. bishops in which he identified religious liberty as urgent led them to issue a formal petition to put the SCU's draft on the council's agenda. Adding leverage to this American petition was the intervention by the new pope, Paul VI, to have Ottaviani's commission approve the SCU's schema for evaluation by the entire body of delegates.

At the third session, which began on September 14, 1964, Émile-Joseph M. de Smedt, bishop of Bruges, Belgium, appointed Murray and Pietro Pavan, a priest who taught social economy at Rome's Lateran University and another *periti*, to draft a statement on religious freedom for the council. De Smedt was a member of SCU and led the proponents of a revised understanding of religious liberty throughout the bishops' meetings. Murray's selection may have looked strange since he had so recently been silenced by Ottaviani. But during the summer of 1964, the American priest had written an article for the Jesuit magazine *America*, in which he contrasted the two understandings of religious freedom. The older conception, the church's formal position, maintained that only truth had rights and governments had an obligation to preserve and defend truth. The newer idea, in contrast, had emerged in modern times from a greater "sense of personal freedom."[24] To keep anyone from misrepresenting his view, Murray insisted that the proponents of religious liberty "with all Catholics" acknowledge "an obligation to profess faith in God" and that "to worship him is incumbent on society." But such a duty could not come from "legislative or executive action." A society's religion was evident "on so-called state-occasions—the opening of the legislature and judiciary, national days of thanksgiving and prayer." Such acts should be organized by the church since the state "has no competence in liturgical matters." Nevertheless, such instances of public worship involved "no legal coercion." Religion was accordingly voluntary but not a "purely private affair."[25]

While Murray explained the place of religion in modern society in a way he believed conformed to church teaching, he also appealed to the idea of historical development to justify the new arrangement. For the American Jesuit the recognition that historical context shaped the discernment of truth was crucial to the new idea of religious freedom. The church's task was "to discern the elements of the tradition that are embedded in some historically conditioned synthesis" of what is "at once new and also traditional." "The signs of the times," Murray believed, were on the side of the church arriving at such a synthesis, and this awareness of historical development was as much a part of his reflections (even inspiration) as his exposition of papal teaching.[26] The view of religious freedom he advocated "presents itself as the contemporary stage in the growing stage of the tradition." An understanding of society, Murray emphasized, could "not be found in ecclesiastical documents of the nineteenth century." Indeed, the notion of "religious freedom as a human and civil right, personal and corporate, is not to be sought in the theologians of the nineteenth century." The reality of religious freedom as an aspect of "limited constitutional government" "only became available" in the twentieth century through the "growth of the personal and political consciousness" of Pius XII and John XXIII. In other words, "what history obscured, history would also clarify." The "totalitarian society-state" implied by *The Syllabus of Errors* (1864) gave way to Leo XIII's restatement of the "question of public care of religion." The task of theologians was to "trace the stages in the growth of the tradition as it makes its way through history."[27]

Although these historicist sentiments were ones that had merited condemnation as modernism only five decades earlier, Murray's reading of the tea leaves of time was vindicated by the historical developments of which he was part. The article, translated in four languages, went to bishops throughout the world. Although Pavan contributed as much to the draft document on religious freedom that the council's bishops eventually studied in the fall of 1964, Murray received much more credit thanks to the attention his article received. Murray had also won over the U.S. bishops, much to Fenton's annoyance. Fenton wrote in his journal that the bishops had "mouthed M's nonsense, as they have been told to do by Meyer" (i.e., Albert Cardinal Meyer, archbishop of Chicago).[28]

Once the bishops at the third session of the council began to inspect the schema that Murray and Pavan produced, differences of opinion were sufficiently prominent (though the American bishops almost to a man lined up behind Murray) for Pope Paul VI, who succeeded John during the council itself, to appoint a commission to draft a compromise position. The committee consisted of four members from Bea's secretariat and four from Ottaviani's TC. Murray was part of the process and chosen as "first scribe." The draft did not stop debate among the bishops and failed to mollify conservatives. The pope's determination to postpone a vote on November 19, 1964, a concession to conservative bishops, became known among Murray's supporters as "Black Thursday," though Murray himself called it the "Day of Wrath." Although Pope Paul promised a return to the subject at the council's next session, the fate of religious freedom looked uncertain. The historical tide in favor of Murray had not yet turned.

But sea levels continued to rise through the assistance of the French church. After the conclusion of the council's third session, Pope Paul sent two of his advisers to consult with Jacques Maritain, an old friend, and a frequent contributor to discussions about church and state. In the spring of 1965 Maritain sent an essay to the pope in which he described the relationship between the state and church as one of autonomy. Political authorities had no legitimate right to intervene in religious matters except in cases of the larger common good. Maritain's basis for this claim was human nature. Because humans were inherently "directed . . . to God," they transcended the "territorial and temporal order of things."[29] Murray himself had a meeting with Pope Paul in May, where evidence of different emphases between the French and American churches emerged. At the final session of the council, which opened on September 14, 1965, French and American bishops elaborated their differences with the former wanting a deeper theological justification for freedom of conscience than what Murray had proposed. If the eventual document lacked some of the rationale that Murray had supplied, it owed to his having to be hospitalized on October 5 with a collapsed lung (he had already suffered two heart attacks within eleven months of each other, in January and

December 1964). On December 7, 1965, the final draft of the council's decree, *Declaration of Religious Freedom* (*Dignitas humanae*), passed the delegates' approval by a vote of 2,308 to 70. The Second Vatican Council closed the next day.

The legal historian Leslie Griffin has compared the final text approved by the council to "the U.S. Constitution," a "brilliant politico-legal document."[30] Her point is to highlight the concern for limited government and individual rights in the *Declaration of Religious Freedom*. Rather than using the "rights" language that came so readily to Pope John in *Pacem in terris*, the *Declaration* affirmed, as the Latin title indicated, the dignity of human beings. As the bishops tried to discern the "signs of the times," a recurring refrain throughout the council's documents, they understood that "the dignity of the human person has been impressing itself more and more deeply on the consciousness of contemporary man." The times also "demanded" that "constitutional limits should be set to the powers of government, in order that there may be no encroachment on the rightful freedom of the person and of associations." These perceptions did not alter the church's affirmation that it possessed the capital-T truth. "This one true religion subsists in the Catholic and Apostolic Church," and the "binding force" of its claims still fell on the consciences of all people.[31] The declaration, as such, refused to enter the weeds that cluttered debates about freedom of conscience. Its aim was limited, namely, to affirm that people should be free "from coercion" in their pursuit of religious truth and that government power should be limited constitutionally.

The *Declaration* located this freedom not in the truth the church taught but in the dignity of the human person. "Religious freedom has its foundation in the very dignity of the human person as this dignity is known through the revealed word of God and by reason itself." This was also the foundation for the civil right whereby constitutional law recognized religious freedom as fundamental to social order. Prior to the council, the church had regarded freedom of conscience chiefly in the context of truth, which resulted in the common notion that "error has no rights." If truth was the gold standard for freedom, then the people with erroneous beliefs had no legitimate social standing, at least according to the logic of Christendom (either Roman Catholic or Protestant). By moving to human dignity, the council found a way to argue against both coercion and restraint. The church had taught historically that belief needed to be freely chosen, though in some cases coercion of heretics was in order. The question was whether its teaching about truth could make room for error.

The council declared clearly that even those who failed "their obligation of seeking the truth and adhering to it" could not be "impeded" from exercising the right to religious freedom (2). Without explicitly embracing freedom of conscience, the decree affirmed it practically: "In all his activity a man is bound to follow his conscience in order that he may come to God, the end and purpose of life. It follows that he is not to be forced to act in a manner contrary to his conscience. Nor, on the other hand, is he to be restrained from acting in accordance with his conscience, especially in matters religious. The reason is that the exercise of religion, of its very nature, consists before all else in those internal, voluntary and free acts" (3). Such rights extended to "religious communities" and families (4–5).

The *Declaration*'s checks on power were less prominent than its affirmations of religious freedom, but the restraints on authority applied to both civil and ecclesiastical rulers. On the one hand, an essential responsibility of government was the "protection and promotion of the inviolable rights of man." As such, the state should encourage the religious lives of citizens, protect the rights of religious institutions, and ensure that belief not be a barrier to equal protection before the law. Governments should also prevent freedom of religion from being abused. The measure for such determinations was "the common welfare of all" (6–7). On the other hand, the church needed to be content with spiritual authority. The way that Christ and the apostles extended their authority over believers was not through the sword:

> From the very origins of the Church the disciples of Christ strove to convert men to faith in Christ as the Lord . . . by the power, above all, of the word of God. . . . They showed respect for those of weaker stuff, even though they were in error, and thus they made it plain that "each one of us is to render to God an account of himself" (Romans 14:12), and for that reason is bound to obey his conscience. . . . Therefore they rejected all "carnal weapons": they followed the example of the gentleness and respectfulness of Christ and they preached the word of God in the full confidence that there was resident in this word itself a divine power able to destroy all the forces arrayed against God. (11)

That distinction between the coercive powers of the state and the spiritual rule of the church was in effect the closest the *Declaration* came to addressing the relations between church and state. On the matter of an ecclesiastical establishment, the decree left room for the state to support a specific church body by virtue of its responsibility to "create conditions favorable to the fostering of religious life" (6). Murray understood that by allowing for established churches he was departing from the provisions of the U.S. Constitution, but he also had no interest in advocating religious disestablishment in ways that would alter the status of the church in Roman Catholic nations.[32]

Americanism Vindicated

Although the *Declaration* did not conform exactly to U.S. notions of liberty, the decree was, as Gerald P. Fogarty has concluded, "the American contribution" to the Second Vatican Council. It was *the* issue with which the American bishops and *periti* had had "long practical experience" and could thereby explain to European bishops and Vatican officials. And with the *Declaration*, the American church, Fogarty adds, no longer lived in the shadow of inferiority because its host society did not meet Roman Catholic standards.[33]

However the observers from the United States may have influenced the *Declaration*, it was a momentous development for the Roman Catholic Church. Never before had the church's hierarchy recognized the legitimacy of religious freedom. In fact, since at least the French Revolution, Rome had condemned adamantly political liberalism, free speech, freedom of association, and the separation of church and state. Pope Pius XII in the context of post–World War II Europe had shown signs of softening on democracy but only in an ambiguous way. Even so, as democratic governments in Europe during the 1950s began to prevail over totalitarian ones, church officials hoped to participate with other religious groups in social reconstruction. The older church-state theory of Roman Catholicism would not allow such collaboration because cooperation implied indifference to religious truth. A corollary was that as the only true religion, Roman Catholicism should be the religion of the state. Such a position obviously hampered the ability of bishops, laity, and religious to cooperate with non-Catholics in social and political reform. Such common endeavor was automatically, according to pre–Vatican II theory, an indication of tolerance for all faiths and the consequence of separating church and state.

For Roman Catholics in the United States, however, no matter how forceful anti-Catholicism might be, the experience with political liberalism was different if not opposite from Europe's clergy. Roman Catholic institutions thrived in America, and lay church members and clergy participated in political and social life in remarkable ways. The patriotism of American Roman Catholics was most notable in times of war. John Courtney Murray's early formulations of religious freedom unsurprisingly emerged during World War II when he tried to find a theological basis for "intercreedal cooperation." Murray's position made sense to many Americans, but for bishops (especially in Europe) and older theologians, his views contradicted church teaching. The novelty of his arguments explains the attempts during the 1950s to silence him. But those same disciplinary measures looked increasingly anachronistic in the context of postwar Europe. Maintaining Christendom's church-state relationship looked especially foolish as Protestants themselves in 1948 had rallied to form an ecumenical agency headquartered in Geneva, the World Council of Churches. Even as these Protestants drafted a statement on religious freedom that called for legal safeguards for "the right of all men to hold and change their faith . . . and to decide on the religious education of their children," officials of the World Council also looked to the Vatican to alter its position on religious freedom if Roman Catholics were going to participate in ecumenical relations.[34]

If circumstances were leading Vatican officials to reconsider church-state relations, to what degree was the Second Vatican Council's teaching on religious liberty the product and vindication of the Roman Catholic experience in the United States? The reasons for raising this question arise not simply from the history of the council's proceedings themselves but also from the shift in papal posture that John XXIII signaled during his relatively brief tenure. At the council differences between French and American approaches to religious freedom emerged, with the former possibly gaining the upper hand thanks to Murray's poor health and hospitalization. That difference stemmed in part from Murray's own reliance on the American founding and the French *periti*'s reflection on broad theological themes. In his article for *America,* distributed widely to bishops and cardinals during the summer of 1965, Murray contrasted the American founders' understanding of negative liberty (freedom from) with the Puritan and Roman Catholic idea of positive liberty (freedom to). The rhetoric of a "city upon a hill" was synonymous with freedom from error and the flip side of "error has no rights." But the American framers regarded religious freedom as a safeguard from coercion. The French influence from Yves Congar, for instance, stressed revelation and salvation, and during the drafting process the French *periti* added more biblical and pastoral considerations than Murray's legal and constitutional approach allowed.[35] In fact, Gerald Fogarty concludes that Murray, along with American bishops before him, drew on a tradition of British and American common law that was alien to and misunderstood by European Roman Catholics. As such, some of the resistance to Murray's ideas and the American contribution at the council owed to a fear that the U.S. delegates were introducing a foreign element into the church. According to Fogarty, "American speech about 'freedom' . . . frequently sounds to the European like a plea for that type of democracy reminiscent of the French Revolution."[36]

In which case, the real precedent for the *Declaration of Religious Freedom* may have come from Pope John's *Pacem in terris*. Not only did Murray and Pavan rely on that encyclical when drafting the decree for the council, but Pavan himself explained to French bishops that Pope John had set the terms of debate. *Pacem in terris* asserted that only God "has the right to judge our conscience." Persons must decide for themselves what they believe. Public authorities, with support from the church, needed "to create conditions favorable to the expression of the rights of citizens." Leslie Griffin concludes that Pope John's encyclical "provided the best precedent for those worried about drafting a document that was faithful to the Church's prior teachings on religious freedom."[37]

Be that as it may, the Second Vatican Council afforded Roman Catholics in the United States the opportunity to come out from under the cloud of suspicion. Murray's involvement at the sessions also allowed the church in the United States, too often perceived as the stepsister by those who still walked in the shadows of Christendom, to achieve a measure of pride in the way American Roman Catholicism helped redirect the church and its understanding of the modern world. That high estimate of the United States, which Murray himself cultivated, not only meant an end to Americanism as a heresy. It also opened the way for Roman Catholics in the United States to regard their nation as Kennedy had said, as a city on a hill, a country as decisive in world affairs as Rome had once been.

4

LIBERAL CATHOLICS, AMERICAN CONSERVATIVES

For Garry Wills, the Second Vatican Council was less about religious freedom than liturgical anarchy. In his 1972 book *Bare Ruined Choirs*, the former contributing editor for *National Review*, who had been in training to be a Jesuit, assessed the effects of the council and judged them pernicious in the main. Most egregious was the reform of the Mass, by which the council launched Roman Catholicism into "the agony of lost symbols and debased associations." Wills did not accept that changes in outward forms had little bearing on internal doctrine. He quoted John Henry Newman: "Nothing is so frivolous and so unphilosophical as the ridicule bestowed on the contest for retaining or surrendering a rite or an observance . . . such as kneeling at the Lord's Table." But the introduction of new observances created for the layperson "a strange house, cluttered with signs of an alien occupancy." Even the seemingly small matter of not touching the communion wafer was part of "a hierarchic dance arranged around the Host, bowings, blessings, kneelings, liftings, displayings, and hiding of It." To eat the host, communicants had to abstain from food in a fast that began at midnight the night before the Mass, reduced in 1953 by Pope Pius XII to three hours before the service (in the Apostolic Constitution, *Christus Dominus*). As Wills described the practice, an "unconsidered mechanical swallow after brushing one's teeth meant no communion that day." This rule also applied to priests.[1]

The significance of these details conveyed a theology of the sacrament that the council destroyed by introducing vernacular languages, turning the priest around to face the congregation, and placing the communion wafer in the hands of recipients. For Wills this was another signal of the bishops' affirmation of freedom. But it had little to do with liberating the laity. Liturgical reforms actually liberated the priests "from the years of theology (and retrospective partial philosophy) learned in Latin by rote." These were part of a "revolution" led by the theologians, the *periti*, the "expert consultants" against the curia. The introduction of sermons was arguably just as difficult for a laity that had "been trained to distrust 'lectures' in church."[2]

The council's reset of the church's outlook on social pluralism and secular politics was a feature that was already evident, according to Wills, in American Roman Catholicism before the bishops and cardinals assembled in Rome. For the better part of a half century, Roman Catholic liberals had appropriated papal encyclicals along the lines of the Democratic Party's New Deal liberalism. John A. Ryan was the principal spokesman for such Roman Catholic political liberalism. And by understanding papal teaching as Democratic policy, these liberals could readily defend themselves against the charge of "lax Catholicism." "The Pope was with the Democratic Party," Wills observed, "even though much of the American hierarchy found itself going to Republican businessmen for donations." When political conservatives, as Wills was prior to the agitations surrounding Vietnam, criticized the civil religion of the Democratic Party, they heard from any number of Roman Catholic editors and spokesmen how the "over-all direction of papal teaching on political-social problems" was liberal.[3]

That identification of party politics and papal power did not sit well with Roman Catholics who wrote for *National Review*, William F. Buckley's flagship periodical for movement conservatism. When Buckley himself questioned John XXIII's *Mater et magistra*, he found himself on the receiving end of liberal-inspired papolatry. The Jesuit magazine *America* even refused to print advertisements for *National Review* after the latter's criticism of the pope. Wills could not resist noting the irony of liberals appealing to "central authority, binding documents, and imposed propositions" against American conservatives such as Buckley.[4]

Although the Second Vatican Council did little to alter debates among American Roman Catholics about the character of their country and the responsibility of the federal government at home and abroad, its deliberations did make life harder for those Roman Catholic conservatives who grew up around Buckley and *National Review* during the 1950s. To be sure, as Wills would often point out during shouting matches with *America*, Buckley's magazine was not a Roman Catholic publication. In effect, Buckley was paving the way for John F. Kennedy's relegation of religion to the private part of his life. As Buckley indicated in one of his exchanges with *America*, *National Review* was "no more a Catholic magazine because its editor is a Catholic" than the Kennedy administration is Catholic because "its head is Catholic."[5] Unlike Kennedy, however, Buckley and his associates were not committed to the separation of church and state, barring government funding of parochial schools, or opposing a U.S. ambassador to the Vatican. Those were American political tropes that appealed to a wide swath of the electorate.

Buckley's following among readers was of a different sort, a conservative audience that opposed the growth of government, defended a shared moral order, and was eager to fight communism, "the century's most blatant force of satanic utopianism."[6] In other words, Kennedy and Buckley each might draw on aspects of their Roman Catholic upbringing, but in their public roles they were taking their cues first and foremost from terms dictated by their American setting. Unlike Kennedy, Buckley's understanding of American interests put him and his magazine on a collision course with the Vatican's *aggiornamento* (updating). Instead of adapting to "the signs of the times," Buckley's brand of conservatism evoked the papacy's older style of standing athwart history and yelling, "Stop!" Making the case that such a conservative pose was part of the DNA of a nation that broke with European politics was another matter, perhaps an argument best suited for someone still loyal to the Latin Mass.

Orthodox Libertarianism

William F. Buckley, Jr., was anything but a typical Roman Catholic. By national standards he was hardly average. He grew up in a devout family of ten children, the son of an oilman who had made a fortune in Mexico and Venezuela. That wealth was a shelter against the storm of the Great Depression, which started in 1929 when Buckley was four years old. The Buckleys lived comfortably in Sharon, Connecticut, and traveled extensively. In fact, in the same year as the crash of Wall Street, the family moved to Paris, where they resided for two years. The Buckleys were also devout. If the clannishness and access to privilege of the family resembled the Kennedys, the piety of both father (Will) and mother (Aloise) set the Buckleys apart from Rose and Joe Kennedy. Buckley's father's faith was aristocratic, private, and militant. Aloise's devotion was much more on the surface and experiential. Faith at home mixed with an odd assortment of schools to separate Buckley further from the world of the average American. When the family was in England during the late 1930s, Buckley attended a Roman Catholic school, but back in the United States for high school he was graduated from Millbrook School, a relatively new private institution in Dutchess County, New York, that for the children's father created space from the pretentious bigotry of the Protestant establishment and the narrow outlook of parochial schools.

After his graduation, Buckley left his privileged surroundings and was drafted into the army. During basic training at Camp Wheeler (Georgia), he became aware that "intelligence is neither recognized nor appreciated." His trick for survival was friendliness. He resolved to be "quiet, kindhearted, generous, interested in other people's problems, and *inconspicuous.*" "It works like a charm," Buckley explained in a letter to his mother.[7] It did help him qualify for Officer Candidate School, which he barely passed, and from which he served in counterintelligence in San Antonio for the last months of World War II.

When Buckley enrolled at Yale in the fall of 1946, he reentered the elite world in which he had grown up but again with a measure of distance, not only because of his faith and cosmopolitanism but owing also to wartime experience. He distinguished himself as a debater and editor of the *Yale Daily News*. John B. Judis writes that Buckley "might have excelled as a student at Yale, but he was not interested in scholarship or even the play of ideas."[8] As someone given to debate and editorializing, Buckley was arguably more attuned to intellectual life than your average American. But several of his ideas were firm and would not budge no matter what he studied. Buckley was decidedly anticommunist and, as a Roman Catholic, convinced of the importance of religion to the West. His encounter with

Willmoore Kendall, a political science professor who also relished the role of provocateur, put some polish on his guiding convictions.

By the time of his senior year, Buckley had carved out a reputation as someone who easily belonged at Yale—he was the first choice of Skull and Bones, Yale's secret honor society—and who relished unsettling conventions. The administration rewarded Buckley's achievements by asking him to give the Alumni Day speech, scheduled for February 22, 1950. He overestimated the request by thinking he could use the occasion to continue to provoke. Buckley prepared a text that faulted Yale for sowing confusion among its students. Socialists and atheists were equal to capitalists and Christians in the classroom at Yale. After receiving an advance copy and asking Buckley for revisions to a speech that was supposed to promote Yale's atmosphere and accomplishments, the university's administration finally accepted Buckley's offer to withdraw the speech. He had not expected such a turn of events, and it put Yale on Buckley's list of "most wanted."

Buckley's speech did not wind up in the wastebasket. After graduating from Yale, he married Patricia Taylor and applied to the CIA. Before returning to intelligence work, Buckley taught Spanish at Yale and turned his Alumni Day speech into a book. *God and Man at Yale* became one of the classics of intellectual conservatism, and its publication in 1951 foreshadowed the rise of a conservative movement that refused to be bound by the constraints of the political establishment. The book displayed Buckley's brashness and youth. On the former score, he went through the faculty and courses at Yale and showed how the university undermined its responsibility to further the convictions that made the West tick, namely, Christianity and individualism (which stood in effect for free markets and against collectivism). Buckley's youth was evident in his prescription for the alumni, not the administration or faculty, to control the university. He did not want Yale to be a Christian university in the sense that it constituted a "company of scholars exclusively or even primarily concerned with spreading the Word of the Lord." The question was whether Yale was a secular institution, indifferent to religion, or if it fortified "the average student's respect for Christianity."[9]

The history of Yale as an institution founded by devout colonial Puritans gave Buckley leverage throughout his comments on the university's religious atmosphere. He did not seem to notice that when Yale had been the most Protestant, it had also been a university most unlikely to admit

Roman Catholics. When it came to individualism, Yale was far more explicit. Buckley's survey of courses, textbooks, and professors indicated that Yale students learned how capitalism was an antiquated system that produced inequality and needed state action to redistribute wealth.

God and Man at Yale was a curious book for many reasons, not to mention its proximity to the publication of Paul Blanshard's *American Freedom and Catholic Power*. Buckley espoused an understanding of freedom that from Blanshard's perspective would have been proof of the Roman Catholic preference for authoritarianism. What would have caught Blanshard off guard was Buckley's appeal to Protestant forms of religious despotism. The tension between Buckley and Blanshard was not simply in the world of book publishing. Blanshard's twin brother, Brand, was chairman of Yale's Philosophy Department, and Buckley did not hesitate to identify the philosopher as an "atheist" who "never made a secret of this, even from Corporation members."[10] If this meant Buckley opposed academic freedom, so be it. It was a "superstition." What made this academic ideal a fiction were the numerous ways in which Yale assumed a posture of sheer neutrality all the while cultivating liberal convictions—especially about democracy and American society. The president of Yale until 1951, Charles Seymour, was on record that the university refused to hire communists, and Buckley also noted that different departments when conducting job searches had certain outlooks or specialties in their selection of new faculty. The problem, as Buckley argued, was that a professed commitment to academic freedom was also at odds with the not-so-open-ended character of administrative policy and classroom teaching.

The solution he proposed was twofold. The first component was a distinction between teaching and research faculty at Yale. Those conducting research could attempt the sort of academic freedom—read intellectual indifference—that had taken hold at Yale. But no students would take courses from such faculty. Instead, the teaching professors responsible for transmitting Yale's "spiritual values and individualism" would be the ones with access to students. The second part of the solution was for Yale's alumni to run the school, or at least influence the administration by withholding support. If the university's graduates "cannot support an institution that encourages values they consider inimical to public welfare," they should not "contribute to Yale so long as she continues in whole or in part to foster contrary values."[11]

Buckley's book was a direct challenge to Yale's place in the nation's liberal society and launched a controversy that seemingly pitted Roman Catholic intolerance against (modernist) Protestant openness; of course, most academics regarded fundamentalists and evangelicals as intolerant. Part of the reason for the public notoriety was the $16,000 that Buckley's father spent on publicity for the book, which was sent free of charge to a wide swath of the university's graduates. President A. Whitney Griswold appointed a blue-ribbon committee of alumni, chaired by the prominent liberal Presbyterian pastor Henry Sloane Coffin, to study Yale in light of Buckley's charges. Coffin could not help but notice the disparity between Yale's Puritan heritage and Buckley's Roman Catholic point of view, an observation that also implied the author's temerity in suggesting how Protestants should operate their own institution. Coffin even stooped as low as to suggest a love-it-or-leave-it response to Buckley when he opined that Fordham University might have been a better place for the author to study. A close associate of Yale's president, who obviously did not have much confidence in the school's instruction, thought that Buckley's proposal for alumni control of Yale would turn the university into "a small town parochial academy."[12]

McGeorge Bundy, a Yale graduate and professor at Harvard, one of the academics that John F. Kennedy would lure to Washington for advice on foreign policy, drew the assignment of responding to Buckley in the pages of the *Atlantic Monthly*, in an article vetted point by point by President Griswold. For Bundy, Buckley's evidence was slight, his estimate of communists much overdone (they were "rare"), and his assessment of religion flat-out wrong. Yale was more religious than it had been a generation before, and the people responsible for religious life on campus (as if their judgment was impartial) completely disagreed with the book's assessment. But Bundy sensed he had Buckley figured out because the latter was not of the right faith:

> Mr. Buckley, who urges a return to what he considers to be Yale's true religious tradition, at no point says one word of the fact that he himself is an ardent Roman Catholic. In view of the pronounced and well-recognized difference between Protestant and Catholic views on education in America, and in view of Yale's Protestant history, it seems strange for any Roman Catholic to undertake to define the Yale religious tradition (and Yale has

thousands of Catholic alumni and friends who would not dream of such a course); it is stranger still for Mr. Buckley to venture his prescription with no word or hint to show his special allegiance.[13]

Bundy clearly echoed Blanshard's anti-Catholicism. His point was also fair since most Yale graduates would have known enough about religion to think it odd that an observant Roman Catholic was instructing Protestants on running a school founded by Puritans.

The most telling criticisms of Buckley came from very different quarters and argued a similar point, namely, that Buckley's politics had undermined his faith. Among Roman Catholic reviews, the reaction in the Jesuit magazine *America* was indicative of the division between the Roman Catholic left and right that would emerge in the 1960s and 1970s and become reliably firm after the 1980 election of Ronald Reagan. The reviewer for *America* faulted Buckley for not evaluating Yale's economic instruction in "the light of Catholic social doctrine." Although Buckley received praise for endorsing Christian education, his "unawareness of the moral authority of the state to regulate economic society seems fairly complete." From another portion of the U.S. church, *Catholic World*, came the observation that Buckley's book showed how "little in common" Jesus Christ and Adam Smith had.[14]

Dwight Macdonald, a Yale graduate who may have proved Buckley's point about the institution's flawed teaching since the literary critic turned out a man of the Left who went from Trotskyism to socialism, thought Buckley's faith was at best tangential to his complaint about their alma mater. *God and Man at Yale* was an "earnest, extreme, and irreverent book" that followed the script of the "campus rebel." The ardor of the author's Roman Catholicism may have contributed to the experience of such rebellion but was in the end "irrelevant." For Macdonald, Buckley's Christianity came across "in Protestant terms, and his economics Calvinist rather than Catholic." For that reason, Macdonald observed, Yale's reaction to Buckley was almost indecent. It had "all the grace and agility of an elephant cornered by a mouse."[15]

The importance of economics to Buckley's brand of political conservatism became even clearer in his next publishing venture, *McCarthy and His Enemies*, a book he co-wrote with his brother-in-law, Brent Bozell, after doing a brief stint at the CIA. That all three of these figures, Buckley,

Bozell, and McCarthy, were Roman Catholic was no surprise since anti-communism had been at least one area of policy debate on which European and American Roman Catholics agreed. Throughout the nineteenth century, the conservative line of the papacy meant that the Vatican rarely distinguished communism from Marxism, socialism, or anarchism. With the rise of Soviet communism after World War I, the church took an even harder line if only because the Soviet system was materialistic and atheistic, and implemented anticlerical policies wherever it expanded. In the United States, the plight of the labor movement and the formation of unions may have provoked second thoughts among Roman Catholics on economics. But by the time that communism became synonymous with the Soviet Union, Roman Catholics in the United States were overwhelmingly anticommunist. Even the reform-minded lay editors at *Commonweal* magazine were convinced of communism's threat to the West and supported foreign policy designed to prevent its spread.

The main difference between the left and right in U.S. Roman Catholicism was over the form such opposition should take. For liberals such as those who wrote for and read *Commonweal*, Joe McCarthy's tactics were antidemocratic and authoritarian.[16] For Buckley and Bozell, who also were ambivalent about McCarthy's tactics, the issues were too important to quibble over implementation. And so, once again, as he had in *God and Man at Yale*, Buckley adopted the position that liberal society could not be "open" to all views but needed to defend aggressively its own orthodoxy. The future of civilization demanded it.

Buckley and Bozell's strategy in *McCarthy and His Enemies* was to distinguish the Wisconsin senator, a devout Roman Catholic who kept his faith to himself in a manner not unlike John F. Kennedy, from McCarthyism. The latter was what the authors hoped to defend and maintain. McCarthyism in their view was first a recognition that the United States was "in a war against international Communism" and second a program of criticism to "pressure the President, Cabinet members, high officials, and above all the political party in power, to get on with the elimination of security risks in government."[17] For the authors, the question was not one of loyalty to the United States but the ability to recognize policies that either supported or hurt national interest. Taken to its logical end, this position might involve embracing McCarthyism as a public orthodoxy and classifying communist ideas as heretical and communist organizations as illegal. Since Bozell and Buckley were also interested in protecting personal freedoms, such opposition to communism hardly looked libertarian. To preserve their liberal credentials, the authors favored social sanctions over legislation aimed at communists.

The book was a failure but did identify the need for a brand of American conservatism alert to the nation's position in world affairs. For those outlets that did review *McCarthy and His Enemies*, Dwight Macdonald captured the impression of many readers when he wrote that the book left the aftertaste of a legal brief for "a pickpocket caught in the men's room of the subway."[18] McCarthy himself did not help. The book's appearance almost coincided with the televised hearings that McCarthy conducted, which soon exposed the senator's failings. His abuse of alcohol combined with a ruthless manner to make the senator an object of public ridicule. Although Buckley remained on good terms with McCarthy and even wrote speeches for the senator, by the time the U.S. Senate censured McCarthy the young conservative author needed to look elsewhere to air his grievances.

Buckley plotted the creation of a magazine that would provide a vehicle for the kind of arguments he had made and that could rally intellectuals of his outlook to counter the moderate, bordering on indifferent, viewpoint of the East Coast establishment that dominated institutions such as Yale and the Republican Party. *National Review* hit the presses in November 1955. It was a publication that Buckley conceived and organized with Willi Schlamm, an immigrant from Austria of Jewish ancestry and a former communist who worked for *Time* magazine and was part of the anticommunist contingent who had the ear of Henry Luce. Buckley's alliance with Schlamm indicated that of the two concerns that had animated *God and Man at Yale*—Christianity and anticommunism—mounting a conservative opposition to the Soviets was more important. Indeed, the original writers and editors Buckley and Schlamm hoped to enlist—James Burnham, Whittaker Chambers, and Russell Kirk—were all outside the church; Burnham had grown up a Roman Catholic but became an atheist before becoming a conservative, Chambers was a communist turned Quaker, and at the time Kirk was a stoic of a kind. What united these figures was not faith but anticommunism, though the godlessness of Soviet communism would force many of its opponents to find the complete answer in an affirmation of the divine.

The early years of *National Review* were energetic even if a bit chaotic because opposition to a common foe rarely yields a coherent set of ideas. The greatest challenge may have been within Buckley himself, namely, how to reconcile a form of libertarianism and its economic implications with Christian belief. Still, that challenge was also evident in Buckley's effort to herd the magazine's anticommunist cats. For instance, as much as *National Review* appeared to be just one more manifestation of 1950s middle-class conformism, the magazine was actually designed to dissent, in a clever and provocative way, from the orthodoxies of the Eisenhower administration. Yet Buckley had trouble identifying the orthodoxy that *National Review* would promulgate and defend. The 1956 Hungarian uprising revealed the first cracks among the magazine's editors when Burnham lobbied for negotiations with the Soviets in the formation of an independent Eastern Europe rather than sending in troops to assist the Hungarian rebels. The editors objected, and Schlamm wanted Burnham's resignation. The conflict led eventually to Buckley needing to let Schlamm go.

The tensions between the magazine's different forms of opposition to communism were also fierce in 1959 when President Eisenhower invited Nikita Khrushchev to visit the United States. Chambers, who had always expressed ambivalence about Buckley's radical streak, eventually resigned over the magazine's opposition to any gesture that might thaw Soviet-American relations. The reason for the differences between Buckley and Chambers, expressed a few years before Chambers's resignation, were telling. Chambers believed that Buckley stood within "a religious orthodoxy" while Chambers did not. The same went for political orthodoxy. Chambers explained that he was a "man of the right" because he tried to "uphold capitalism in its American version."[19] Even so, capitalism could never be squared with conservatism. For Chambers, modernity and medievalism were at odds.

Buckley sought to harmonize the European past and the American present, a traditional society and a modern economy, through a strand of conservatism that one of the magazine's editors, Frank Meyer, identified as "fusionism." Meyer, the book review editor at the magazine and a Jewish American who would at the end of his life convert to Roman Catholicism, followed a blend of Christian teaching on morality and a libertarian approach to economic and political freedom that wound up

functioning, according to John B. Judis, as Buckley's "*de facto* philosophy." What Meyer tried to do was to add a moral and religious dimension
to classical liberalism by identifying a free society as the means "whereby
men can pursue their proper end which is virtue." Judis put it well when
he observed that Meyer's fusion "provided a way to reconcile [Buckley's]
doctrinal legacies from his father: Catholicism and laissez-faire capitalism." It was an updating of Roman Catholicism almost a decade before
the bishops descended on Rome for the Second Vatican Council to do the
same in their official capacity. But for Buckley and the politically conservative Roman Catholics associated with *National Review*, the updating of
Christianity had a distinctly American flavor.

The Americanness of Buckley's Roman Catholic traditionalism became
particularly noticeable during the papacy of John XXIII and the deliberations of the Second Vatican Council. The founding editor of *National Review* was a serious and observant Roman Catholic, which meant precisely
that he went to Mass routinely and took great comfort from the Latin rite,
all of which the Second Vatican Council overturned. Buckley's affinity for
the Latin service reflected at least in part his own aesthetics, traditionalism, and cosmopolitanism. The Latin rite, Buckley conceded when he
later quoted Evelyn Waugh's defense of the old liturgical form, may have
been accessible only to "the educated few," but surely "Mother Church,
in all her charity, can find a place even for the educated few."[20] At the
same time that Buckley's attachment to Latin reflected his own privileged
background, he was typically American in his understanding of church
authority. Russell Kirk observed that Buckley was not an economist, but
that did not matter since the magazine editor's conservatism stemmed not
from economics but faith. In other words, Buckley had accommodated
the social realities of his nation every bit as much as Al Smith, even if
Buckley's experience included sailing yachts and Smith's only riding the
East River Ferry.

Buckley's custom of thinking about economics and politics indepen-
dently of the Vatican became especially evident after Pope John's encyclical, *Mater et magistra*. Although the pope affirmed the legitimacy of
private property, it was a brief endorsement compared to the longer statement of the state's responsibility to establish a just and equitable social
order. When John wrote that the state "must do all in its power to promote the production of a sufficient supply of material goods," "protect

the rights of all its people, and particularly of its weaker members, the workers, women and children," and work "actively for the betterment of the condition of the workingman,"[21] American conservatives such as Buckley read a potential approval for the sort of state-planned economies that communists followed. He dismissed the encyclical in a July 29, 1961, introductory paragraph to the magazine's editorials. It put an exclamation point on the contrast between Buckley's and John's understanding of the world situation: "[*Mater et magistra*] must strike many as a venture in triviality coming at this particular time in history. The most obtrusive social phenomena of the moment are surely the continuing and demonic successes of the Communists, of which there is scant mention; the extraordinary material well-being that such free economic systems as Japan's, West Germany's, and our own are generating, of which, it would seem, insufficient notice is taken; and the dehumanization, under technology-*cum*-statism, of the individual's role in life, to which there are allusions, but without the rhetorical emphasis given to other matters."[22] In effect, the Vatican was still slighting the United States and its newfound importance in world affairs.

Two weeks later, in its August 12, 1961, issue, Buckley let slip a phrase that would generate even more attention and controversy than *God and Man at Yale*. In a section of *National Review* that amassed ephemera from the headlines, the following appeared: "Going the rounds in Catholic conservative circles: 'Mater, si, Magistra, no.'"[23] Not only did the phrase capture Buckley's devotion to the church as mother and express his disagreement with papal social teaching, but it played off a popular anticommunist slogan: "Cuba, si, Castro, no." In less than a decade Buckley proved capable of offending both the Protestant and Roman Catholic establishments in the United States.

American *Aggiornamento*

The editorial comments in *National Review* prompted a skirmish among U.S. Roman Catholics that foreshadowed later fault lines of faith-informed red state–blue state partisanship. On the upside, it also prompted ironically the first (and only) substantial response to the sort of anti-Catholicism that Paul Blanshard practiced. The respondent was Garry

Wills, a thirty-year-old writer for the magazine who had appeared on Buckley's radar seven years earlier by submitting a parody of *Time* magazine, called "Timestyle." In many respects, Wills was a perfect fit for *National Review*. The son of a mixed (Roman Catholic and Protestant) marriage, Wills received the best education Jesuits had to offer (philosophy at Saint Louis University and Xavier University) before deciding against a career as a priest and pursuing a Ph.D. in classics from Buckley's alma mater, Yale. Buckley was so impressed with Wills that he hired the Yale graduate student as drama critic.

The irony of Wills's response to Buckley's Roman Catholic critics was to turn political conservatives into liberal (read: Americanist) Roman Catholics, that is, people who did not readily affirm papal authority and teaching. At the same time, that charge of ecclesiastical liberalism, or cafeteria Catholicism, from Roman Catholics who were politically liberal placed Buckley's and Wills's critics in the unlikely position of appealing to illiberal (clerical) forms of authority against politically conservative Americanists. Protestant onlookers must have been mystified to see traditionalist Roman Catholics (Buckley) defending the Constitution's liberal polity while progressive Roman Catholics who favored New Deal–styled federal policy appealed to a bishop with divine-right prerogatives. But such was the challenge of trying to map Roman Catholicism's hierarchical character onto the U.S. political system.

The editorial dustup between the Jesuit magazine *America* and *National Review* was the occasion for Wills's book *Politics and Catholic Freedom*, a title that recalled and responded to Blanshard's *American Freedom and Catholic Power*. Wills set the stage for a lengthy and learned—likely too much of each for the book to capture a wide swath of readers—estimate of papal encyclicals' status within the church. The barbs that went back and forth between *America* and *National Review* had less to do with the substance of John XXIII's encyclicals than with the flippancy that Buckley had revealed to papal authority. Then a young author with real talent, Wills decided to begin *Politics and Catholic Freedom* with lengthy quotations from the back-and-forth bickering, a decision that may account, despite the insight afforded, for the book's tiny footprint in the literature of papal authority and conservative Roman Catholicism.

Wills began with a quip from Thomas N. Davis, editor of *America*, that it "takes a daring young man to characterize a papal document as 'a venture in triviality,'" but Buckley's long "practice on the high wire" had nurtured such daring. Wills also found similar effrontery in parish newspapers. From William J. Smith came the hyperbolic comparison: "When a spiritual intellectual giant of the stature of Pope John XXIII is ridiculed by a hypercritical pigmy, the sound of protest should be loud and lasting." Another parish editor, Donald McDonald, also thought Buckley had no qualifications "to speak out on the great social problems of our age"; his words simply had no force. "True" Roman Catholic conservatives needed to oppose the "latest display of anti-intellectual temper tantrums." As Wills's report of the exchange wore on, anticommunism surfaced as an important factor preventing reconciliation. In an article for *Ave Maria* in which Buckley tried to explain his criticisms of *Mater et magistra*, he objected to the naive notion that implementing programs of social justice was sufficient to stop the spread of communism. "The Communists would find just as much to criticize in an integrated South," he explained, "as in a segregated South." Davis at *America* replied that such a statement, if eaten "word by word," would incline a person "to skip lunch." In fact, Buckley's anticommunism inevitably boiled down to "individualism" and so contradicted the church's social teaching of solidarity.[24]

The debate had its moments and certainly explained Wills's purpose, but it also added an ephemeral quality to a book with much greater substance than the ad hoc rhythms of editorial bickering. *National Review*'s comments raised the age-old issue that American Roman Catholics had faced since the Americanist controversy: to what degree were church members obligated to adhere to papal teaching? "Buckley's case," Wills explained, "is the ideal one for presenting some of the dangers that threaten Catholic discourse in America." The assumed disloyalty of Buckley in the Roman Catholic press and among devout church members, without anyone being able to explain precisely how Buckley had gone astray, was comparable to assuming people who disagreed with *Brown v. Board of Education*'s reasoning were racist.

Wills used the case of John F. Kennedy. Some conservative clergy and laity had "tried to discredit" the presidential candidate with a loyalty test similar to the one *America* magazine's editors had used on Buckley (41). Wills conceded the sincerity of this test, that Buckley's critics were doing what they thought was in the interest of the church. Wills detected an assumption that good Roman Catholics "cannot disagree on any significant matter without one party's putting itself outside the pale" (42). What particularly reinforced this assumption was the doctrine of papal infallibility and the supreme authority of the pope that always tagged along with that dogma. Was it possible, for instance, after popes having referred repeatedly to the legitimate work of the United Nations, for a Roman Catholic to debate what had become part of the church's social teaching? This dependence on the papacy, according to Wills, "impeded the development of an informed and active laity" and nurtured the idea that Roman Catholics had only "*one* acceptable view on each question" (45). The irony was that at the very moment Wills was calling for the reevaluation of papal authority, the church's hierarchy was doing precisely that at the Second Vatican Council.

One part of Wills's book was an estimate of the exact weight a papal encyclical possessed in the life of the church and the conscience of a church member. Encyclicals had, he conceded, "assumed great importance in the modern world," an expression of the church's corporate "personality" (51). Yet their nature was "shadowy," so much so that theologians were divided (52). Wills contended that they were a recent addition to papal authority and even that the genre in its contemporary form did not emerge until Benedict XIV's letter of 1740. What is more, encyclicals became the device for popes, having lost the mechanisms of temporal authority in the Papal States and needing a way to address the pluralistic societies in which the church existed, to address relations between ecclesiastical and civil authorities. Here, however, the range of papal teaching on the state was so varied—from *The Syllabus of Errors*, which condemned liberalism, to *Mater et magistra*, which showed remarkable openness to a variety of political systems—as to challenge the degree to which encyclicals could ever be binding (let alone coherent).

Further confusion concerned the matter of infallibility. Were encyclicals infallible? What if a pope issued an infallible dogma through an encyclical? Were all encyclicals of equal authoritative standing? All of these were questions that popes had not clarified and on which theologians disagreed. Even more confusing, at least in the way that encyclicals functioned among twentieth-century Roman Catholicism, were statements such as Leo XIII's in *Immortale dei*, in which he declared that in matters "purely political," differences of opinion were "lawful" (69). And then encyclicals occasioned the dilemmas that dogged biblical scholars in the interpretation of scripture. For instance, when a pope asserted that nineteenth-century economic activity was motivated almost exclusively by materialism, did that settle the matter of historical research into the market's origins? Or might the pope be reflecting his own historical circumstances and so employ culturally conditioned assumptions to convey truths that transcended time and place? Wills was offering a thoughtful response to the perennial anti-Catholic complaints about papal authority over U.S. officials who were church members—the kind used against Al Smith and Kennedy—that few Roman Catholics had yet attempted. It challenged the very heart of papal authority. And it was coming from a political conservative.

Wills's objection to papal authority did not rely on American assumptions per se but instead depended on a form of theological reflection that demonstrated a willingness to think within the teaching of the church. The question of papal infallibility, or whether the church could err, was too often a deduction, in Wills's estimate, from mechanical conceptions of the magisterium. He spotted a similarity between claims of papal authority and divine right monarchy. "Because the church is founded on a divine mandate . . . all its *proper* actions are exempted from the laws of nature." This understanding simply "homogenized" the character of authority. According to Wills, the truth was much more complicated and involved the reality that the church could err "*even in the exercise of her divinely granted authority*" in matters of "earthly society" (114). The reason was that church authority played out in the vicissitudes of "human circumstances and accidents." Divine truth and authority could not override human limitations and weakness. In fact, appeals to papal authority often included a belief that popes were protected from error in ways that escaped even those who wrote the Bible.

The preposterousness of that idea led Wills to give examples of the limits on papal insight. When papal encyclicals appealed to historical developments, was it possible for a pope to be wrong about the past? "If the Pope is not guaranteed against error in the description of past events, he can scarcely be granted unfailing insight into the men, institutions, and movements of his own time" (190). The same logic applied, Wills argued, to medicine, economics, and politics. The limits of papal insight were even manifest when popes taught about church matters. When, for instance, Boniface VIII claimed universal jurisdiction over temporal and spiritual matters in *Unam Sanctam*, he overreached in ways acknowledged by most theologians. The church had interpreted Boniface to be restating the abstract truth of papal primacy but not the actual relationship between the bishop of Rome's power and other earthly authorities. In fact, many theologians argued that Boniface's assertion was unwise, which led Wills to claim that "infallibility does not make popes prudent." However interpreted, that famous papal encyclical pronounced an extraordinary truth within a *"misconception of the relation of that truth to the political order"* (193; italics in the original). How such circumstances squared with Roman Catholic confidence in popes to be right about everything was a riddle not even papal authority could solve.

Wills's complaints about infallibility extended to John XXIII, the one whose encyclical had prompted the skirmish between *National Review* and *America*. At issue was the ability of popes to provide good and wise counsel—several rungs below infallible teaching—about social matters that oftentimes eluded the academic experts who studied these subjects for a living. In a survey of papal social teaching about unions, Wills noted that Pope Leo "emphasized the right to form organizations," Pius X and Pius XI stressed "adaptability" of organizations in including Roman Catholics, Pius XII "warned against the loss of human perspective" in organizational scale, and John XXIII recommended the benefits derived from "multiple and flexible 'intermediate organizations'" (200). In each case, popes issued historical judgments that were "more and less adequate." Leo XIII's warning's against "neutral" unions made sense in European contexts where anticlericalism still prevailed, but not in the United States where Roman Catholics had adjusted to religiously indifferent unions well before the encyclical *Quadragesimo anno* (201). For Wills, the doctrine of papal infallibility was not a mechanical solution to the dilemmas of the modern world nor the answer to being a good Roman Catholic. Papal teaching always had to be "combined with historical circumstance, often in a way that was not foreseen by the encyclicals, or even in a way that *canceled* recommendations made on the assumption that other conditions did or would prevail." Such application did not *"involve disloyalty to the papal teaching"* (206).

John XXIII's apparent support for the United Nations in *Pacem in terris* was another instance where logic outran the demands of prudence. Simply because the church's teaching, "discovered by reason and confirmed by

faith," supported inclusive organizations that promoted peace and disarmament, the conclusion did not follow that the United Nations was "the
most inclusive organization," or that Roman Catholics had an obligation
to support the international body. For anticommunists such as Wills, too
many difficult questions surrounded the usefulness of the United Nations
or attempts to prove the papacy's endorsement: "Should complete tolerance, or a minimal courtesy, be given to the evil system, so that contact
may be had with the men enslaved by it?" What happens if such contact
increases "that slavery," decreases "men's hope of liberation from it," and
removes "their very ability to conceive an alternative?" These were not
"easy questions" that an encyclical could determine (241).

In the end, Wills's book was a brief for freedom within the papal system, and his conclusion echoed earlier Roman Catholic arguments for
American ideals but did so in a way that recognized the difficulty posed by
simple assertions of papal supremacy. He concluded the book with a discussion of freedom that attempted to reconcile personal liberty with being
Roman Catholic. The way to do this was to affirm liberty not as freedom from restraint but as self-government. Liberty on this view involved
"a recognition of the freedom and responsibility of others" (276). Wills
believed the church had historically encouraged such liberty even while
rejecting "libertarian" notions of freedom. He observed that the Gospel
of John included Christ's words that "the truth shall make you free" (John
8:32) (281). The role of the Holy Spirit in guiding such liberty meant that
"external laws and rules of discipline" by the church were "supplemen-
tary and subordinate" to the Spirit's "action in the soul" (282).

This nonlibertarian and spiritual understanding of liberty had important consequences for thinking about the place of Roman Catholicism in
the United States. On the one hand, the personal nature of liberty meant
that requiring religious fidelity from the state was misguided. "The state
does not serve God. . . . It has no soul to save," Wills asserted. " 'America'
will not go to heaven or hell." On the other hand, the Roman Catholic notion of liberty truly freed Roman Catholics to serve American ideals. Wills believed John F. Kennedy well exemplified the Roman Catholic
contribution to national life when he explained that as a Christian he
"acknowledged laws that are prior to political laws" (288). The capacity
to recognize a higher law, one that provided "moral moorings that can
ride out the passionate and anarchistic tidal waves that sometimes wreck

whole nations," was the sort of freedom that Wills defended. These moral obligations were perfectly consistent with the tradition of constitutional government and with the papacy's capacity to provide moral teaching that transcended time and place. Papal authority, as such, was variable according to "all kinds of regimes" (290). The Paul Blanshards of the world were just as wrong as the editors of *America* to use papal authority in a mechanical way that missed the moral nature of liberty and the flexibility of church teaching.

Tradition Reversed

The reception of *Politics and Catholic Freedom* was virtually opposite that of Paul Blanshard's *American Freedom and Catholic Power*. The foes of Buckley and *National Review* in the Roman Catholic publishing world ignored the book. Indeed, if the policy during the spat between *America* and *National Review* at the Jesuit magazine had been to refuse any submission from a person on Buckley's magazine's masthead, giving Wills publicity through a review was no less egregious. This was not the case for *National Review*, where the book received positive coverage. Will Herberg, a Jewish academic who wrote about the sociology of religion and contributed regularly to *National Review*, explained that the significance of Wills's book lay in the explanation of an encyclical's authoritative status. Herberg grasped that a pope was infallible in cases of doctrine and morality when speaking *ex cathedra*. But what about the rest of the pope's and the hierarchy's statements? A Roman Catholic was obligated to follow a universal standard of charity. Did such love involve opposition to a "foreign aid policy geared primarily to an over-all strategy for the defense of our country and mankind against Soviet totalitarian tyranny?"[25] That question—the United States' battle against Soviet communism—was the one that animated American political conservatives and raised the stakes for conservative church members such as Wills and Buckley.

Wills himself had barely mentioned communism or the Cold War in his book. His treatment of papal authority went far beyond the incident that had touched off the debate with *America* and tried to solve a perennial problem for lay Roman Catholics in an age of papal social teaching: namely, were church members obligated to follow the pope on all papal instruction? Wills's great contribution, for Herberg, was to loosen papal authority and quasi-infallibility from "certain ideologies and policies." In other words, rather than losing Roman Catholic opposition to communism thanks to papal idealism about a new age of cooperation and mutual understanding, Wills provided a way for individual church members to maintain a measure of fealty to the hierarchy while also honoring their obligations as citizens of a nation engaged in a cold war. The "pre-eminent position of the Roman Catholic church in the West" was too consequential for the clash of free and totalitarian civilizations.[26]

When Murray Kempton, the respected journalist then attached to the *New Republic* and a friend of Buckley's, commented on Wills's book, he spoke less about Roman Catholicism than about Americanism. For Kempton, Wills represented a "cafeteria Catholic," a phrase that one of Kempton's friends had applied to Buckley after reading *God and Man at Yale*. "We are a nation," Kempton wrote, "whose theological diet is catered by short-order cooks." The limited diet of the nation and its Roman Catholic citizens meant that the reception of Pope John's encyclicals would fall along not dogmatic but political lines. For Buckley's fellow believers at *National Review*, the church stood (or should stand) foursquare against communism, while his critics read John's encyclicals through the lens of "the brotherhood of man." Kempton believed the point of the church was to stand above the times, to resist the spirit of the age. He encouraged his friend, Buckley, to remember that Christianity does not "grow or diminish to the degree that its Supreme Pontiff can be read as soldier or slacker in the Cold War." The same lesson applied to Buckley's clerical critics. A man was not in danger of hell for failing to support labor unions. "Hell is a place with more serious standards for admission," Kempton concluded, and to suggest otherwise was "to lose all proportion about the wages of sin."[27]

Of course, the problem for political conservatives such as Buckley was that the church seemed to be shifting from its long-standing opposition to the modern world. For American conservatives, the point of identifying with the Right was to "stand athwart history and yell stop."[28] Being Roman Catholic was a natural part of such resistance to modernity, since for almost four centuries the papacy and curia had registered verdict after verdict on the modern West's departure from medieval Europe's Christian civilization. Yet Pope John and the ecumenical council he called was softening its conservatism. Not only did John's ecumenism hedge the church's earlier opposition to communism, but his desire to open the church to the modern world seemed to do precisely the opposite of that for which the times called—"yelling stop."

The problem for American political conservatives went beyond Rome's receptivity to left-leaning politics to the matter that Wills's book examined head-on—namely, papal authority. He later admitted that appearing as it did during the Second Vatican Council, *Politics and Catholic Freedom* was "an instant anachronism." After the council, Wills explained, the old left-right antagonisms among Roman Catholics in the United States "faded or were effaced." The work of the bishops who gathered during the early 1960s in effect destroyed the ecclesiastical mechanisms that had silenced John Courtney Murray and the liberal identification of Roman Catholicism with the Democratic Party. Wills contended that Paul Blanshard had a point about papal supremacy since Rome had silenced Murray "precisely for saying that there could be no church-established politics." The Second Vatican Council vindicated Murray and demonstrated that the 1950s Vatican had been "aberrant."[29] The domestication of the church for national politics had also contributed to an odd amalgam of liberal discomfort with papal restrictions and enthusiasm for progressive-sounding social teaching. "Some Catholics wanted to prove that they not only *could* be democratic with a small 'd,' but *had* to be Democrats in the party sense. Older liberals remembered the Al Smith campaign, and charges that a Catholic could not be a true American. In the general superpatriotism of the cold-war years, they started saying only 'true Americans' could be Catholic!" That construction of patriotism left out Bill Buckley, according to Wills. When *National Review*'s editor opposed the "welfarism of Pope John's *Mater et Magistra*," priests and lay theologians accused Buckley of "schism, Heresy, defection from the faith." "For a heady moment, the victims of heresy hunts" became "heresy hunters themselves."[30]

To be sure, the Second Vatican Council's openness to modernity signaled an end to the kind of close reading of political arguments that Murray had experienced, but it hardly resolved Wills's questions about papal authority. In fact, the bishops' discussion of the hierarchy and church power only increased the potential for disputes among U.S. Roman Catholics about loyalty to Rome and betraying such fealty with either American patriotism or nationalism. In *Lumen gentium*, a Second Vatican Council statement (dogmatic constitution) on church governance, delegates conceived the ecclesiastical hierarchy in ways more collegial or reciprocal than previously. The bishops appealed to the example of the apostles, the early church, and the period of conciliarism (fifteenth century) to argue that the papacy and the bishops share "a bond of unity, charity, and peace" that called for them to settle "profound issues" in common. In other words, the episcopate possessed a "collegiate character."[31] John O'Malley, in his impressive history of the Second Vatican Council, argued that *Lumen gentium* reproduced ways of thinking about the church more "rhetorical and poetic" and typical of the first millennium of Christian history than the "juridical, political, and agonistic language" that prevailed in the High Middle Ages and that characterized Rome's responses to modernity. A minority at the council opposed collegiality because it seemed to contradict the First Vatican Council's assertion of papal infallibility and exhibited a form of collegiality that was "unworkable, unacceptable, dangerous, and perhaps even heretical."[32]

As much as *Lumen gentium* affirmed greater cooperation among the bishops, it nevertheless reaffirmed a hierarchical approach to church power that left the pope in charge and the laity at the bottom rung of the ecclesiastical ladder. For instance, the document was adamant about papal supremacy: "The college or body of bishops has no authority unless it is understood together with the Roman Pontiff, the successor of Peter as its head." In sum, papal authority "over all, both pastors and faithful, remains whole and intact."[33] Meanwhile, though *Lumen gentium*'s instructions on the role of the laity included church members in the mission and work of the church, it also reaffirmed submission to the church hierarchy. Members should "promptly accept in Christian obedience decisions of their spiritual shepherds." The council acknowledged that church members, "by reason of the knowledge, competence or outstanding ability," had permission and sometimes were even obligated to express their opinions about the good of the church. But when communicating in such a manner, the laity needed to work through "organs erected by the Church" and to express their views "with reverence and charity toward those who by reason of their sacred office represent the person of Christ."[34]

By those criteria, Buckley's quip (after Wills) "Mater si, magistra no" still fell short of the standards erected by the updated church for submission to the hierarchy. Not only had he challenged the capacity of Pope John to understand the world that the Vatican wanted to engage, but Buckley had done so without the requisite reverence and charity, or even in the proper forum. As much as the Second Vatican Council may have reduced tensions between national and church loyalties, especially by recognizing religious freedom, the hierarchical conception of the episcopacy still imposed restrictions implicitly on what church members might say. This was especially true in a context where popes decided to weigh in on political and economic subjects under the rubric of the church's social teaching.

Wills may have thought that he answered Paul Blanshard's anti-Catholicism and that the Second Vatican Council opened a new stage of Roman Catholic history. But for Roman Catholics who esteemed the U.S. political and economic system and the nation's role in world affairs, what used to be called Americanism could still wind up at odds with papal pronouncements or church members who appealed to those statements. In that case, American political conservatives would have to forge a politics that took its direction not from the old world order that had historically shaped the Vatican but from the ideals of a nation conceived as a "new order for the ages." That outlook meant taking cues about the United States more from Ben Franklin, Thomas Jefferson, and John Adams than from Popes Pius IX and Leo XIII.

5

THE EXTREMITIES OF
DEFENDING LIBERTY

When Barry Goldwater chose William E. Miller as his running mate in the 1964 presidential election, the Republican nominee's advisers regarded Miller's church membership as an asset rather than a liability. The grandson of German American immigrants, Miller was reared in the Roman Catholic Church and graduated from the University of Notre Dame before attending Albany Law School. At the time of the 1964 campaign, Miller was a congressman from New York State (Niagara County) and chairman of the Republican National Committee. None of those positions helped him overcome obscurity. Many knew Miller best for his constant sniping at John F. Kennedy. Even so, a common refrain during the campaign mocked the vice presidential nominee's insignificance: "Here's a riddle, it's a killer / Who the hell is William Miller?" That anonymity would eventually pay dividends for the New York congressman. In the 1970s, when American Express ran advertisements featuring unknown figures with the campaign, "Do You Know Me?" Miller was the first person to appear.[1] That was hardly consolation to Goldwater who in the 1964 election lost in one of the worst defeats in presidential history. The Republican nominee won only six states, all in the South, and received a mere fifty-two votes in the electoral college. Miller's eastern and Roman Catholic attributes were no match for his unremarkable status as a national political figure.

Miller's fame was the least of Goldwater's worries. For a candidate who had throughout the Republican primaries endured charges of being an extremist, the contest with the incumbent, Lyndon Baines Johnson, only exposed Goldwater to further accusations. The most publicized was the "Daisy" commercial that juxtaposed the image of a little girl plucking petals from a flower with an atomic bomb exploding while the voice of LBJ said: "These are the stakes—to make a world in which all of God's children can live, or to go into the dark."[2] That sentiment echoed more the call of Pope John XXIII to peaceful coexistence than it did taking a hard line against the Soviets. Even so, it spoke to many Republicans who opposed Goldwater's candidacy.

On the eve of the 1964 Republican National Convention in San Francisco, Goldwater appeared on *Meet the Press* with a party rival, William Scranton, the governor of Pennsylvania who had gained momentum among the East Coast Republican establishment—Milton Eisenhower, George Romney, and Henry Cabot Lodge. Goldwater and Scranton were friends, and the Arizonan had considered tapping the Pennsylvania governor as his running mate. But that was impossible after Scranton informed the nation how leaders in the GOP thought of their fellow Republican: "Goldwaterism has come to stand for a whole crazy-quilt collection of absurd and dangerous positions that would be soundly repudiated by the American people in November." Goldwater's campaign responded, with the help of Harry Jaffa, a political science professor at Ohio State University, by trying to present the senator's conservatism in the aura of Abraham Lincoln. According to a press release, if the first Republican president were alive in 1964 he would have called himself a conservative. Goldwater himself tried to turn Scranton's accusations into an asset. His most memorable line in his acceptance speech in San Francisco was: "I would remind you that extremism in the defense of liberty—is—no—vice." His corollary was that "moderation in the pursuit of justice is no virtue."[3] What the press and the American public failed to notice was that the pugnacious and vociferous conservatism that Goldwater voiced bore the fingerprints of Roman Catholic neo-Americanists.

The 1960 book that identified Goldwater with the conservative movement and that challenged the GOP's East Coast establishment, *Conscience
of a Conservative*, was the ghostwritten product of L. Brent Bozell. The
brother-in-law of William F. Buckley, Jr., and coauthor of *McCarthy and
His Enemies*, Bozell grew up in Nebraska a nominal Protestant who converted to Roman Catholicism before enrolling at Yale University, where he
met Buckley and began their friendship. Bozell's politics were even more
aggressive than Buckley's, and the two men eventually parted over *National Review*'s effort to keep libertarians and traditionalist Roman Catholics together under conservatism's tent. Whether that difference with
Buckley made Bozell extreme in the sense that Richard Hofstadter popularized with the phrase "paranoid style" was the question that haunted
the brand of conservatism being developed by Roman Catholics such as
Bozell. (In 1964, soon after Goldwater secured the Republican nomination, Richard Hofstadter, a Columbia University historian, published an
essay with *Harper's* magazine, "The Paranoid Style of American Politics,"
an early attempt by a Pulitzer Prize–winning historian to understand and
explain the rise of political conservatism.) Another voice that gained the
ear of a Republican presidential hopeful was Patrick J. Buchanan, a senior
adviser and speechwriter for Richard M. Nixon. Bozell and Buchanan by
no means shared the same outlook, nor did their political convictions line
up unequivocally with their religious beliefs. Even so, both rendered an estimate of the United States that resonated with the older Americanism that
the Vatican had once regarded suspiciously. Although the Second Vatican
Council signaled a different relationship between the church and the modern world, conservative Roman Catholics such as Bozell and Buchanan
suggested that local circumstances like national origin and personal convictions did more to color perceptions of politics than the church's social
teaching.

Conscience Freed

L. Brent Bozell was an unlikely person to ghostwrite for a presidential
candidate. Born in 1926 to an Episcopalian family in Omaha, Nebraska,
Bozell's parents sent him to Creighton Preparatory School, an institution
that planted the seeds of Roman Catholicism and also prepared him for

admission to Yale. In 1944, after graduating from Creighton Prep and before using an American Legion scholarship for oratory to acquire an Ivy League education, Bozell joined the merchant marine because he was too young to join the navy. Once he turned eighteen he joined the navy and served for two years before enrolling at Yale. That was the same year that Bozell joined the Roman Catholic Church, a decision that his father was also planning before his death in 1946. The conversion likely had more to do with William F. Buckley, Jr., than with Bozell's father. Indeed, Bozell's ties to the Buckleys included more than religion. Through their friendship, Bozell turned from the idealism of one world government—he had been president of Yale's World Federalists—to political conservatism. Bozell also married a Buckley, Patricia, Bill's sister who attended Vassar College. Buckley credited Bozell with being the superior student of the two friends. Buckley also said that Bozell was "the most incisive political orator I ever knew."[4] After Yale, Bozell attended Yale Law School, and on graduation in 1953 he moved to Washington to become a speechwriter for Sen. Joseph McCarthy, a position that afforded an insider perspective for the book he coauthored with Buckley, *McCarthy and His Enemies* (1954). From there the transition to being a founding contributor to *National Review* and editor after 1957 was fluid. Bozell was on the ground floor of the conservative movement.[5]

The route to ghostwriting a book for a presidential hopeful was less circuitous than working for his brother-in-law. Here the world of Roman Catholic anticommunism afforded Bozell a straightforward even if hidden path. The person who put Bozell on that trail was Clarence "Pat" Manion, a Roman Catholic from a Democratic family in Kentucky who became a lawyer and dean of the University of Notre Dame's Law School. Before assuming the reins at the Law School, Manion had taught law at Notre Dame and also ran twice unsuccessfully for Congress, once for the House (1932) and once for the Senate (1934). A critic of progressivism and the New Deal, in 1940 Manion opposed FDR's plans to intervene in the war in Europe and joined America First, a coalition of liberals and conservatives who opposed U.S. entry into another European war. With objections as well to the growth of the federal government, Manion adopted a decidedly antistatist outlook. By the time he retired in 1952 from Notre Dame, he began to work for the Republican Robert Taft in that year's Republican presidential primaries. When defeat looked imminent and Taft agreed to support the Eisenhower-Nixon ticket, General Eisenhower pledged to use Taft supporters in his administration.

Under Eisenhower, Manion chaired the Intergovernmental Relations Committee, a position that allowed him the opportunity to spot federal programs that unconstitutionally increased Washington's power over national life (even if the Constitution may have reserved such tasks for the courts). Not long into his tenure on the committee, Manion was fired by Eisenhower for supporting the Bricker Amendment (discussed in the next section). The former dean returned to South Bend, where he devised strategies to reduce the federal government's scope and Wall Street's access to Washington. By 1958, after the off-year elections saw Democrats drub Republicans, Manion drew up a scheme to dislocate the party's eastern establishment and looked to writers at *National Review* for help. Drafting the junior senator from Arizona, Barry Goldwater, was crucial to that plan. Manion also recruited Brent Bozell to raise funds for the Draft Goldwater campaign.

Because Bozell himself had suffered defeat in the 1958 Maryland election for the state's House of Delegates, he must have figured he had the time to work for Manion, who hoped to shake up the Republican Party. Contributions to the Draft Goldwater movement were meager. Bozell managed to raise only $1,667 that year. The problem was that major donors wanted to know whether the campaign could count on support from the South. Another difficulty was an unrealistic estimate of the American public. The leadership behind Goldwater's campaign assumed that most of the country shared their conservative outlook. Bozell, however, thought a conservative constituency needed to be cultivated. He wrote in *National Review* that the "great majority" of the American public were not ideological and cast their votes for Democrats or Republicans without serious consideration of the implications. The task before political conservatives was to educate the public "and organize them."[6]

Whether a magazine or a booklet from the candidate was a better pedagogical strategy was up for debate, but by 1959 Manion had secured from Goldwater permission to write under the senator's name a hundred-page booklet on conservatism. The former law school dean had also persuaded Bozell to write the book. The hope was that businesses and corporations would purchase the title and distribute it to employees, customers, or anyone associated with their companies. Once Goldwater agreed to the book,

Manion discovered that Bozell was in Spain where throne-and-altar conservatism had begun to turn the Roman Catholic convert's head. But once back in the United States, Bozell devoted his energies to the Goldwater book, and by the time of the next meeting of the Draft Goldwater forces in January 1960 at Chicago's Union League Club, *The Conscience of a Conservative* was ready for the senator's inspection. Goldwater approved, and Manion turned the manuscript over to Victor Publishing, a vanity imprint that Manion had created specifically for the book, which by March had printed fifty thousand copies.

The Conscience of a Conservative functioned as playbook for post–World War II American conservatism. All the themes that have animated conservative political candidates from Goldwater to recent Republicans were present—limited government and its constitutional provisions, protection of freedoms for individuals, suspicion of federal programs, and national military prowess. The book began by establishing the proper relationship between people and government. Goldwater (via Bozell) insisted on the dignity and variety of individuals. Government's duty was to protect personal freedoms and so nurture the diversity of people. From here it was a short step to the idea of limited government. The balance between freedom and order was a "delicate" one. The predicament that America faced in 1960 was an expansive government that restrained freedom. Federal spending was too large, taxes to pay for the federal budget were too high, and the government increasingly regulated private business, whether the farmer who received instruction on "how much wheat he can grow," the worker who was "at the mercy" of union leaders empowered by federal legislation, or a business owner "hampered by a maze of government regulations." All of these interventions in the economy were at odds with both the spirit and the letter of the Constitution. That document reflected the lessons taught by history, namely, that "the natural tendency" of power was "the acquisition of *all* power." The design of the Constitution, accordingly, was to specify the federal government's powers, reserve for states and citizens those authorities not "delegated" to federal power, and limit federal government's power through a system of checks and balances among the executive, legislative, and judicial branches. As significant as Soviet communism's threat to the United States was, "ignoring the Constitution and disregarding the principles of limited government" were no less menacing.[7]

Goldwater's affirmation of states' rights was appealing to Americans who both celebrated the Constitution and were still smarting from the New Deal's expansion of the federal government's administration. According to Goldwater, the Tenth Amendment was not merely a "general assumption" but a "prohibitory rule of law." The virtue of the states' sovereignty was first to restrain central government and second to affirm that "local problems are best dealt with by the people most directly concerned." The conservatives' preference for localism might have looked less objectionable when in 1960 it came to funds for a proposed Federal Department of Education. Spending on public education through the federal government would obviously raise taxes and "inevitably means federal control of education." Standardization of public schooling was the next domino to fall, and with it came John Dewey's philosophy of "progressive education," an outlook that helped students "adjust to their environment" and tried to make education "fun," instead of stirring "the ambitions of our best students." States' rights was less pronounced in Goldwater's argument when he addressed labor unions, which needed to be restored "to their proper place in a free society." That meant making union membership voluntary, confining union activities to collective bargaining, and ensuring that the employer would be directly involved in contract negotiation.[8] So too when Goldwater discussed welfare, he questioned whether the federal government was the proper vehicle for addressing poverty. Here the remedy was not the states. It was private humanitarian agencies such as churches, hospitals, and community charities.

Through Bozell, Goldwater foreshadowed most of the arguments that conservatives would make over the next fifty years, but on the subject of race and civil rights the senator's political philosophy was the most glaringly suspect piece of his proposal. The phrase "civil rights" was commonly associated, Goldwater claimed, with "human" or "natural" rights. But the precise definition of civil rights was one incorporated explicitly in the law. As such, the right to vote was a civil right protected by the Fifteenth Amendment. Enrollment at a mixed-race school, however, was not a civil right but a matter of prudence. "It may be just or wise or expedient for negro children to attend the same schools as white children," Goldwater explained, "but they do not have a civil right . . . protected by the federal constitution." The senator clarified that he was himself "in agreement with the *objectives* of the Supreme Court in the *Brown* decision." Goldwater believed that integration of public schools was "just and wise." But he was not prepared to "impose that judgment of mine on the people of Mississippi or South Carolina." The challenge of race relations, like most of society's problems, was "best handled by the people directly concerned."[9]

Race relations revealed the weakest link of conservatives' states' rights outlook. Not only did many Americans interpret it later as code for protecting white supremacy in southern states. It made also conservatism appear to have no policy for an enormous social injustice that had direct bearings on the rest of the states in the union. Indeed, reasserting states' rights in the midst of the civil rights movement was a strategy that tied political conservatism to the South and the region's infamous past. But to readers of the *National Review*, sympathy with the white South was not surprising, since William F. Buckley, Jr., had written three years earlier that white southerners were justified in taking "such measures as are necessary to prevail" because whites were "for the time being" the "advanced" race. For conservatives in the Goldwater camp, "the claims of civilization supersede those of universal suffrage."[10]

The greatest inconsistency in the argument that Bozell laid out for Goldwater was the gap between protecting local government and fighting international communism. How could local authorities possibly carry on a battle of that scale? Goldwater gave almost no attention to the chasm between reducing the federal government domestically and increasing its international presence in the chapter on "The Soviet Menace," the book's longest. It was a full-scale rejection of U.S. foreign policy and left the sort of paper trail that Johnson's campaign could use to portray Goldwater as trigger-happy. The basic problem of the nation's policy was its ideal of peace and appeasement when the threat of communism required a strategy of confrontation. Goldwater rejected alliances as ineffective, foreign aid as expensive and counterproductive, negotiations with the Soviets as dishonest, exchange programs as naive, disarmament as foolish, and the United Nations as compromised.

The book's complaints about disarmament and the United Nations were not yet but would become particularly sensitive for Roman Catholics such as Bozell once Pope John XXIII's encyclical, *Mater et magistra*, predisposed the Vatican to treaties that banned nuclear testing and cooperation through international organizations. *The Conscience of a*

Conservative appeared a year before the encyclical, but the contrast between Goldwater's convictions and papal teaching explained the controversy that erupted over Buckley's line, "Mater si, magistra no," and Garry
Wills's subsequent account of papal authority's limits. Even so, Goldwater's concluding argument was a call for victory over communism. Appeasement risked war as much as the pursuit of military superiority. But
only one strategy could defeat communism and preserve American liberty.
For Goldwater, the "hard counsel" of confronting the Soviets varied little
from the "risks that were taken to create our country," when the founding
generation of Americans "staked their 'lives, fortunes, and sacred honor' "
for the sake of procuring liberty.[11]

The Conscience of a Conservative was not sufficiently effective to
put Goldwater on the 1960 Republican ticket for president, but it was
responsible for adding spice to the party's national convention held in
Chicago. The vice president, Richard M. Nixon, ran in the primaries virtually unopposed, though in states such as South Dakota and West Virginia, governors (James M. Lloyd and Cecil H. Underwood, respectively)
won local primary elections before withdrawing from the race. The Draft
Goldwater remnant remained strong and vocal in Chicago. When Nixon
arrived at his hotel for the convention, he saw hundreds of "Goldwater for President" placards held by demonstrators on the street. Those
supporters were also responsible, along with organizers such as Manion,
for nominating Goldwater for president on the penultimate night of the
convention. The nomination came from the Arizona delegation but had
much support from southern Republicans and a raft of college students
for whom Goldwater had become a political phenomenon. After the delegates heard Goldwater's name placed in nomination, they witnessed
the senator's supporters march around the convention hall while the or-
chestra played "Dixie." Goldwater tried to stop the wave of excitement,
but the crowd ignored his raised hands. When movement conservatives
finally quieted down, Goldwater asked the chairman of the convention
to remove his name from nomination. He explained that despite differences with Nixon, the "Republican platform deserves the support of every
American over the blueprint for socialism presented by the Democrats."
Goldwater encouraged his supporters: "Conservatives have made a splen-
did showing at this Convention," but it was time to "put our shoulders
to the wheel for Dick Nixon and push him across the finish line." When

Bozell heard the senator fall in line with the party establishment, he said, "That son of a bitch."[12]

The Conservative's Dilemma

When politically conservative Roman Catholics such as Bozell were putting their hopes in the Republican senator from Arizona, they were not only snubbing the GOP East Coast establishment but also the Roman Catholic senator from Massachusetts. In fact, if John F. Kennedy stood out for his willingness to say that his religious convictions were private and had no direct bearing on his understanding of policy or the presidency, politically conservative Roman Catholics were equally untethered to church teaching in their case for Goldwater. In some cases, the Roman Catholics who spearheaded the campaign to draft Goldwater exhibited a form of Americanism even more decidedly nationalist than that of Kennedy, Al Smith, or even the most patriotic U.S. bishops. The Democratic Party, after all, had been the political home for immigrants, had cultivated public assistance programs that mirrored Roman Catholic charities, and, as Kennedy showed, could be as anticommunist as the best Cold War warriors. To embrace small government platforms, to see socialism in any federal government program, to endorse personal freedoms in ways that bordered on Lockean liberalism, and to do so by exalting the American founding and the powers enumerated in the U.S. Constitution was to sow serious confusion within the priests and laity. For devout Roman Catholics to be at the forefront of such an outlook was breathtaking. Many critics of Kennedy could account for his views about politics and religion by explaining that his attachment to the church was weak. But for those such as Buckley devoted to Rome's liturgy, tradition, and hierarchy (to some extent) and also partial to a set of arguments about the United States that showed little attention to the Vatican's social teaching, that combination represented a riddle that few church historians were prepared to solve (and most ignored).

Support for Goldwater from Roman Catholics who wrote for *National Review* showed no signs of tension between national ideals and religious tradition. In fact, the subject of faith rarely came up in connection with the Arizona senator's conservatism. When Brent Bozell first wrote about a Goldwater candidacy in 1959, he did invoke the religious language of modernism and conservatism to describe the division within the Republican Party. The backers of Nelson Rockefeller and those of Goldwater stood in two "unreconcilable factions," each "morally certain" that coexistence was impossible. But aside from details of party leadership in the Senate or finding the right policies on organized labor, Bozell's regard for Goldwater was strictly pragmatic. He identified the senator as the best hope for political conservatives.[13] Most of *National Review*'s early support for Goldwater demonstrated more the need for an identifiable standard-bearer than proving the cogency of the senator's governing philosophy. He was tough on communism, opposed to foreign diplomacy that compromised the nation's autonomy and power, and read the Constitution in a manner that put restraints on the federal government in line with the founders' intentions. Those items on Goldwater's résumé were largely responsible for Bozell's disappointment over the senator's concession speech in Chicago. Bozell thought Goldwater would have been wiser to speak as the leader of a "Loyal Opposition" than to "wash away the differences that give the party's conservative faction its identity." Indeed, by "fuzzing over the differences" between Goldwater and Nixon, the Arizona senator "did the damage" of weakening conservatism. Conservatives could not afford "to support uncongenial candidates while muting its voice."[14]

If Bozell and Buckley could not secure the tie between Christianity and conservatism—and Bozell's ghostwritten book for Goldwater was also godless—Clarence Manion was the man to the rescue. Even before John Courtney Murray began to search for the metaphysical underpinning of the American founding, Manion was charting the way, though without the theological sophistication. In his 1939 book *Lessons in Liberty*, written when Manion was teaching constitutional law at the University of Notre Dame and published by the university's press, the law professor strictly interpreted the U.S. Constitution to oppose the New Deal. To do that, however, Manion also supplied a brief for the divine-right origins of American rights. The book opened with an image of the "tree of liberty," which featured branches of the state and federal governments growing out of a trunk composed of both state and federal constitutions that was firmly planted in the soil of "God's creative purpose." In the most theological part of the book, Manion surmised that God's design in creation was for human beings to "love and serve [God] in this world" and thereby merit "happiness with God throughout eternity." Such love and service was only genuine if voluntary. As such, the point of human existence required a political order that encouraged freedom, "an indispensable part of every human being," an "inalienable right." Governments that restricted liberty ultimately interfered "with the design of God."[15] Materialists and atheists, consequently, posed a threat to free society.

Manion also argued for the Christian origins of the United States by commenting on the political significance of Christ's life and ministry. In his interactions with his followers, Christ had clearly taught the "spiritual dignity of each individual person." Pagan governments rejected such teaching because they regarded people as mere "things," objects by which to obtain more wealth and power. By introducing "humanitarianism" into the West, namely, the idea that "a human being is entitled to more respect and consideration than a chair," Christianity cultivated the notion that rulers needed to give heed to the God-given rights of every human being.[16] The Roman emperors who persecuted Christians, of course, rejected this new understanding of human dignity. For them, Christianity was a threat to absolute power. But over time, Christian anthropology triumphed. How long that victory would take was a subject that Manion avoided, since the Christian rulers that emerged after Constantine in the ancient and medieval worlds did not provide the lessons in liberty that only came to students of the American founding.

American independence, according to Manion, derived its significance not from English legal precedents but from the "rights of man." When after a decade of debates with Parliament about the rights colonists had by virtue of the English constitution, Americans "sought higher and firmer ground" for freedom. They abandoned the British constitution and looked to "their rights as men and as creatures of God." Many Roman Catholics associated the phrase "rights of man" with the French Revolution, a political upheaval that hurt the Gallican church and prompted the papacy's resistance to political liberalism. But Manion did not even hint that assertions of human rights might turn anticlerical because the Declaration of Independence rested such freedoms on "God-given rights." Manion added a helping of American exceptionalism to his interpretation of the founding: "*Never before had a new government been formed for the sole and only purpose of protecting the God-given rights of the individual person.*" America abandoned the "old field of orthodox political science" and formed a government based on the *"direction and consent of the governed."*[17]

Manion not only draped the American founding in the cloak of God-given rights but also added the halo of faith. The Declaration of Independence's assertion of self-evident truths implied that these basic convictions required faith. Here Manion's logic wobbled since he likened these special, epoch-making self-evident truths to something as common as "the air that we breathe." Such vagueness also characterized Manion's assessment of the founders. For him, they were men not simply of courage but also faith. The American enterprise, in other words, was steeped in religion, a recognition that prompted Manion to sermonize: "Good Americans today must likewise have faith. If we enjoy the good fruits and protective shade of the Tree of American Liberty, we must have faith in the self-evident truths that constitute its roots. We are proud of American independence; we are proud of the fruits of the American Revolution; we are proud of our traditional liberty and democracy. Therefore, let us likewise be proud of the faith that made these blessings possible . . . [and] inherit and share the faith of the Revolutionary fathers." In sum, the American system of government, as codified in the Declaration, presupposed three principles that each stemmed from belief in God. First, since humankind was created, the founders acknowledged a "debt of gratitude to God who gave us life," an obligation that excluded the materialist and atheist. Second, being "created equal" meant that the "God-given" life of every person was "precious and sacred," regardless of "worldly station." Last, American principles of government included the inalienable rights of life, liberty, and the pursuit of happiness, "endowed" by God and to be respected by rulers. Indeed, this part of American political theory elevated the United States above all other nations because America denied emphatically the " 'all-powerful-state' theory" of government.[18] This was divine-right limited government.

Manion may have found God in the Declaration of Independence, but the real object of his apologia for America was the Constitution. The Declaration may have affirmed limited government implicitly, but the U.S. Constitution codified the constraints that protected Americans' God-given rights. The Constitution was especially important to Manion and fellow conservatives for providing leverage against the expansion of the federal government that Franklin Delano Roosevelt had instigated under the New

Deal's programs. In his 1939 book *Lessons in Liberty*, the expansion of the federal government was especially fresh in Manion's mind. The wedge that had led precipitously to the hegemony of Washington in the U.S. federal system—aside from an unprecedented economic collapse—was the "general welfare" clause of the Constitution.

For Manion, the federal government's duty in maintaining the general welfare of the country was to protect equally the God-given rights of all citizens. But the federal government had no power to actually improve the welfare of Americans directly. For instance, Congress could create funds for all citizens to acquire smallpox vaccinations but could not require Americans to be inoculated. This distinction had already become fuzzy, but with the New Deal it vanished. National poverty relief programs had given untold power to the federal government. With the New Deal, Washington "launched a spending program too great for the full comprehension of the average citizen." Under the guise of Congress's interstate commerce power, the National Recovery Administration attempted unprecedented regulations of the economy. Promoting the "general welfare" became the constitutional grounds for these programs' legitimacy. Manion conceded that responding to the Depression's devastating circumstances was "*essentially conservative*" because where the government's task was the protection of the people's God-given rights, the federal government needed to "take responsibility for preventing starvation and destitution."[19] Even so, Manion wondered where the money for the New Deal came from and what these programs would do to the balance of powers between federal and local governments articulated in the Constitution.

With the hindsight of twenty-five years, Manion's negative opinion of the New Deal and its legacy had coalesced to define the political conservatism responsible for Goldwater's candidacy. In his 1964 book *The Conservative American*, a companion piece as it were to Goldwater's (and Bozell's) *The Conscience of a Conservative*, the turning point of modern U.S. history was 1932, the date when "self-proclaimed 'liberals'" had taken over American government. This was a system of government—"statism"—interested not in preserving liberty but in protecting the "irresponsible force of our federal government." As such, modern liberalism was fundamentally at odds with the American constitutional system, "*the most effective protection for human liberty ever devised by the brain and purpose of man.*" Modern conservatism, consequently, stood in a place comparable to the American founding. Manion could cite " 'a long train of abuses and usurpations' which 'evince a design to reduce them under absolute despotism.' " Unlike the founders, who sought autonomy for colonists from an excessive government, Manion's conservatism looked for a restoration of the political order that had made the United States great—namely, "national independence and constitutional government." Conservatives hoped to remind Americans of what they had forgotten, that "this is the only place on earth where human liberty has been protected by a constitutional government built upon the principles set forth in the American Declaration of Independence."[20]

New Deal liberalism for Manion was actually little more than socialism. He reproduced parts of the Democratic Party's 1932 platform, contrasted it with Norman Thomas's socialist program, and concluded that FDR had abandoned his own party's program and adopted instead a series of policies on unemployment, labor, agriculture, and taxes that only eighty-nine thousand Americans favored when they cast votes for Thomas. Also revealing of Roosevelt's socialist impulses was his decision to do what no previous president had done and open diplomatic relations with the Soviet Union. At this point, Manion's argument began to unravel. As an advocate of "national independence" or what some also called isolationism, Manion resented both Woodrow Wilson's and Roosevelt's decisions to insert the United States into the European wars of the 1910s and 1940s. At the same time, Manion and his conservative compatriots (including Goldwater) were hard-line cold warriors who were determined to fight and defeat communism around the world. The book's concluding chapter was an extended brief for ending the "red menace." And yet, Manion regarded America's entries into the two world wars as further manifestations of the federal government's unconstitutional and growing girth.

Manion judged that the United States' entry into the First World War "worked a tragic turn in our national history and it likewise marked an unfortunate day in the history of the whole world."[21] The reason had less to do with the horrors of war or the dangers of unwise foreign policy than with the nation's constitutional order. Manion feared that international treaties, such as the 1913 agreement with Canada about protecting migratory birds, could upset the delicate balance of federal and state power. Wilson's hopes for an international order after the First World War only raised the stakes for binding the United States' legal norms to those of other nations. Manion celebrated the isolationist spirit that prevailed in the 1920s. But the debates over Germany's aggression during the 1930s pushed the United States back into the international arena and prompted organizations such as the America First Committee to defend the nation by keeping it out of the European war. Once President Roosevelt, who Manion believed was looking for ways to provoke Germany and Japan to justify America's entry into the war, brought the United States into the conflict, the America First Committee disbanded and "subsidiary considerations" such as the Declaration of Independence and the Constitution "would have to wait."[22] Again, the problem posed by the war was not one of justice or international peace but what America's increasing involvement in international politics would mean for the God-given liberties asserted and protected by the nation's founding documents. What would treaties with allies and the terms of peace do to the constitutional form of government that was the prize possession of the United States?

The import of this question helps explain Manion's decision to devote an entire chapter to the Bricker Amendment, the 1950s legislative attempt by Ohio's Republican senator, John Bricker, to protect the power of the U.S. government from restrictions imposed by international treaties. The specific occasion for the amendment was a United Nations policy to impose on members the 1948 Declaration of Human Rights. Republicans who balked at the Soviets' veto power in the UN and who feared the infiltration of communists such as Alger Hiss in the State Department wanted to protect U.S. prerogatives. Bricker was uncomfortable with the isolationist profile of some fellow Republicans, but he also worried about the increasing ability of the president to act unilaterally both domestically and in foreign negotiations. His proposed amendment called for the invalidation of any foreign treaty that conflicted with the Constitution and called for Congress to enact domestic legislation implied by any international agreement involving the United States. Bricker's sentiments were sufficiently plausible for his amendment to receive support from the American Bar Association.[23] Manion, who had already objected to U.S.-Canada treaties that set policies for migratory birds, regarded the Bricker Amendment as yet one more responsible attempt to shore up the Constitution and its powers to protect the rights of Americans. The proposal "drew a sharp line" between "those who believe that personal rights . . . should not be sacrificed to international plans and purposes" and those who were willing to sacrifice Americans' rights "in the interest of international cooperation."[24]

The role that President Eisenhower played in orchestrating the defeat of Bricker's proposal was the last straw for conservatives such as Manion. Already alarmed at the liberties Roosevelt had taken with the Constitution through the New Deal and betrayed by the Republican Party establishment's backing of Dwight Eisenhower over Robert Taft in the 1952 presidential primaries, they could take no more. The president's opposition to Bricker and continued commitment to internationalism provoked Manion and fellow conservatives to look for presidential alternatives. Taft had gained concessions from Eisenhower in the Republicans' 1952 platform—a commitment to reduce federal spending and a resolve to root communists and their sympathizers from the State Department. But the president had reneged on the most important provisions, even "fatally" blighting the anticommunism of Vice President Nixon. When Eisenhower left office, "the conservative Republican leadership that had flourished so militantly with such bright promise in 1952 had all but disappeared," Manion lamented. Only Barry Goldwater was left, and in party leadership "no uncompromising conservatism" remained.[25]

Manion's conservatism, the one he recognized in Goldwater's militant opposition to the Soviet Union, was a mélange of American exceptionalism and anticommunism. On the one hand, the first priority of American conservatism was perpetuating "our national sovereignty." This conviction pitted conservatism against proposals for world peace through international laws, treaties, and the organizations such as the United Nations. To those who suggested that a union of Earth's nations could function as the global equivalent of the original union of American states, Manion offered a lesson in U.S. history. The formation of a federal union of states did not create a government that could transfer power to a "supranational body" or with authority to "subordinate the reserved powers of the states to any international alliance." The states of the union still possessed all of the powers of "sovereign nations that were not delegated to the federal government" as specified in the Constitution.[26] For Manion, states' rights were not simply a matter for restraining government officials in Washington, D.C., but also with foreign policy implications that gave the citizens of the United States as much authority as the nation's allies and foes.

On the other hand, American exceptionalism was the last best hope for defeating communism around the world. "Conservatives are convinced," Manion wrote, that the chances for freedom and the "advancement of men and nations everywhere" depended on a "strong, constitutionally governed nationally independent United States of America." The best way to defeat communism and so liberate humanity was for a strong and independent United States to challenge and fight the Soviet Union. Manion's survey of U.S. history since the Russian Revolution was one of good-faith American negotiations with the Soviets that all the while unintentionally had allowed "the Communist contagion" to infect "the entire human race." Four decades of negotiations had hardened into a policy of avoiding confrontation and produced optimism that communism was "mellowing." For Manion, only the United States possessed the convictions to defeat communism, and on top of that, only conservative Americans understood the fundamental antithesis between communism and Americanism. The United States stood for "four basic" affirmations: the existence and power of God, personal responsibility, limited government, and private property. "The Communists," he concluded, "have never hesitated to proclaim this generic incompatibility of their institution with ours." This meant that only the United States, not international organizations that recognized the legitimacy of communism, could prosecute the fight against the Soviets. Barry Goldwater, accordingly, was the model for American conservatives if only because he was willing to assert that "we should declare the world Communist movement an outlaw in the community of civilized nations."[27]

Two difficulties hampered Manion's brand of conservatism, neither of which he addressed head-on. One was the tension, if not contradiction, between an affirmation of states' rights and a commitment to a hard-line anticommunist foreign policy. The latter depended precisely on federal powers and a military-industrial complex that required the consolidation of authority in the executive branch of U.S. government and left the states with almost no voice in international affairs except for their federal representatives. Of course, that was the Federalists' intent, the way by which the states would function within the national government. But power to plan, prepare, and fight a war placed American sovereignty within the hands of federal officials. Manion's notion of the American states as sovereign in international affairs was a fairy tale.

The other difficulty was the faith that informed Manion's conviction. His affirmation of God was generic and could well appeal across Christian communions and extend to other monotheists. But he failed to address the tension between his opposition to internationalism and the Roman Catholic Church's own brand of political catholicity. Not only was the papacy, with its apparatus in the Vatican, one of the oldest of bodies that tried to broker international relations. But John XXIII had given a papal imprimatur in *Mater et magistra*, even if only in a small way, to recognizing communist countries as legitimate interlocutors in finding a just and equitable social order. Obviously, Buckley and his colleagues at *National Review* understood the implications of the pope's encyclical. Manion, though, failed to distinguish permissible from impermissible forms of internationalism—a curious oversight for a devout Roman Catholic.

Goldwater Still

Barry Goldwater may have disappointed conservative leaders in 1960 when he endorsed Richard Nixon and deflated conservative optimism, but by 1964, as Manion's book indicated, the senator from Arizona was the choice of conservatives. More surprising was Goldwater's popularity with the nation's young people. The collective memory of many Americans about the 1960s and college students runs to images of protestors who joined the ranks of the civil rights movement and opposed the Vietnam War. But even before Students for a Democratic Society adopted its Port Huron Statement in 1962, college students were enthusiastically supporting Barry Goldwater. Their institutional outlet was Young Americans for Freedom (YAF), an organization that drew much of its initial coherence from the ideas and energy of Buckley.

YAF originated technically at the 1960 Republican national convention when a small group of students constituted Youth for Goldwater for Vice President as a way to give conservatism a voice in the party's presidential campaign. Goldwater had encouraged those students to form YAF, an effort that received support from Marvin Liebman, a New York City publicist. In 1960 he issued a call to more than a hundred student activists and journalists to take *"political action."* Liebman also persuaded Buckley to host a gathering of young conservatives at the Buckley family estate in Sharon, Connecticut. According to Rick Perlstein, these young people had come to their political convictions by reading *National Review* and *Human Events*, and they had participated in programs sponsored by the Intercollegiate Society of Individualists (later Intercollegiate Studies Institute) and the Foundation for Economic Freedom. He adds that a "disproportionate number . . . were serious Catholics" who had drawn inspiration from Pope Pius XII's opposition to communism, which filtered down to parish pulpits and church publications during the 1950s. "They saw how John F. Kennedy was unthinkingly lionized by their parochial school peers (and New Dealer parents)." Perlstein also observes that these young conservatives "viewed the Democratic Party as a moribund establishment" that relied on urban political machines every bit as much as the South's segregationist machinery.[28]

The young Republicans' set of convictions, the "Sharon Statement," summarized the ideas that had animated Roman Catholic conservatives in the orbit of *National Review* and Clarence Manion. The author was M. Stanton Evans, the twenty-six-year-old editor of the *Indianapolis Star*, who had also graduated from Yale University and served as an associate editor at Buckley's magazine, beginning in 1960. The Sharon Statement was an affirmation of "eternal truths," which included "foremost" the individual's "use of his God-given free will, whence derives his right to be free from the restrictions of arbitrary force."[29] This invocation of religion was actually controversial among those gathered at the YAF event and passed by the narrow margin of 44 to 40, thanks to the strong presence of Roman Catholics at the conference. Evans himself believed, according to Gregory L. Schneider, that freedom and belief in God-given rights were axiomatic even though some young conservatives were not religious and others of a more religiously doctrinaire persuasion thought the statement gave too much room to classical liberalism and personal autonomy.[30] The statement included an affirmation that government's purpose was to protect these freedoms and that the U.S. Constitution was the "best arrangement yet devised" for restraining the state's powers and for dividing power among the federal government, "the several states, or . . . the people."

The conflict with communism was also at the forefront of concerns animating these conservatives. Not only were the "forces of international Communism the greatest single threat" to God-given liberties, but the cause of freedom depended on "the national sovereignty of the United

States." Some present wondered how combating communism with the diplomatic and military apparatus of the federal government meshed with the preservation of personal freedom. Still, the statement received broad support both at the conference and from conservatism's leaders. According to William Rusher, the Sharon Statement was the distillation of the conservative movement's "original principles."[31]

Goldwater was still the standard-bearer for self-conscious conservatives, and YAF threw its support behind efforts to nominate the senator as the Republicans' presidential candidate even if the older members of the Right had misgivings. Between 1960 and 1964 YAF's leadership promoted Goldwater by sponsoring events on university campuses where the senator sometimes spoke and by instructing heads of local chapters on fund-raising strategies designed to counteract the money that Goldwater's likely competitor, Nelson Rockefeller, had at the ready. Writers and editors at *National Review* also supported Goldwater but showed more political savvy than the idealism of YAF might allow. Brent Bozell, for instance, cautioned that a successful Goldwater campaign would force conservatives once again into an uneasy relationship with the Republican Party. He worried that party leaders might use the conservative movement to enlist support for either Rockefeller or Nixon. Consequently, Bozell insisted that conservatives make "the party a reliable instrument of conservatism, not the other way around."[32]

Keeping their eye on the prize was also prominent in Buckley's delicate maneuvering with the John Birch Society. The organization's founder, Robert Welch, had taken anticommunism a bridge too far when he accused Eisenhower and his administration of not only being soft on but espousing communism. Buckley's strategy for adding moderation to conservatism was to distinguish Birch Society members from Welch, the leader whose books members had not read. Buckley's rebuke to Welch also involved trying to save Goldwater from being tarred with the brush of the Birchers. Russell Kirk, one of the regulars at *National Review*, quipped that "Eisenhower isn't a Communist. He is a golfer."[33] Buckley assured readers that Goldwater had never been a member of the Birch Society and had also consistently repudiated Welch. If Goldwater had not also done the same with rank-and-file Birchers, he was no more guilty of the society's views than President Kennedy was of racism for failing to reject the Democratic Party's southern leadership.

The editors at *National Review* not only had to shield Goldwater from associations with Robert Welch; they also tried to protect the candidate's reputation from caricatures. Buckley explained that "being soft on Communism," a remark that Democrats used against Goldwater, was a perfectly reasonable worry to have about U.S. foreign policy. Buckley as well as the publisher William Rusher also ran interference for the candidate on charges of racism in which they explained the realities of doing political business with southern conservatives and the need for the South's support for electoral victory.[34]

Sometimes the magazine's writers employed caricature for their own purposes, such as Russell Kirk's piece on the "mind" of Goldwater. Kirk conceded that the senator was not an intellectual, but Goldwater knew "*how* to think; . . . he seems able to leap mentally, in the course of a conversation, from premise to conclusion, even though the particular ground may be unfamiliar to him." Kirk also complimented Goldwater for the "resoluteness" he displayed in *The Conscience of a Conservative* and for a capacity to "confront hard truths" in *Why Not Victory?* Still, the real measure of the man came in "his humorous extemporaneous speeches" and "private discourse" where he showed "toleration and prudence and generosity." Indeed, "no politician of our time is less of an ideologue," Kirk concluded, "that is, less governed by what Burke called theoretic dogma and abstract doctrine," than Goldwater.[35]

Such positive estimates were easier to come by when the conservative movement's leaders had access to the Republican candidate, but that changed when people closer to the campaign tried to protect Goldwater from the extremes that seemed to accompany Buckley and his colleagues. At a somewhat famous meeting with Buckley and Bozell in the spring of 1963 in Washington, D.C., Goldwater's chief advisers and campaign manager, Dennison Kitchel and Bill Baroody, dismissed most of the *National Review*'s writers' suggestions about campaign strategy. The *New York Times* reported on the meeting, using an "unnamed source," likely Baroody, and indicated that what Goldwater needed least "is more support from the far right." The *Times* story said that Buckley and Bozell emerged from the discussion "with no share of the Goldwater command and wondering if they wanted any."[36]

The meeting and news story soured Buckley's relationship with Goldwater. Although the candidate apologized to Buckley and attributed the

events to Baroody, Goldwater also proved incapable of managing his supporters. When a campaign event at Madison Square Garden cosponsored
by *National Review* dropped Buckley from the roster of speakers at the
last minute, Goldwater's lame explanation was to include only "active
Republican political figures," even though the event included a speech
from a supporter of Chiang Kai-shek.[37] At first, Buckley seemed not to
notice the bad treatment despite fuming over the *New York Times* story.
He continued to strategize on behalf of the Goldwater campaign and was
for a time quite confident that his idea of adding Eisenhower to the ticket
as the vice-presidential nominee was brilliant. As the 1964 Republican
primaries played out, however, Buckley lost his enthusiasm for Goldwater.
To his colleagues he sent a memo that questioned whether Goldwater's
heart was in it or if he was qualified to run for president. Once those questions started, Buckley's strategy became finding a way to save face for the
conservative movement.

Those reservations became particularly pronounced at the YAF conference two months before the general election, where Buckley may have
finally had the chance to retaliate for some of the slights the Goldwater
campaign had inflicted on him. During the second night of the Republican national convention, at a YAF-sponsored event emceed by Ronald
Reagan, campaign officials pulled Buckley from the list of speakers.
At the fall YAF gathering, Buckley disaggregated the conservative movement and the Goldwater campaign: "The nomination of Barry Goldwater,
when we permit ourselves to peek over the euphoria, reminds us chillingly
of the great work that has remained undone; a great rainfall has deluged
a thirsty earth, but before we had time properly to prepare it, I speak of
course about the impending defeat of Barry Goldwater."[38] According to
John B. Judis, "a sepulchral hush" fell over YAF's thousands. When Buckley finished his speech, in which he reminded the audience about the point
of being conservative—which was different from electing a Republican—
he received a smattering of applause. YAF's leaders decided not to print
the speech in their magazine. (They later published it after the November 4 election.)

A month later Buckley explained to conservative leaders in New York
that conservatism was a resistance movement. "In America," he explained, "we are *dragging our feet*; kicking, complaining, hugging on to
our ancient moorings."[39] That was a curious way for a Roman Catholic

who celebrated the United States to parse a "new order for the ages." After all, the Roman Catholic Church was ancient, and the United States and its Constitution were thoroughly modern. Yet for Buckley and fellow conservatives, the United States' ideals of government represented truths steeped in the history of the West. In contrast, the hierarchy of the church appeared to be breaking with the past in order to join the modern world. This was arguably the most surprising aspect of Americanism for Roman Catholic political conservatives: not the church that Christ founded or its diplomatic and ecumenical efforts but the United States, its political traditions, and its conflict with Soviet communism was the hope for saving the world.

6

THE LIMITS OF AMERICANISM

It was one thing to invest in Barry Goldwater and lose the 1964 presidential election—the Republican candidate did perform better than Democrats George McGovern in 1972 and Walter Mondale in 1984, but
conservatives were not fortune tellers. It was another thing to lose so deci-
sively while also sensing that the country was coming apart. Conservatives
knew what was best—a federal government to limit itself to the powers
enumerated by the Constitution and military and diplomatic measures
to defeat Soviet communism, which constituted a dire threat to Western
civilization. But the emergence of the radicals, feminists, black separatists, free love advocates, and antiwar protesters that huddled under the
banner of the New Left rendered irrelevant debates over big government,
states' rights, and the Bill of Rights. As Andrew Hartman describes the
conflict that erupted during the 1960s, "normative America" stood for
"hard work, personal responsibility, individual merit, delayed gratifica-
tion, social mobility," heterosexual marriage, well-defined gender roles,
and national greatness.[1] Democrats, establishment Republicans, and

conservatives might disagree about the responsibilities of the federal government and its programs, but practically no one disputed these cultural expectations.

That was not so with the protest culture that arose on college campuses during the 1960s and eventually found a home in the Democratic Party. The New Left embraced a transgressive outlook that challenged practically all sides of the American way. According to Theodore Roszak, the "counter culture is the embryonic cultural base of New Left politics, the effort to discover new types of community, new family patterns, new sexual mores, new kinds of livelihood, new aesthetic forms, new personal identities on the far side of power politics, the bourgeois home, and the Protestant work ethic." Hartman concludes that the students and faculty who identified with the New Left "pushed the envelope of American norms." But for conservatives, the Left's "rejection of authority," "transgression of rules and standards," and "antipathy to anything mainstream" left Americans without an envelope to push.[2]

Conservatives were hardly alone in not seeing campus radicalism coming. Even so, for those who took their bearings from debates about the New Deal in domestic affairs or combating communism in foreign policy, the identity politics that took hold among a segment of the nation's student population was as astonishing as it was disorienting. For some, the radical Left was truly new. According to Jeffrey Hart, book review editor for *National Review* and literature professor at Dartmouth, it was a "cultural explosion." The combination of "LP records, Mailer and Genet 'covering' the Democratic Convention," "the op-art and pop-art and porno phenomenon," along with the growth of "government action" and the assumption that all Americans should go to college, had "given rise to a vast student proletariat." That college population was the audience for America's adversary culture. Some thought, however, that the New Left was simply the fruit of New Deal liberalism. M. Stanton Evans wrote that the Left's premises included "a vague commitment to collectivism, permissiveness in morals, militant egalitarianism, hostility to patriotic sentiment, and strident pacifism." These were not new but "the root premises of Liberal orthodoxy," and the New Left was simply "American Liberalism writ large."[3]

That notion that the United States was coming apart, not simply from specific circumstances of postwar society but owing to fundamental weaknesses in American political ideals, haunted a number of Roman Catholic conservatives. So challenging was the dilemma that it led the likes of Brent Bozell and Garry Wills to break faith with the Americanist fusion of faith and conservative politics. Whether they heeded carefully the instructions of their bishops was not the question as much as the resources that church tradition provided for a critique of the United States. No matter how important their nation may have been to defeating Soviet communism, the events of the 1960s revealed the bankruptcy of a country founded on modern ideas about individual liberty and limited government. In effect, they came to understand that Americanists had overestimated the United States and undervalued the church.

Founders Built Worse Than They Knew

Bozell's standing in the conservative movement grew increasingly shaky after the 1964 defeat of Goldwater. The reason had less to do with disappointment over the Republican loss than discomfort over American society more generally. He tried to maintain the conservative line about the nation's founding and the fundamental harmony between classical liberalism and Roman Catholicism. But he sensed in ways that few of *National Review*'s contributors did the basic tension between traditional faith and modern politics.

That recognition first set in after Bozell finished the book for Goldwater, *The Conscience of a Conservative*. In 1961 he had moved to Spain, and for the next two years he began to entertain ideas about the restoration of Christendom. Even if Spain under its prime minister, Francisco Franco, represented a fascist regime to most Americans, whether libertarian or progressive, for traditionalist Roman Catholics the country evoked a society in tune with the "throne and altar" conservatism that had animated the European church. Bozell was likely too steeped in American assumptions to be taken with Franco, but Spain's Christian traditionalism did take root in his imagination. He gained an awareness of Carlism in particular, a strain of Spanish Roman Catholicism that stood against the excesses of the French Revolution and for a well-ordered monarchical society in which the church functioned as the check on the crown. Carlists took their name from a group of Spanish traditionalists who during the

1830s hoped that Carlos Maria Isidro would succeed his feeble brother, King Ferdinand VII, to the throne. Though the king's wife thwarted those hopes, Carlism was a source of inspiration to Spanish conservatives all the way down to the Spanish Civil War. For Bozell and his conservative colleague Frederick Wilhelmsen, who also wrote for *National Review* and overlapped with Bozell in Spain, the Carlists were the last great examples of Christians fighting for Christ. In one piece on the Carlists, Wilhelmsen extolled Carlist units that during the Civil War had "Christ the King on their lips, rosaries, around their necks, Sacred Hearts on their tunics," and he described following a soldier "whose duty was to carry a tall cross into battle."[4] Bozell's time in Spain was pivotal for his reassessment of conservatism's prospects in the United States.

Back in the United States, however, Bozell remained part of the politically conservative world that Buckley had cultivated, and those ties sent him back into the world of the Right's veneration of the Constitution. If conservatives had wanted a mainstream source for their opposition to the growth of the federal government since the New Deal, the Constitution was a ready debating point because the careful balance of enumerated powers in the federal government was essential to the nation's constitutionalism. To be sure, the changes in American society between 1789 and 1960—demographic, economic, geographic—had revealed limits in those legal provisions and the need for adaptation. Two of the chief mechanisms for adjusting the Constitution to later developments were either through amendment or the courts. The latter approach, a Supreme Court that smoothed out the seeming discrepancies between small government and mass society through federal agencies, was the subject that occupied Bozell's attention when he resumed his place among American conservatives on the eve of the 1964 national elections. In addition to running for U.S. Congress in Maryland, Bozell also worked on a book he had been contemplating for a number of years, a study of the Supreme Court during the tenure of Chief Justice Earl Warren.

The Warren Revolution, published in 1966, was yet another study in American constitutionalism from the Right. Bozell began with the theme of "crisis" and spelled out the way constitutions operate. Some were fixed (United States), some were fluid (England), but all reflected a consensus in their respective societies. Bozell conceded that constitutions adapt as they reflect the emergence of a different consensus. He noted that at the turn of the twentieth century, the power of Congress to "wage war on poverty" would have caused many Americans to laugh. By 1960, however, Americans recognized "a congressional *power* to undertake any welfare measure that can be accomplished by the appropriation and allocation of public funds." Here Bozell recounted some of the history of New Deal legislation, how the courts had ruled the first recovery acts unconstitutional, how Congress had used the vague powers of the Commerce Clause, and how the Supreme Court had capitulated to "community sentiment."[5] For conservatives, the changes to American government under FDR had left a bitter taste.

But the real problem of the Warren court was a new kind of constitutionalism. For 165 years the nation had carried on a tradition that distinguished between provisions originating from the "fixed" constitution and those best suited to the nation's "fluid constitution." Notable exceptions were the sectional crisis that led to the Civil War and Prohibition. But during the twelve years of Justice Warren's tenure, a new idea of the Constitution had taken hold, one that transferred "*the solution of some of the most momentous problems of contemporary public policy from the fluid constitution to the fixed constitution—by judicial decree.*" After a survey and assessment of the Constitution's amendments—the Eighteenth exemplifying "the kind of problem that should never be thrust into rigid prescriptions of a fixed constitution"—Bozell concluded that until 1954 the Constitution had survived and worked well under the "framers's [sic] original plan." Major policy decisions emerged from the "organic tensions" among "the wills of all branches of government." The Warren court's great defect was to resolve matters "about which a hard constitutional consensus did not exist" as though "such a consensus *did* exist." Decisions of the court had achieved "the same dignity" formerly attached to "the Constitution's formal amendment procedures." Instead of following earlier patterns of jurisprudence where the court provided the forum for discovering "working consensuses in areas not covered by the fixed constitution," the Supreme Court had become the "*umpire*" whose judgments were "final and binding." In sum, the court's verdicts had become "*the equivalent to a provision of the fixed Constitution,*" its decisions the product of "*a nine-man tribunal.*"[6]

Bozell used the book to discuss various decisions from the Warren court. One case in particular—prayer and Bible reading in public schools—may have been an indication of Bozell's budding Roman Catholic traditional-ism. He offered little comment about the devotional practices that New York, Pennsylvania, and Maryland legislators had included in their school systems. The issue was primarily legal. Bozell did not understand how the exercises that the Warren court ruled unconstitutional reached the level of religious establishment since in all cases school districts had made provi-sions for conscientious objectors. Even more perplexing for Bozell was the court's application of the Bill of Rights (the original ten amendments) to the states through the Fourteenth Amendment. The First Amendment, he argued, was clear in limiting its scope to a national church. Congress could not establish religion, but the rest of the Constitution, including the Tenth Amendment specifically, delegated to the states power to decide religious life at the local level. He appealed to Joseph Story's *Commentary on the Constitution*: "*The whole power over the subject of religion is left* [by the Amendment] *exclusively to the state governments to be acted upon according to their own sense of justice and the State Constitutions*," thereby leaving "the Catholic and the Protestant, the Calvinist and the Armenian, the Jew and the Infidel" to sit down at "the common table of national councils" without any reference to their religious status. For that reason, the only liberty the Establishment Clause protected was "freedom from a national church." Bozell believed that someone did not need to be a professor of constitutional law to understand that a "State [was] hardly in a position to jeopardize that liberty, if only for reasons of geography."[7]

Bozell blamed the court's rulings on religion and education, includ-ing its language of a "high and impregnable" wall separating church and state, on a bias against "theistic religion." According to the Warren court's logic, all public expressions of religion—from the mention of God in the Pledge of Allegiance and on the nation's currency, to public ceremonies that included religious songs—constituted "*a prima facie case of uncon-stitutionality*." If true, then the Supreme Court had vacated a pose of neutrality and had become antireligious in the same way that Christ had warned that "those who were not with Him were perforce against Him." The court's understanding of religion left the public schoolteacher in the impossible position of not being able to answer in the classroom whether "human rights come from a Creator-God as asserted by the Declara-tion of Independence." The cumulative effect of the Warren court was to "neatly" replace "our traditional public affirmation of God and His law" with a new "non-theistic public creed."⁸ This was but one instance of the way by which the Warren court laid down a constitutional consensus on its own without negotiating with the other branches of U.S. government.

The book failed to attract attention either critical or positive, and Bozell may not have cared. As his biographer, Daniel Kelly, observed, Bozell had analyzed the court in almost "wholly secular" terms and showed no awareness of the "better world" the author had discovered in Roman Catholic Spain. For those who did take the time to write reviews, Bozell's book was, as for Martin Diamond, a Claremont College historian, an "unconvincing" explanation of judicial review that verged "dangerously" close to a populist understanding of constitutional consensus. Another review in Russell Kirk's *Modern Age* by James McClellan, a legal scholar, opined that the Warren court was only half the American judicial system's problems. The largest concern was the way the Fourteenth Amendment gave the federal courts standing in deciding state legislation, an opening that the Warren court clearly used but as part of an older constitutional framework. A third review, this time from George Carey, who taught government at Georgetown University, praised Bozell for his critique of the Warren court but also thought the author had an overly sanguine regard for appropriating the constitution through a " 'consensus' machinery."⁹

Bozell had originally conceived of the project as a two-volume enterprise, but he lost interest after the first book. By 1968 he faulted himself for ignoring religion in his analysis. According to his biographer, Daniel Kelly, *The Warren Revolution* was Bozell's "swan song" within the old anticommunist, pro-Americanist, Roman Catholic conservatism. From here on, Bozell refused to dilute his faith with American politics.

The problem for someone of Bozell's religious convictions, however, was finding an outlet for a traditionalist Roman Catholic perspective. The major magazines for American Roman Catholics were *Commonweal* and the Jesuit *America*, but these were left of center both politically and ecclesiastically. That left *National Review*, a publication where Bozell could vent on both national and church affairs. As late as 1965 Bozell was still using Buckley's magazine as the platform from which to promote his brand of Roman Catholicism. Already in 1964 he drew criticism from mainstream Roman Catholics in the United States for noticing a "strange drift" in the church that easily floated from support for liberal government assistance programs to endorsements of communism. The object of his critique was an essay in *America* by the priest George H. Dunne that called on Americans to consider the way the rest of the world viewed their nation. Dunne had argued that American superiority was dubious to people in struggling parts of the world economy because it proved to be as prone to social inequality as any other economic system. The problem with this way of interpreting communism, for Bozell, was its implicit acceptance of Marxism's materialist premises. "If the issue between East and West becomes, merely," he warned, "which side can provide more material satisfactions," then the West would need to match the "zeal and single-mindedness" that communists claimed. That might be a reasonable expectation for public policy experts. But Bozell was concerned for the church and what Dunne revealed about the American clergy. The struggle with communism called not for a debate about equitable distribution of goods but a reaffirmation of human nature and man's relationship to God. "The West," he wrote, "asserts a God-given right and thinks of it as a God-imposed duty, to conserve and spread its truth, to judge political and economic and social systems according to its lights, to change and improve them under *its* authority."[10] The church had a duty to "fight" for Western civilization.

Of course, the problem facing Bozell was larger than priests such as Dunne but extended to those bishops planning to gather in Rome even while he complained about *America*'s Jesuit editors. The early returns on the Second Vatican Council were discouraging to Bozell if only because the idea of *aggiornamento* seemed to set the church on a course of accommodating "Christianity's enemies, so defined both by history and theology." He did not care for "bringing the liturgy down to the meeting house level" any more than he approved of revising church life to make it "acceptable to Protestants." The council's propensity to blur distinctions under the banner of ecumenism, Bozell believed, owed less to Protestantism than Hinduism. If the reforms of the council now opened the church to greater flexibility and rejected a top-down command structure, then surely the formation of the Catholic Traditional Movement, of which Bozell approved, was only a confirmation of the bishops' collective affirmation that "obedience can never be unquestioning."[11]

Bozell's own identification with nascent Roman Catholic traditionalists was primarily responsible for his break with Buckley and *National Review* and his decision to start *Triumph* magazine. He had already shown signs of independence by running for Congress from Maryland in the 1964 Republican primaries (and losing overwhelmingly to Charles Mathias), and then proposing to Buckley and others at the magazine the formation of a new political party. A cool reaction to such a plan pushed Bozell to launch a new publication. The overlap between *National Review*'s writers and the institutional network of the conservative movement was apparent. To Bozell's credit, he was able to attract a number of Roman Catholic authors who were as alarmed by the trajectory of secularization in America as he was. Among his sympathizers were Garry Wills, Russell Kirk, E. Victor Milione (who ran programs at the Intercollegiate Studies Institute), Willmoore Kendall, Edwin J. Feulner (who went on to preside over the Heritage Foundation), and Lee Edwards (one of the founding members of Young Americans for Freedom and director of information for the 1964 Goldwater campaign). Throughout 1965 and 1966, plans for the magazine went ahead with the inner circle usually using meetings of the Philadelphia Society, a conservative intellectual organization founded in 1964, to recruit colleagues.

By March 1966, Bozell had founded the parent organization for a magazine, the Society for the Christian Commonwealth. The editorial committee took *Commonweal* and *National Review* as their models—commentary and analysis on culture and politics but from an explicitly conservative Roman Catholic outlook. At one of the planning meetings, Bozell brought a mock-up of the publication to Russell Kirk. Kirk's reaction was, "Well, Brent, this is quite impressive, but there is already a magazine just like this. It is called *National Review*." Kirk believed *Triumph* was intentionally "anti-*National Review*." Yet Buckley supported *Triumph* by giving Bozell contacts for fundraising and praising the addition of a conservative Roman Catholic magazine to the shelf of American publications. Despite this support, Bozell still regarded Buckley's politics as too pragmatic for the good of faith. An editorial in which Buckley had warned against efforts to criminalize abortion prompted Bozell to write a letter to *National Review* in which he accused Buckley of "relativism." According to John Judis, Bozell's letter "stung" his brother-in-law.[12]

Expectations for *Triumph* were mixed from the outset. One group, consisting primarily of the magazine's donors, were committed to a more overtly Roman Catholic version of *National Review*. According to one of the magazine's longtime editors, E. Michael Lawrence, Bozell's readership believed that American political conservatism and orthodox Christianity went hand in hand. Where *National Review* was less willing to devote extensive coverage to church matters, *Triumph* would defend Roman Catholic traditions, an enterprise especially necessary in the early days of the postconciliar church when all that had been solid appeared to be fluid. Readers, accordingly, wanted the magazine to defend the Latin Mass, critique the trendy qualities of vernacular translations of liturgy and scripture, put pressure on weak bishops, expose liberal theological follies, and reassert the traditional ethics of marriage and procreation. This dual commitment to American ideals and Roman Catholic orthodoxy may explain John B. Judis's observation that *Triumph*'s politics "became" theocratic at the expense of conservatism.[13] Many of *National Review*'s thirty thousand readers shared that evaluation.

And yet, Bozell not only wanted space from his brother-in-law; he also desired a faith uncompromised by political liberalism. A good indication of the evolution of his view came in a 1968 article Bozell wrote on the Warren court in which he essentially repudiated the arguments he had made in his 1966 book when still promoting the conservative cause. He admitted that he had originally projected a second volume. Now he conceded that such an endeavor was futile. One reason was that no one (at least in the political establishment and mainstream media) cared about the provisions of the Constitution: "What did you read about today [in the morning newspaper]? Vietnam? The OEO's war on poverty? A congressional debate on open housing? Milton Friedman's negative income tax? . . . These day-to-day developments in the establishment of national policy are convincing, not because they are fraught with constitutional implications over which their movers are determined to run roughshod; but because the constitutional implications—whatever else, pro or con, may be said about the policy—are never spoken of." The last time anyone had "intruded" these considerations "on the public mind" was Barry Goldwater's 1964 run for the presidency.[14]

Even Goldwater, however, failed to capture Bozell's newfound loyalties. The reason was the conviction that civil government derived its legitimacy exclusively from God. Social contract notions of the governed's consent were antithetical to a Christian understanding of politics. Bozell insisted that "divine authority must be kept in view as a *limitation* on the sovereignty of 'the governed,' on *their* claim to authority." He did not refuse to connect the dots: "The American commonwealth, even in its early days, rejected this view of the matter." Bozell did concede that the authors of the Declaration of Independence—"especially those with ties to the Puritan theocracies"—did not believe they were repudiating God. They appealed to "the Supreme Judge of the world" to give their undertaking legitimacy. In fact, God was present in the American founding in ways comparable to saints functioning as patrons of Roman Catholic countries. The problem, however, was that as much as God was in the air at the time of the founding, what would American officials have done in the event "of a *conflict* between the will of the governed and the will of God as revealed in Christian doctrine?" Bozell's reading of the nation's early history indicated that Americans were not prepared to submit to divine will. "The republic came into being as an autonomous entity answerable only to itself." That the Constitution failed to mention God was no surprise. Still, the "ultimate defect" of the founding was not simply that they derived their legitimacy from an "illusory power." The fundamental problem was that American government lacked access to "divinely ordained restraint on civil power and the only source of civil virtue." Writing a second book about the deficiencies of the Warren court was to apply a mere Band-Aid to a metastasizing cancer.[15]

Instead of writing a second volume, Bozell opened wide his critique of the United States and used *Triumph* to give space to other critics who did so precisely on Roman Catholic grounds. On the one hand, writers for the magazine often placed U.S. history in the sweep of narratives of the West and veered toward apocalyptic conclusions. Warren H. Carroll, a Columbia University–trained historian who also worked for the CIA before writing for *Triumph* (after converting to Roman Catholicism), asserted that "ours is an age of apostasy—the most widespread thorough-going apostasy since the Church was founded." The woes of the age went beyond mere heresy. They included "the total abandonment of Christ and mockery of God." The 1960s had been decisive for the redirection of the West, which was odd for Carroll since the decade had begun with Roman Catholics holding high office: John F. Kennedy, Charles de Gaulle (France), Konrad Adenauer (Germany), Francisco Franco (Spain), and António de Oliveira Salazar (Portugal). Of those five, Kennedy was the most disappointing because his renunciation of the church as a guide in public duties was "explicit." Even so, as a group, these Roman Catholics yielded no evidence of "carrying out an explicitly Christian policy designed to repair the enormous damage done" by the twentieth century's apostasy. Carroll bordered on despair but rejected calls for the revitalization of Christianity among Africans or communism's martyrs. Such a development would be "a disaster for the West."[16] That meant American Roman Catholics needed to continue to work for renewal in the West within its existing structures.

Sometimes writers for *Triumph* tried to cut through problems that specifically confronted conservative Roman Catholics in the United States. Some traditionalists were more concerned with putting the church's house in order or amplifying its moral teaching. W. H. Marshner, another historian who moved in Bozell's circles, argued that the most important task for Roman Catholics was to reinstitute the politics that could resolve the dilemmas of liberalism (whether classical or contemporary). Roman Catholics "alone have a tradition which transcends the fatal American dialectic." The fundamental flaw in the U.S. system was "the attempt to put the state above religious differences." That produced a state "at our throats" because it "is constitutionally incapable of agreeing to Catholic morality." This left Roman Catholics to return to "confessional politics," an arrangement that would put everything else into place—"abortion, drugs, pornography, ecology, nuclear arms, economic justice—even Catholic dissidence."[17] Marshner may have been guilty of a form of American exceptionalism, as if fixing the United States could also remedy the post–Vatican II church. But it was a decidedly different Americanism, one grounded in Roman Catholic priorities.

What finally accounted for Bozell and company's break with Americanism was abortion. As early as 1969 the editors at *Triumph* were calling attention to the growing gap between the U.S. government's policies on family planning and church teaching on sexual reproduction. Of course, these Roman Catholic traditionalists took encouragement from Paul VI's encyclical, *Humanae vitae*, a statement that left Roman Catholic progressives wondering if the pope understood the definition of *aggiornamento*. In an editorial about the 1968 encyclical, Bozell found himself having to work through material that Garry Wills had already covered on papal infallibility. *Triumph*'s editor had no problem finding papal precedent for the explicit ban on contraception (including the pill) and even asserted that submission to the encyclical was required of all church members thanks to even the Second Vatican Council's understanding of papal authority.

Bozell quoted the council's Dogmatic Constitution on the Church, *Lumen gentium*: "Religious submission of will and of mind must be shown in a special way to the authentic teaching authority of the Roman Pontiff, even when he is not speaking *ex cathedra*."[18]

Although that was not the attitude of *National Review* editors when John XXIII was pontificating about nuclear arms or international relations, Bozell now recognized a life-and-death matter that distinguished the church clearly from the nation. In a follow-up editorial on *Humanae vitae*, he praised Paul VI for staking out the "battleground" on which the church's "fate will be decided." The church's vocation was to "draw the connections between the senses and the spirit, between nature and supernature." This mission was no more apparent than in the "mighty mystery of sex, which unlocks the door to the even more awesome mystery of life, which in turn reveals the reality of the supernatural." In contrast, the United States, under the direction of President Nixon, was traveling in the opposite direction by adopting federal programs for making family planning services available to every citizen that could not afford them. According to Bozell, here was proof—well before *Roe v. Wade* (1973)—that the "most fundamental tenet of the Christian morality—the holiness of human life—is now under direct attack by the American government."[19]

At the same time, traditionalist Roman Catholics needed to appropriate church teaching carefully since the Second Vatican Council sounded modern on church-state relations. For instance, John Courtney Murray's "Americanism" came in for special critique in the magazine because he had abandoned the old ideal that placed civil government under the authority of Christ's church. Bozell and his colleagues believed Roman Catholics in the United States still had a duty to evangelize American society and reconstitute the federal and state governments as confessional political authorities. In response to whether the Second Vatican Council introduced a new and modern understanding of church-state relations, Hannah Fraser, one of *Triumph*'s writers, responded in ways that demonstrated Bozell's abandonment of Americanism because of its inherently secular character. She asserted that continuing to insist "on penetrating and perfecting the temporal order with the spirit of the Gospel" was impossible if it also included ruling out "in advance any question of the restoration of Christendom on twentieth-century foundations."[20]

To be sure, the reconciliation of church teaching and American pluralism was a herculean feat for any believer who took his or her bearings from ancient writings (scripture) or institutions (magisterium), and the Second Vatican Council may have cleared some room for Roman Catholics residing in the United States. But the questions raised by unbelief had always posed a challenge to the ideal of Christendom, and affirmations of human dignity did little to resolve the particular conundrums posed by a society such as the United States in which not only did religious pluralism prevail but movements to overturn conventional morality were acceptable and popular. Bozell's turn to Roman Catholic traditionalism in response made some sense. It did not, however, add to the plausibility of a faith-based political conservatism derived from loyalty to Roman Catholic traditionalism and teachings about natural law.

The Limits of Anticommunism

Bozell and Garry Wills did not share much in common except their friendship with William F. Buckley, Jr., their work for *National Review*, and their coincidental departure from the world of political conservatism. During an early skirmish in 1961 between Buckley's magazine and the liberal Roman Catholic press, Wills and Bozell had joined arms behind the banner of anticommunism. The latter had criticized liberal church members and clergy for insufficient vigor in defense of the West in the context of the Cold War. Of Europe and its offshoots Bozell claimed "a God-given right" and duty "to conserve and spread *its* truth, to judge political and economic and social systems according to *its* lights, to change and improve them under *its* authority." The conflict with Soviet communism possessed redemptive significance because the West was "*God's* civilization." When Roman Catholic critics accused Bozell of blasphemy for confusing Western civilization with the church, they also added a lesson about Christ's assertion that his kingdom was not of this world. In fact, the editors of *Commonweal* insisted that Christ's kingdom did not "rely on secular means to bring about its fulfillment."[21]

Wills rallied to Bozell's side. He explained that *Commonweal's* opinion would have surprised Joan of Arc, who understood something of divine ways employing "secular means to protect a Christian civilization." Wills himself offered a lesson on sacramental theology. The scandal of Christianity was the embedded character of the divine in the world. A sacramental view of life demanded that Christians reject a segregation of "Christ's work" and "secular means."[22]

Bozell appreciated Wills's support, but by 1967 the former Jesuit was a chief reason for abandoning *National Review* and starting *Triumph*. In a piece written to sort out questions surrounding contraception and family planning on the run-up to Pope Paul's *Humanae vitae*, Wills crossed the line that Bozell believed to be firmly drawn between God's ways and civilizational decay. Wills's piece, "Catholics and Population," was as modest as it was thorough. With experience at interpreting the significance and limits of papal authority, he acknowledged and respected papal and magisterial power. Wills also insisted that no infallible utterance was before the church, but he understood that a firm "papal directive" from Pius XI (*Casti connuubii*, 1930) had condemned any use of sexual relations within marriage that "deliberately frustrated . . . natural power to generate life." Even so, the bishops had not rendered any "extraordinary" teaching about contraception. Meanwhile, Roman Catholic moral theologians, although all accepting that to frustrate the natural purpose of sex was contrary to divine will, also conceded that sometimes couples could legitimately engage in sexual intimacy with the intent of not conceiving. Sex during pregnancy and menopause were two instances that no longer drew condemnation from the church. So too the acceptance of the "rhythm" method of family planning demonstrated a willingness to separate sex from its procreative consequences.[23]

An additional factor in Wills's assessment was global overpopulation. Although he felt the weight of objections that opposed adapting spiritual teaching to material circumstances, Wills also believed that rearing children with adequate physical resources was a spiritual matter that church officials should weigh. Aside from questions about papal authority, the evolution of moral teaching, or difficult circumstances confronting political leaders, Wills believed it was imperative for the church to maintain its traditions and to tinker with them at great peril. Roman Catholicism, he argued, was "a continued meditation" on redemptive history and divine revelation that united and intertwined in ways that prevented isolating certain subjects such as sex or contraception from a much more profound set of truths. Roman Catholic "resistance" to North American and

European assumptions about contraception was not an accident.[24] It was part of a millennium and a half of teaching and piety. To try to separate contraception from the wider set of norms, habits, and expectations was to miss the inherent conflict between an accepted part of Christian piety and the modern experience of hedonism. If Wills was not a reactionary Roman Catholic, he was certainly no modern believer on whom tradition clung lightly. He wanted a modern expression of the faith but on traditional terms.

Fears of the "population explosion," popularized in Paul and Ann Ehrlich's *The Population Bomb* (1968), in fact led many of the authors at *National Review* to question church teaching on contraception. Even before that book, the magazine had published an article by Alan Guttmacher, then president of Planned Parenthood Federation, when in 1965 contraception was still distinguishable from abortion. At the same time, worries about a crowded planet along with the Second Vatican Council's recognition of freedom of conscience gave Buckley room to speculate that abortion could be an option for those "left free to practice the dictates of their own consciences." If Roman Catholics opposed abortion, as well they should, Buckley insisted that the means they used be "suasive rather than coercive." Openness to abortion as a matter of conscience would change for *National Review* conservatives after *Roe v. Wade* (1973), but Buckley, who only had one child, remained open to family planning that included artificial means, and Wills did as well. In a 1969 interview, for instance, he conceded that contraception was not "an obvious violation of the marital ideal." If couples desired to limit the size of families, Buckley was open to "any collective endeavor to suggest means" for such regulation "subject to prior consent by the Church."[25] No wonder Bozell, who saw procreation as the line in the cosmic sand, broke ranks with fellow conservative Roman Catholics.

Wills's exit from Buckley's ranks had less to do with moral theology than anticommunism, though an awareness of the persistence of racism cracked open the door. After failing in 1967 to receive tenure at Johns Hopkins University in classics, he worked as a staff writer for *Esquire* magazine. His experience as a journalist functioned as a conversion. "After going from Jesuit seminary to graduate school and from there straight into the classroom," Wills later confessed, "I suddenly found myself in strip joints, police helicopters, black nationalist headquarters." He was even a hostage to a black radical "madman" who held Wills at gunpoint for the better part of an afternoon and allowed the journalist to experience that "authentic sixties feeling."[26]

Wills's encounters with race, from Martin Luther King, Jr., to black separatists, led him in 1968 to write *The Second Civil War*, a book about race riots, how police departments armed themselves to combat crime, and how African Americans perceived liberal reformers and law-and-order city officials. Hanging over Wills's reportage was a sense that on the domestic front the United States was using a strategy similar to the arms race. Race riots and urban police efforts to avoid them were "a test of nerves, a series of feints" that needed to remain symbolic so that antagonists could save face and avoid resorting to weapons. "It is good to know about, and fear, the guns we all live under," Wills opined. "Otherwise, God help us, we may use them." Even so, Wills hoped that if Americans could look beyond the units of police and black nationalists, they might see remarkable persons, resilient urban blacks, decent officers, inspiring community leaders, people who made it difficult "to imagine our being such idiots as to go to war with ourselves."[27] Wills had come a long way from Young Americans for Freedom.

In *Nixon Agonistes*, Wills established himself, in the words of Patrick Allitt, as "one of the most gifted nonfiction writers" in America, firmly in the ranks of Norman Mailer, Tom Wolfe, and Joan Didion.[28] Wills also proved himself to be a thinker who thought outside the lines of left and right as Americans understood those categories. Rather than using his faith as a vantage from which to stand outside the nation's political divide, as in his book on papal authority, Wills stood within America's reigning political ideals, tried to find coherence, and saw only basic and destructive tensions. In point of fact, he devoted himself less to the formal thought of Americans than to "a huge sunken body of historical aspirations" implicit in "half-forgotten dreams," "goals we hardly aspire to any more," "meaningless" words. From this perspective, President Richard Nixon was hardly conservative but the embodiment of American liberalism, a Lockean outlook that located society on a "contractual tie" among "sovereign" individuals. Persons entered society for the advantages of "human commerce" and recognized the need for an "umpire-state" to protect citizens' civil liberties. In turn, citizens looked to the "best men" to adopt the best policies for society.[29] Yet Americans received their Locke not from

Edmund Burke but from Horatio Alger. This made Nixon the "most authentic voice" of American liberalism.

A comparison to Eisenhower, the Republican that movement conservatives thought compromised by the establishment, showed Nixon's authenticity: "He was more self-made than Eisenhower. He was more religious—Ike started going to church when he sought office. . . . He was more competitive, *much* closer to the common man and full of that resentment our emulative ethic breeds. . . . [He was] more deeply and consistently liberal than Eisenhower. Phrases like 'equal opportunity' and 'self-determination' meant something to Nixon. To Eisenhower, they were just phrases." For Wills, Nixon's election in 1968 was also the last gasp of American liberalism. It reflected the country's desire to rehabilitate its odd mix of market logic and self-determination in the face of social realities that displayed the limits of liberalism. "Self-government" was the nation's political philosophy only because politics depended on personal morality. Without self-government, Americans would need a king, "like recalcitrant ancient Israel." With it, democracy was safe. Yet this left all social problems at the level of personal morality. Resorting to government programs was a confession of dependence, of "weakness." From this perspective, the student uprisings and the civil rights movement were an affront to Americans' "insistence on self-regulation." "Law and order," consequently, was code for racism. But it was also much more basic, the DNA of liberalism. "American liberalism has always been based on this . . . the ideal of self-government, of the self-disciplined self-made man."[30]

This understanding of the market, the nation, and human nature left the distinctions between Democrats (liberals) and Republicans (conservatives) in shambles. Wills conceded a difference between American and British classical liberalism. While proponents of the latter were willing to countenance the survival-of-the-fittest dimensions of laissez-faire, Americans were much more good-hearted about the market. Capitalism within the American creed was not simply an affirmation of the system's efficiency but also its moral ethos. "Business molded character." This created a tension in American liberalism between the ideal of "business competition" and capitalism as a "morally uplifting system."[31]

One more aspect of American liberalism that caught Wills's eye was the connection between markets and constitutionalism: "Individual initiative is . . . a check on the ambitions of those in authority." FDR may have had doubts about market efficiency, but he maintained his beliefs in the moral and small-government implications of free markets. Indeed, the Left in Wills's estimate "continued to be individualist in its attitude toward civil liberties, suffrage politics, academic freedom, and international determination." But the Right was simply "impoverished." The dynamics of a two-party system pushed defenders of "Market fundamentalism" such as Milton Friedman into "the mishmash of Right-Wing forces behind Barry Goldwater" that exalted "unfettered individualism" to the point of "philosophical anarchism." Wills conceded that "moral orthodoxy, social conformity, and community solidarity" had always placed limits on civil libertarianism in the United States. Nevertheless, the incoherence was palpable in the Goldwater campaign when the Republican nominee received the support of Ayn Rand individualists "*and* racists, states-righters, monarchists, and God knows what else." Of course, Goldwater disappointed conservatives when for practical policy he turned to traditional liberals— "Milton Friedman and Warren Nutter and Harry Jaffa."[32]

Frank S. Meyer drew the assignment of reviewing *Nixon Agonistes* for *National Review*. Right out of the blocks, he announced that Wills's book was "strange." It was not about Nixon as much as it was about the nation "about which there is nothing good to be said, an America seen from a point of view similar to, if not identical with, that of the revolutionary forces intent upon our destruction." Here Meyer meant black nationalists, leftists, and, more broadly, "the counterculture." Worse, Wills's book was filled with bile for "the America of self-reliance, individualism, aspiration, self-made man." *Nixon Agonistes* was also strange because Wills's contempt for America came in the medium of "the New Journalism," which possessed "all the straightforward openness to rational discourse of the TV commercial." Clearly, Wills had hit a nerve. Although Meyer appreciated Wills when he skewered Woodrow Wilson, the *National Review* editor was not so sanguine when Wills failed to distinguish New Deal liberalism (with its "corrupt degeneration toward socialism") from classical liberalism. Wills was guilty, consequently, of attacking "the American constitutional tradition, the heart and soul of contemporary American conservatism."[33]

Meyer had no trouble accounting for the source of Wills's loss of faith. It did not owe to Roman Catholic social teaching or his earlier flirtation with the distributism of G. K. Chesterton but to his empathy with "the rebel kids." Meyers discerned that Wills had discovered the truth about America's flaws through "militant blacks and student revolutionaries." For Meyer, neither the discontent of the nation's youth nor the harrowing events of 1968 could diminish "the glory of our constitutional tradition," which was responsible for creating "the most effective system yet known to man to minimize injustice and maximize opportunity and freedom."[34]

If *Nixon Agonistes* revealed Wills's apostasy, his opposition to the Vietnam War was evidence of heresy. The book already offered a peek into the author's change of attitude about the way the United States was prosecuting the Cold War. The plight of Daniel and Phillip Berrigan and the rest of the Catonsville Nine, who protested the war by breaking into a local draft board, taking files, and burning them in public, struck a nerve in Wills. He empathized with the Berrigans even if he maintained reservations about breaking the law. Nevertheless, their protest was understandable because Vietnam had revealed that the United States was "unwillingly, half-wittedly at war." The official rationale—self-determination for the South Vietnamese—conflicted with actual self-interest, such as helping the French and maintaining a presence in Asia. By 1968, as the Johnson administration floundered to justify the war, "there was nothing in the long war's lesion of our best youth and self-confidence to satisfy any type of man—not hard anticommunists, nor irenic accommodationists . . . not guardians of our self-interest, not generals looking only to the military aspect, not politicians, not moralists, not anybody."[35]

Least satisfied was Wills himself. About the same time that *Nixon Agonistes* appeared, he submitted pieces to *National Review* against the war. Buckley rejected them as "unnecessarily provocative." Wills did not take the rejections well. He wrote Buckley that although his respect for the editor "continues undiminished," he believed the magazine's "standards of veracity and honor are scandalously low." Wills and Buckley continued to spar. The former urged the latter to distinguish between Daniel and Phillip Berrigan, Daniel being not as provocative as his brother (although Wills failed to make much of a distinction in his book). Buckley shot back that Wills needed to distinguish between Nixon and Satan. Wills responded that such a distinction was "easy. . . . Satan's brighter." Buckley finally went public with Wills's inability to tell the difference between the "hysterical repression" of the Berrigans by J. Edgar Hoover and a political system that produced Joseph Stalin and Mao Zedong. Buckley confessed that the "historical frivolity" of "confused" and "confusing men" such as Wills was simply overwhelming.[36] With that, the bond that had held Roman Catholics within the conservative movement broke.

The Limits of Fusionism

Wills, Bozell, and Buckley may have diverged from the path they had taken between 1955 and 1965, but each of them continued to cling to conservatism. That was a harder sell for Wills because his criticisms of the United States, the conservative movement, and the church indicated an independence of mind that apparently undermined group loyalty. In *Bare Ruined Choirs* (1972), an autobiographical reflection on the significance of the Second Vatican Council, Wills praised the bishops worldwide for finally forcing the church to adjust to contemporary society and raising the stakes for church members so that faith could be genuine, not the product of "pretending out of deference to others." The preconciliar church had prospered and grown "fat." "Bringing that thing down—if the Council really accomplished this—was not a work of confusion, but a holy task, the destroying of idols."[37]

Yet Wills was dubious about how much the work of the council had trickled down to parishes in the United States. The American preconciliar church had made its peace in a "delicate balance" between faith and nationality. "Catholics grew up 'safe,' trusted as fully American; yet they had their own little enclave of comforting familiar things, some borrowed, some adapted, some preserved, all forming a distinctive texture." The Berrigans' protests against Vietnam and their criminal activity had "destroyed" this accommodation. Consequently, Roman Catholics in the United States were split. "One part . . . is captive of the state; and the other is trying to free it."[38]

Here is where Wills's conservatism became topsy-turvy and revealed the dilemma for Roman Catholics in the United States more generally. In his understanding, the new face of the U.S. church, the Berrigans, had "a greater sense of identity, of continuity with the past," a rendering that would suggest the Second Vatican Council's opening to modernity was actually a return to the past. Meanwhile, for Wills the preconciliar American church had been the real source of friendliness to modernity, full of a "mishmash of styles, all forced and unfelt."[39] In other words, young was old and traditional was modern. That may have rendered great insight to the dilemmas of Roman Catholicism in the United States, but it also suggested how far out of sync the American church was from Europe, where the Second Vatican Council represented an unprecedented attempt to modernize the church.

Even as Wills may have found solidarity with Roman Catholics on the Left, he continued in 1979 to think of himself as a conservative. In another memoirish book, *Confessions of a Conservative*, Wills had no trouble self-identifying with conservatism, but he distinguished his version from the "right wing" and the movement of which he had once been a contributor. For Wills, conservatism was an outlook that endeavored to preserve "the cohesion and continuity of society—what makes people band together and remain together with some satisfaction." He invoked Augustine to describe society as a *"common* possession" that included language, a shared history, "a concrete set of loyalties." And because conservatism valued continuity, conservatives were not opposed to change because it was inevitable. Avoiding change would only make society brittle and destroy social cohesion. As Carl T. Bogus observed, Wills may have thought he was appropriating Augustine, but "much of what he said sounded like Edmund Burke."[40]

In ways surprisingly similar, Bozell also soured on American conservatism and the church in the United States. In ecclesiastical matters, Bozell took the turn that many traditionalists did by defending and advocating the Latin Mass. For instance, he (with fellow editors) tapped Dietrich von Hildebrand to defend the old liturgy on the grounds that it cultivated true piety better. The new liturgy threatened an encounter with Christ because "it discourages reverence in the face of mystery, precludes awe, and all but extinguishes a sense of sacredness."[41] That was clearly a different posture from Wills, who welcomed changes in the church, but when Bozell and fellow conservative Roman Catholics at *Triumph* turned to American society, race relations and the Vietnam War provided reasons for breaking with political conservatives. In 1967, as neighborhoods in Detroit and Newark, New Jersey, burned thanks to an explosion of race riots, Bozell opined that the protests were welcome indications of secular liberalism's failure. "Our ignorance of the problem posed by the Negro is," Bozell lamented, "simply appalling." Legislation, court orders, free markets, and integration had all failed, and conservatives did no better by thinking the collapse of liberalism would vindicate Republicans. The only approach that might unite whites and blacks was to recover the Christian truths that had undergirded Western civilization.[42]

Meanwhile, the Vietnam War was another sign of the United States' departure from the moral and religious truths that had contributed to its power and goodness. In 1968, after President Johnson agreed to withdraw troops from Khe Sanh, Bozell wrote that the United States had become "a *formerly* great power." If the nation were to ever recover its greatness, it needed to rediscover "its mission in history." In contrast to Wills, who when confronting difficult truths about the United States recommended adjustments to faith and politics, Bozell proposed the traditional Roman Catholic faith and a nationalism based on submission ("bending the knee") to divine purpose.[43]

That left Buckley to carry the water for many Roman Catholics in the conservative movement and calculate their relationship to the Republican Party. With Richard Nixon as the candidate in 1968, Buckley decided to endorse the man who had been vice president under the too-moderate Eisenhower. It did not hurt that Buckley had emerged as an influential political figure (his debates with Gore Vidal billed as analysis on network television during the national conventions were partly responsible). Buckley rallied conservatives who read *National Review* not to vote for George Wallace but to back Nixon. He even secured pieces for the magazine from Barry Goldwater and John Ashbrook, a Young Republican leader, to help readers understand properly the contrast between Nixon and Wallace. By 1972, after Nixon's opening to China with its implications for going soft on communism, Buckley understood why conservatives might have mixed feelings about Nixon. He knew the president was not ideal. He refused to look at support for George McGovern as a way to teach the GOP a lesson, but he also tried to allow fellow editors and contributors to voice dissent within the magazine. When William Rusher wanted to write that conservatives would be better off with McGovern, Buckley refused on grounds that the "position was eccentric."[44] The lesson that many of Buckley's fellow travelers were learning was the same that had provoked the magazine's founding, namely, the Republican Party needed to be purged of the Rockefellers and Nixons.

Could Buckley have steered a better course if Wills and Bozell had remained on his team? According to John Leonard, another writer at *National Review* who left because he was too liberal, Wills's departure was the most devastating to Buckley:

> Garry was the future. He was religious. He was the genius they were waiting for. This was the real thing; this was their angel. His defection was the defection of their greatest hope. When Garry said what was happening to blacks was more important than what was reflected in the magazine, and it hurts me personally, morally, he spoke to that best part, that most vulnerable part of the Buckleys. It went from blacks to Nixon to Vietnam. He was saying not simply I disagree with you, but I am closer to God. A real moral issue was being thrown at them. . . . Garry was a soul. And Garry's burned soul scared the shit out of them.[45]

Even if they were scared, in the end Buckley still held out for America and its political traditions. As Frank Meyer explained in his review of *Nixon Agonistes*, Wills was raising the same questions that Bozell had with the founding of *Triumph*, though traditionalist Roman Catholics spoke "from an older, more intellectually coherent, if rather fanatical, standpoint." Meyer also conceded that Bozell and Wills were right that much was wrong with the nation. But their diagnosis blamed the wrong source. The United States' problem was not the Constitution or its political traditions but "the destruction of our Constitution and our tradition." Meyer added, "It is the glory of our constitutional tradition that it created the most effective system yet known to man to minimize injustice and maximize opportunity and freedom."[46]

Americanism still animated conservatives. However, some Roman Catholics, such as Wills and Bozell, sensed that the turmoil of the 1960s, from race to sex, was not an aberration but a consequence of U.S. political ideals. For them, Americanism was wishful thinking.

7

AMERICANISM REVIVED

By 1974 the prospects for American conservatism looked grim. Having invested in the Republican establishment sufficiently to embrace Richard M. Nixon, conservatives themselves could only regard Watergate and the president's subsequent resignation as catastrophic. (At least Garry Wills and Brent Bozell did not have to worry about defending or condemning Nixon.) William F. Buckley, Jr., observed on his television show, "Mr. Nixon's policies were so confusing as regards conservative priorities domestically and internationally that he has left the conservative movement scattered, slightly incoherent, and perhaps even emasculated."[1]

The next year, 1975, at the twentieth-anniversary party for *National Review*, Buckley sounded even more pessimistic. Conservatism was a small remnant that every once in a while sang "the old song, free of the tormented introspections of the new idiom; ignorant altogether of the litany of reasons why we should hate our own country; axiomatic" in the Left's "demand for human freedom." Sometimes those old choruses even stirred conservatives' emotions so that "the heart stirs," "the blood begins to run," and "the effort continues." With the approach of the nation's bicentennial, Buckley concluded, "We have stood together for one-tenth the life span of this Republic, and we must resolve to stand with it, and its ideals, forever."[2] America was still exceptional, still the outpost of the West and so part of the heritage of Christendom, still a nation worthy of Christians' hopes and industry. But the relatively short history of conservatism had yet to recruit more Americans than a remnant. It continued to subsist (perhaps "thrive" is more apt since *National Review* held its party at New York City's Grand Plaza Hotel's ballroom) on the margins.

By 1975 as well, the hopes for fusing American ideas of small government and personal liberty with traditional Christianity looked less than promising. The mainline Protestant churches, just like the guardians of Yale University with whom Buckley had first done battle, were coming to terms with the 1960s mix of political reform and moral indifference in ways that were more radical than traditional. Conservative (or born-again) Protestants had yet to emerge as an identifiable political constituency, and their concerns were generally too pious and moral for the urbane and worldly ethos of movement conservatives. Meanwhile, the Roman Catholic Church was in the midst of sorting out the reforms of the Second Vatican Council while also needing to defend papal teaching on sex and contraception; if the council had opened the church to the modern world, *Humanae vitae* had set limits on how far. During the 1976 presidential election, that sifting had produced an ecclesiastical voice with a pro-life reputation. In August the executive committee of the U.S. bishops met with Jimmy Carter, then the Democratic nominee for president, to explain their call for a constitutional amendment that gave "maximal protection" to the unborn. They hoped to appeal to the candidate's personal opposition to abortion (despite his party's pro-choice platform). Carter tried to reassure the bishops that he was not opposed to a constitutional amendment per se, but he simply could not support any of the ones proposed so far. Press coverage indicated that the bishops had interrogated Carter and that the Democrat's staff felt "sandbagged" since they had hoped for a discussion about policies other than abortion. President Gerald Ford capitalized on the bishops' pro-life reputation and met with leading bishops in the White House weeks after Carter's meeting. Ford assured the bishops that he opposed abortion and supported an amendment.[3] Those encounters with Carter and Ford were arguably the best gauge of the church's leverage in presidential politics.

The other challenge to movement conservatives was the emergence of neoconservatism. The voices associated with this outlook had been advocates of government programs for equality and racial harmony during the 1960s, but after the disruptions of 1968 some became increasingly frustrated with liberalism's promise. To sustain this "revisionist liberalism," as Irving Kristol called it, neoconservative magazines such as the *Public Interest* became outposts for critiques of liberal government programs. This version of conservatism resonated with the older version Buckley had constructed. Neoconservatives were responding to a perceived collapse of tradition in American society as well as a departure from what Kristol called the "animating principles" of the United States.[4] And just as the conservative movement had been friendly to religion, especially Roman Catholicism, neoconservatives also saw the crisis of the 1960s as one where secularization had harmfully displaced religion. The neoconservatives' Jewish backgrounds were mainly foreign to the conservative movement. But both groups were friendly to a religion-based morality in ways that liberals, who feared religious authoritarianism, were not.

Still, George Nash has maintained that neoconservatism "should not be equated with orthodox *National Review* conservatism."[5] Many of the neoconservatives continued to identify themselves as liberal and favored federal programs in ways that conflicted with the constitutionalism of movement conservatism. For a time, though, neoconservatism infused vigor on the Right in ways that Buckley had fifteen years earlier. The question was whether a Roman Catholic version of conservatism could keep pace. The answer to that query came from an entirely unexpected direction—former critics of U.S. domestic and foreign policy who came to recognize in Roman Catholicism the best way to restore American greatness.

The Odd Couple of American Conservatism

If patriotic Roman Catholics were looking for reinforcements for the defense of American political ideals, Michael Novak and Richard John Neuhaus would not have made the first cut. Throughout the 1960s neither man could be found supporting the causes that animated the Right, but in fact each had sided with the nation's most pointed critics. Born within three years of each other, Novak in 1933 and Neuhaus in 1936, each grew up in religious homes that made plausible a career in the church. The former, a cradle Roman Catholic, grew up in Johnstown, Pennsylvania, among the Slovak Americans who worked in the region's mill towns and coal mines, though Novak's father was an insurance salesman. His education in preparation for the priesthood included studies at Stonehill College, a small liberal arts institution in Massachusetts run by the Congregation of Holy Cross, the Gregorian University in Rome. After experiencing questions about his vocation and grief over the murder of his brother, a missionary priest, he pursued graduate studies at the Catholic University of America and Harvard University in religion and philosophy. Novak never completed a doctorate and began a writing career during the early 1960s, which included two novels and coverage of the Second Vatican Council for *National Catholic Reporter*.

While for Garry Wills journalism had been a fallback after being denied tenure, for Novak reporting led to an acquaintance with the Presbyterian theologian Robert McAfee Brown, who taught religion at Stanford University. Brown recruited Novak to the California university, where the young intellectual became the first Roman Catholic to teach in Stanford's humanities program. From Stanford, Novak moved in 1969 to the State University of New York at Old Westbury, and in 1973 from within the empire of Rockefeller he went to head the humanities program at the family's foundation. Novak went on to teach at Syracuse University and University of Notre Dame while also gaining a foothold in the think tank world at American Enterprise Institute.

Neuhaus's career was not as straightforward, even though it landed him in a position similar to Novak's as a Roman Catholic public intellectual. The son of a Missouri Synod Lutheran pastor in Pembroke, Ontario, Neuhaus aspired to the ministry but not to its constraints. That semirebellious spirit sent him to a Lutheran prep school in Texas, where he dropped out. Despite not receiving a diploma, Neuhaus moved to Saint Louis to enroll at the Missouri Synod's Concordia Seminary. His first call in 1961 took him to a congregation in Brooklyn, New York, with primarily black and Hispanic members. As a pastor, Neuhaus was active in the civil rights movement and helped form, with Daniel Berrigan and Rabbi Abraham Joshua Heschel, Clergy and Laity Concerned about Vietnam.

On two occasions, police in New York and Chicago arrested him as part of protests against segregation in public schools and the Vietnam War at the Democratic National Convention. Neuhaus's interest in public policy continued throughout the 1970s while he continued to serve as a pastor and as he moved from the political left to the right. The following decade he left the ministry to devote his energies as a public intellectual to the Institute on Religion and Public Life. Those transitions took Neuhaus from Lutheranism to Roman Catholicism. In 1991 he became a priest.

Novak and Neuhaus were not avid readers of *National Review* while they were finding their way professionally during the 1960s. To describe them as part of the political left is accurate but not the whole story. Nevertheless, the concerns that animated support for Barry Goldwater—constitutionalism, anticommunism, U.S. sovereignty—were distant from the causes that fueled the next stage of Roman Catholic political conservatism.

The issue that separated both from conservatives was the war in Vietnam. While teaching at Stanford, Novak served as a faculty adviser to an antiwar student association. He later recalled that he was an odd fit because he occupied "the right wing of the radical movement."[6] That he viewed the matter as an American rather than an international one may have foreshadowed where he would land. For the time being, though, he raised serious objections against the church's history of anticommunism while also faulting the United States for failing to adhere to the 1954 Geneva Accords. Novak visited Vietnam in 1967 and wrote articles that contrasted the humanitarian work of agricultural and medical workers to the destructive character of the U.S. military. He also joined Neuhaus in forming Clergy and Laity Concerned about Vietnam.

Opposition to the war was also the defining moment for Neuhaus in national politics, though he had dipped his toes in the pool of New York City politics as soon as he had arrived at Saint John's in 1961. Race relations were another factor that kept the former Lutheran pastor several steps removed from conservatism. He functioned as the liaison in the city for Martin Luther King, Jr. Neuhaus's oppositional stance had much more of an edge than Novak's. This likely owed to disgust with the federal government's perceived indifference to inner-city conditions. On the eve of the 1968 Democratic national convention in Chicago, Neuhaus was ready to challenge all political authority, a resolution that prompted him to join a protest during the convention. That act of defiance also landed him in jail.

Two years later, Neuhaus coauthored with sociologist Peter Berger a book on the possibilities and challenges of political insurrection, *Movement and Revolution*. In the book Neuhaus revealed sympathy for the Left's radicalism but also wondered aloud about the real danger (physical and moral) of revolution.

By the early 1970s, Neuhaus and Novak had become increasingly uncomfortable with critics of the United States on the left. That discomfort emerged when both recognized the weakness of elites in American society and especially intellectuals' indifference toward, if not disdain for, religion. The failure of the 1960s protests and the subsequent ferment of the 1970s—defeat in Vietnam, economic weakness, and Watergate— prompted Neuhaus to blame secularism particularly for the nation's woes. The U.S. ruling intellectual class had embraced a "secularized liberalism" that was "cut off from its religious roots and robbed of its power to provide meaning."[7] As such, an alleged gap existed between the people and elites, with the former experiencing alienation from most of the proposals that officials offered as remedy for reform. The sense that "real" Americans were at odds with the political and cultural establishment was partly responsible for drawing Neuhaus into the world of conservatism where such discontent paved the way to reconsider national identity. Rather than looking to the founding or the Constitution for bearings, though, Neuhaus turned to biblical accounts of a nation's obligations to God as the remedy for America's spiritual crisis.

Novak too took a populist turn, as evidenced by his popular book, *The Rise of Unmeltable Ethnics* (1972). During a tour of the country with Sargent Shriver in 1970, Novak observed the decency and stability of regular Americans. That experience evoked a certain nostalgia for Novak's own hyphenated American past and the values of his immigrant ancestors. The flip side of Novak's appreciation of ethnicity was suspicion of the WASP establishment in both the Democratic and Republican parties. It also led to a recovery of both his Roman Catholic heritage and the immigrant work ethic, which included a reassessment of capitalism and its capacity to improve the living conditions of the poor. From the mid-1970s until the 1982 publication of *The Spirit of Democratic Capitalism*, Novak strove to give free markets a theological justification.

These shifts for Novak and Neuhaus landed them a regular column in *National Review*. In 1979 Novak began to write for Buckley's magazine at a page called "Tomorrow and Tomorrow." The forerunner to this regular page-long essay came in September 1979 when in a piece called "Illusions and Realities" editors introduced Novak as a resident scholar at the American Enterprise Institute and the author of a novel (*The Guns of Lattimer*), a book on athletics (*The Joy of Sports*), and *The Rise of Unmeltable Ethnics*, a book then almost a decade old. In his first article, Novak zoomed in on the theme that made him a mainstay in the world of conservatism—the superiority of democratic capitalism to socialism. What made Novak's maiden voyage particularly noteworthy was its display of theological erudition. In ways that echoed Garry Wills's services to conservatism, Novak attempted to explain and overcome the Roman Catholic Church's objections to capitalism.

For instance, he summed up traditional Roman Catholic moral theology this way: "For several generations, the Roman Catholic Church has taken a dim view of capitalism, indeed, regarding it from faraway Italy as a Northern heresy, Protestant, individualistic, materialistic, and based upon 'Manchester liberalism.'" Novak threw in that until the Second Vatican Council, Rome had also "condemned" liberalism, democracy, and even religious liberty. As much "progress" as the church had made, theologians were still hostile to capitalism and preferred socialism, an inclination that Novak could not fathom. If critics faulted capitalism for creating a system where 6 percent of the world's population used 40 percent of the world's energy, they seldom observed that "this same 6 per cent *produces* 60 to 70 per cent of the world's energy and resources." Democratic capitalism, in fact, supplanted the older forms of energy—wind, sun, water, and beasts of burden with oil, electricity, and nuclear power. Without those advances, Novak argued, no "wealth of nations."[8]

Why Novak insisted on modifying capitalism with "democratic" became clear as he developed his column for *National Review* readers. He regarded socialism as authoritarian and "biased toward the interests of experts and intellectuals," another indication of the populist strain in Novak's appeal to conservatives.[9] At the same time, he suggested that socialism represented a false religion, "a surrogate for Christianity and Judaism." Even in the West, the conflict between statists and conservatives was "morally unequal." The reason was that conservatives, in advocating democratic capitalism, were "closer to the inner meaning of history" than statists. To be sure, socialists and statists evinced a compassionate concern for the poor and less fortunate. But they translated "compassion into taxes, and taxes into budgets, and budgets into agencies, and agencies into federal forms." At each step, "greed, self-interest, and profiteering" invaded statist transactions. In contrast, in the private sector, markets were "imaginative, energetic, efficient, practical, and public-spirited." Democratic capitalism had greater capacities than socialism for improving material conditions, channeling human freedom into productive outcomes, and generating wealth. Novak conceded that capitalism permitted "sin to flourish, along with virtue." It was not a system for "mass-producing individual saintliness, self-realization, or collective happiness." It did, however, follow the "Creator, Who so loved liberty as to permit its awful desecrations." Or, as Novak explained the moral implications of socialism and capitalism, the former's egalitarianism assumed that envy was the "most powerful passion in the human breast" while the latter thrived on "rational self-interest," a motivation "not quite a sin" but also necessarily virtuous.[10]

Novak likely did not need to convince many *National Review* readers of capitalism's advantages, but his columns did offer a Roman Catholic–inflected argument for conservatism's animating convictions. For instance, in a column critical of the Carter administration's foreign policy—insufficiently anticommunist and too passive—Novak was especially critical of the idea that the president's policies were "born-again," as if opposition to the administration implied infidelity. Was any national leader, Carter included, Novak asked, willing to follow the path that Christ walked and lead a nation to "crucifixion and death"?[11]

Novak also used his columns to take issue with the U.S. bishops' increasing support for the foreign and domestic policies of the Democratic Party. Particularly alarming was the rejection of Roman Catholic just-war theory by a majority of theologians and some bishops. The danger was not simply the politicization of the church but "excessive clericalization." Were bishops really competent to make all "the key political judgments," more so than one-fourth of Congress (the number of Roman Catholics in the federal legislature)? Novak feared that these developments were "on the road that Vatican II" traveled. His criticisms were not reserved for U.S. bishops. Novak also mildly faulted Pope John Paul II in his encyclical on work (*Laborem exercens*) for failing to recognize the positive contributions of British and American classical liberalism. In the main, the pope's criticism of Marxism was thorough and welcome, but it missed the genius of John Locke, Adam Smith, Montesquieu, Jefferson, and Madison. Novak's own version of patriotism sprang from the nation's history of free markets and the work ethic of its people. "Few are the individuals who have come to the United States from any other culture on this planet," he asserted, "who do not find greater opportunity here than where they were." Novak added that the poor "seemed to know [this] better than the privileged."[12]

A pro-American voice familiar with the teachings of the church was also useful when bishops weighed in on domestic and foreign affairs. In 1983 the U.S. Conference of Catholic Bishops did just that when they delivered the third and final draft of their pastoral letter on nuclear weapons, "The Challenge of Peace." Novak brought *National Review* readers up to speed by pointing out just how much the bishops had avoided the shipwreck of pacifism and a condemnation of first use.

The source of sanity about the nature of the Cold War and the church's traditional understanding of just war was, in addition to New Orleans archbishop Philip Hannan, "who fought alone and bravely against the Left," the Vatican itself. Earlier drafts had entertained ideas so distressing that certain European prelates and the Vatican secretary of state needed to provide caution. For instance, the Vatican faulted the U.S. bishops for not distinguishing adequately between matters of prudential judgment and doctrinal truths on questions surrounding the first use of nuclear weapons as well as "counterpopulation warfare." Vatican officials also objected to parts of the draft that gave episcopal blessing to pacifism and reminded U.S. bishops that just-war theory was a long-standing conviction of the church. Novak understood that American bishops would still present the aim of their letter in ways that ignored the Vatican's directives. But the fingerprints of Rome were all over the document, and Novak advised readers not to be intimidated by episcopal authority but to "hold to [Vatican instruction] as to a rock." In those parts of the text where the Vatican's instructions on just war and deterrence were "valiant," the U.S. church had a reliable statement on nuclear war and deterrence.[13] In the 1960s criticisms such as this might sound insubordinate. By the 1980s they were standard fare.

Another assembly of bishops was the occasion for Richard John Neuhaus's first sustained contribution to *National Review*, though in that same year—1986—he also filled in for Novak in the "Tomorrow and Tomorrow" column before receiving his own under the title "Pilgrim." Neuhaus also began as the magazine's religion editor, even while overseeing three other publications, *Lutheran Forum*, *This World*, and *Religion and Society Report*. This time *National Review*'s readers received instruction on how to regard the Extraordinary Synod of 1985 that witnessed bishops and cardinals assess the meaning of the Second Vatican Council. Neuhaus, still a Lutheran pastor, let Roman Catholics render the final verdict. According to one of his sources, Pope John Paul II had recognized a crisis of authority in the church, and the synod, with the pope's hearty approval, had given conservatives the victory. "It was a clean sweep for us," a traditionalist leader told Neuhaus. "Now we'll have to convince our people not to crow about it too much." Instead of opening the church to the world, one now seen as secular and morally unsettled, the synod had responded to the challenge of modernity with a "return of the sacred." Talk of a new catechism that would inform instructional materials throughout the entire church was further evidence to Neuhaus of Rome's recovery of its footing after decades of uncertainty. The Extraordinary Synod, under the direction of John Paul II, was "the real beginning of the renewal proposed by Vatican II," one that spoke to the modern world but used the church's own resources.[14]

From there Neuhaus's columns featured for conservative audiences the standard themes that animated the religious Right. Those conservatives rallied behind opposition to abortion. In fact, Neuhaus's very first "Pilgrim" column faulted the Supreme Court for overturning Pennsylvania laws that regulated access to abortion. Here Neuhaus introduced what became a oft-repeated contrast between the "democratic morality" of the people and "the judgment of a transient majority of an imperial court." When the same court ruled that sodomy was not a "fundamental right" and so upheld state laws that banned certain homosexual behavior, Neuhaus welcomed the justices' recognition of the rights of the people's representatives. He also alerted readers rather predictably to the dangers of divorce and teenage pregnancy, not on grounds of sanctity so much as on the basis of public policy. Sex outside marriage was merely a symptom of a much larger problem, one that Daniel Patrick Moynihan had highlighted almost two decades earlier. Neuhaus spoke of his own experience while ministering to black parishioners in Brooklyn and warned of the collapse of the African American family, a demise furthered by "welfare policies," "anti-family propaganda," movies and television, and "the failure of black churches."[15]

Neuhaus used his space in *National Review* to sort out his relationships with Christians in the United States. Although a pastor with ties to an ethnic communion, the Lutheran Church Missouri Synod, Neuhaus by instinct was drawn to mainstream Protestantism, the so-called Protestant establishment. In addition, he sided with the wing of Lutherans that rejected the Missouri Synod's parochial theology and formed the Lutheran portion of the Protestant mainline. Still, Neuhaus grew weary of the mainline's predictably liberal pieties that lurched in an anti-American direction. He was prone to use the following as a test of political sanity: "On balance, and considering the alternatives, American influence is a force for good in the world." Neuhaus sensed that the oldest Protestant churches increasingly had abandoned this conviction. Too many academics and clerics harbored affection for socialism, partly, he speculated, because they needed "an alternative to the way things are." What Neuhaus could not believe was the church's blindness to the dangers of socialism. Accounts such as Whittaker Chambers's from the 1950s or that of Armando Valladeres, who escaped from Cuba after twenty-two years in jail and documented his torments in *Against All Hope*, revealed "an evil thing that is the greatest continuing assault upon humanity in our time." The Protestant mainline, through either its National Council or World Council, could not acknowledge such evil but only "the idea of historical misfortune and mistake."[16] For that reason, Neuhaus increasingly looked beyond the Protestant mainline, to evangelicals and especially to Roman Catholics, as better allies for combining American patriotism and Christian conviction.

Neuhaus was aware of the challenges that Roman Catholicism in the United States posed to conservatism, yet he alerted readers to important American voices within the church. In one column, Neuhaus tried to parse the disagreements between Mario Cuomo, governor of New York, and John Cardinal O'Connor, archbishop of New York City. Although sympathetic to Cuomo's arguments against capital punishment, Neuhaus was less than impressed by the coherence of the governor's appeal to the "seamless garment" of the church's social teaching on abortion. Nevertheless, the real culprit in the apparent conflict between civil and spiritual authorities was not Roman Catholics (lay or clerical) but the *New York Times*, whose writers had tried to create a controversy. Here Neuhaus defended the prerogatives of bishops, not newspaper editors, to define Roman Catholic identity. In fact, for all the difficulties that Rome may have experienced in coming to terms with democracy, the church seemed unlikely to "accept the idea that questions of faith and morals are to be decided by opinion polls." The Congregation for the Doctrine of the Faith still mattered more than the *Times*'s editorial offices.[17]

As impressive as episcopal authority was—and Neuhaus became a close associate of O'Connor—even more significant for the defense of traditional morality and civil society were lay Roman Catholic intellectuals. Although Neuhaus had sparred with Novak in the 1970s over the implicit cultural separatism of *Unmeltable Ethnics*, by the second term of the Reagan administration Neuhaus recognized Novak as a fellow traveler. The former believed the latter belonged to the ranks of those who perceived "a natural and assured ordering of things." What particularly impressed Neuhaus was Novak's defense of democracy against socialism or liberationist movements. When its leaders recognized they were "under God," liberal democracy cultivated a sense that politics were not "ultimate" but at best penultimate. This prevented politicians—unlike the liberationists— from trying to immanentize the eschaton. Neuhaus detected a similar perspective in George Weigel, then the founding president of the James Madison Foundation. In Weigel's book, *Tranquilitas Ordinis*, Neuhaus recognized another Christian who was critical of the churches falling into line with the political partisanship of the hour. Instead of segregating religion from politics as the remedy for such partisanship, Weigel proposed, and Neuhaus seconded, that Christianity be repoliticized. Christianity could reinvigorate American politics not by supplying the right policy prescription but by drawing on its "impressive resources" in discussions of "how *ought* we to live together?"[18]

The timing of Neuhaus's appreciation for Novak and Weigel was propitious. Within a year he traveled with sociologist and longtime friend Peter Berger, Novak, and Weigel to Rome to meet with Vatican officials. The Americans had access to Joseph Cardinal Ratzinger, then the prefect for the Congregation for the Doctrine of the Faith, who wanted to lend support to Neuhaus's plans for cooperation between American Christians and the Vatican. After his return from that trip in the spring of 1988,

Neuhaus was a guest at a White House state dinner hosted by President Reagan. The Lutheran pastor was himself under contract for a book on Roman Catholic contributions to national debates on social and foreign policy. Here was a new form of faith-based conservatism. Unlike Buckley, Bozell, and Wills, who worked through access to the Republican Party's leadership, the troika of Neuhaus, Novak, and Weigel not only wrote for the readers of Buckley's magazine but also had the ear of presidents and cardinals. This was a novel form of Roman Catholic conservatism for which many church members and clergy in the United States were unprepared. Neuhaus and his friends' conservatism was still very much in the Americanist mold.

The Catholic Moment

The book that Neuhaus produced for Harper & Row was so long—two hundred thousand words—that his editor thought *The Catholic Millennium* a better title. An abbreviated form of Neuhaus's case for Rome's unique capacity to engage politics and society both in the United States and around the world appeared a year before in a column for *National Review*. There the magazine's religion editor—Neuhaus—distilled the essence of "the Catholic Moment": "This is the historical moment at which Roman Catholicism has a singular opportunity to take the lead in reconstructing a moral philosophy for the American experiment in republican democracy." Neuhaus conceded that this sentence needed careful unpacking. But a crucial piece of the assertion was unstated. The "manifest decline, if not collapse, of Anglo-Saxon Protestant cultural hegemony" in the United States was the most important reason for looking to Roman Catholicism. Neuhaus echoed without realizing it Buckley's complaint thirty-five years earlier about Yale, namely, that the Protestant establishment had in the spirit of toleration lost its nerve and could no longer defend its traditions or contribution to American society.

Neuhaus was aware of the reinvigoration of evangelical Protestantism through the constellation of agencies that comprised the formal and informal moral majority. But he hoped Jerry Falwell and company would not achieve "a monopoly on culture-formative religion" in the United States. Neuhaus did not explain that hope. The evangelical leadership was likely so boorish in its manners and blinkered in its cultural sensibilities that he did not need to explain. What the nation needed was a theologically infused moral discourse that could also defend and maintain the ideals of political liberty and self-government. Roman Catholics were, Neuhaus acknowledged, finally "at home" in America. What he hoped was that such comfort was not of the kind that John F. Kennedy demonstrated when he convinced Protestants he was no threat to the nation. Kennedy was no threat, Neuhaus explained, "because he was not much of a Catholic."[19]

In his book-long case for Roman Catholicism, Neuhaus knew the world of the clergy and theologians well enough to understand that the church in the United States could capitulate to cultural trends the way mainline Protestantism had. He was especially aware of the difficulties posed by the Second Vatican Council and its aftermath. For an older expression of conservative Americanists (Buckley, Wills, Bozell), that council and its resolutions had weakened opposition to communism. For Neuhaus, however, the council provided a setting where the church's administrative sector began to catch up with recent theological advances from the likes of Yves Congar, Karl Rahner, Joseph Ratzinger, and—always dear to Roman Catholics in the United States—John Courtney Murray.[20]

Neuhaus seemed to be convinced of the claim that the substance of doctrine had not changed at the council even if the mode of presenting it had—he did not acknowledge that this was also the way that mainline Protestants had justified their adjustment to modernity. He conceded that Rome had moved to the left on social and political questions, a turn that followed John XXIII's lead, and recognized the wit and truth of Buckley's quip, "Mater si, magistra no." Neuhaus also admitted that the council's optimism about the modern world looked "Pollyannaish" three decades later (53). In fact, a plausible reading of the council might emphasize "the ambiguities and contrasting accents" such that the documents read like "a jumble of notes, occasional disconnected bars, snatches of tunes new and old, from which one can pick and choose to compose whatever song strikes one's fancy" (55). Indeed, Roman Catholicism after the Council of Trent was "a package deal" that the Second Vatican Council undid, which consequently "led to a large measure of confusion" (60). This state of affairs also made plausible the judgment that Roman Catholicism faced a "crisis" (67). Within the church in the United States, according to Neuhaus, the "center of Catholic intellectuality," represented by the

University of Notre Dame's theologian Richard McBrien, was devoted to "nurtur[ing] the continued allegiance of Catholics whose main dogma is the rejection of dogma" (69, 70).

But for all of Rome's challenges, Neuhaus saw in the church resources unparalleled by any other Christian expression. Early in the book he quoted from John Adams's description of a Mass he attended in 1774 in Philadelphia: "Here is everything which can lay hold of the eye, ear, and imagination—everything which can charm and bewitch the simple and ignorant. I wonder how Luther ever broke the spell." Neuhaus disagreed with Adams on the ignorance of Roman Catholics, but he did recognize in Rome a superior expression of Christianity—"the bearer of the marks of present catholicity and historical continuity far more impressively than any other church" (10). What particularly caught Neuhaus's eye, even despite the tribulations of the Second Vatican Council, was Rome's authority. Time and time again, he turned to John Paul II and Joseph Ratzinger for explanations of faith and practice and to determine the direction of Roman Catholicism. When examining discussions among bishops and theologians in the United States, Neuhaus heard debates that were "disappointing in their institutional insularity" (12). But that was not the case when listening to the pope and his top theological aid. At an important transition in the book, from the American church's doldrums to the prospects for the "Catholic moment," Neuhaus wrote of John Paul II and Ratzinger:

> One need not believe that these men are spiritual heroes or the greatest theological minds of the century. One need not think they have transcended temptations to pride and petty self-interest. Both have spoken often and movingly about sin and ambiguity in the lives of Christians, and there is no reason to believe that they think they are exempt from the reality they describe. . . . It is truly odd but it is oddly true that one must today present a defense for taking the Pope and the prefect of the Congregation for the Doctrine of the Faith seriously as theological interlocutors. If someone wanted to understand Roman Catholicism and its prospects for the future, that person should not look to the margins of church life but to "the Pope, the Curia," and the "overwhelming majority of bishops throughout the world." (95)

Neuhaus followed his own advice when he turned from the uncertainties spawned by the Second Vatican Council to the Vatican's own leadership. John Paul II was obviously at the top of the list and impressive to boot. "He is not a pope who happens to be a philosopher; he is a philosopher who became pope," Neuhaus observed (163). For that reason, in addition to his own struggles with communism in Poland, John Paul II had much to teach theologians who sometimes theorized from their university offices. Neuhaus also agreed with Paul Johnson's estimate that the pope was the man of the hour, the one to contain the damage done by the excesses of the council. "With the coming of John Paul . . . [the damage] is being repaired. The instrument is being fashioned for service again," Neuhaus quoted (98).

Also important was the pope's choice of another intellectual, Joseph Ratzinger, to oversee the teaching activities of the church. The cardinal's "jaunty readiness to challenge the hegemony of stifling secularism" alarmed journalists and some clerics. In fact, Ratzinger had become a "symbol of all that is odious and threatening about the pontificate of John Paul" (104). Not to Neuhaus, though, since he believed Ratzinger's candor and intelligence in being "unapologetically Roman Catholic" would enhance the faith's "distinctiveness and attractiveness" (105). One further indication of the "renewal" of Roman Catholicism under John Paul II was the 1985 Extraordinary Council. A great contribution of the synod, which debated and discussed the legacy of the Second Vatican Council, was to come down "strongly in favor of the teaching authority of each bishop in communion with the college of bishops and, of course, with the Bishop of Rome" (117). The synod also avoided the hysteria of political causes and reaffirmed "the way of the cross" (119). All told, John Paul, Ratzinger, and the synod represented an effort, Neuhaus hoped, "to chart a course of faithfulness in the absence of false certitudes that once put their leadership beyond question" (125).

But what did any of this have to do with the United States and its political and social institutions? For a writer whose editorials never lacked punch, Neuhaus's point in *The Catholic Moment* about Rome's prospects for American politics was frustratingly indirect. The United States, he appeared to indicate, needed a better foundation for its understanding of freedom than the one that in the 1960s had allowed liberty to drown social order. The great temptation for Roman Catholics was a liberation theology that collapsed church and state along habits of thought that merged religion and society. Neuhaus called this tendency "monism." The church needed an alternative, one that distinguished between religious and political spheres, which he called "pluralism." The modern theologian to justify such pluralism was John Courtney Murray, who presented a "lively alternative to the habits of monism" (192).

Not only had the American Jesuit prevailed at the Second Vatican Council, but John Paul II, while not following Murray's footprints, was using the American's trail. Neuhaus conceded that the pope was not always clear in his critique of liberation theology. But his record of opposition to Marxism, his positive statements about work and private property, and especially the pope's recognition that "politics is not salvation" and "salvation is not politics" avoided the problems of monism and mirrored Murray's pluralism (207). Also indicative of John Paul's ambivalence about liberation theology was a document produced by Ratzinger's Congregation for the Doctrine of the Faith, "Instruction on Christian Freedom and Liberation," which in strong terms rejected efforts to synthesize Marxism and Christianity (208). Neuhaus acknowledged that providence had not yet finished the chapter on liberation theology. Even so, John Paul's recovery of an otherworldly piety was an indication that the church had rightly balanced the claims of politics and salvation.

In the end, the "Catholic Moment" was the way to find a Christian foundation for the American "proposition about the right ordering of society" (239). Neuhaus acknowledged that Americanism had been a problem for the church in the United States. Aside from Leo XIII's 1899 condemnation, American Roman Catholics had always veered between "progressives who give priority to being true Americans" and conservatives who sided with being "good Catholics." He was also aware of the turn that progressives such as Garry Wills and the "Catonsville Nine" had taken after the Second Vatican Council in adopting the Left's "disillusionment with America" (255–56). He warned Roman Catholics of the Americanized Christianity forged by the Protestant mainline churches in which national politics and the gospel were indistinguishable. The challenge was for the church "to demonstrate a new model of ecclesiastical vitality and integrity within the American context" (263).

Again, John Courtney Murray was decisive and useful. "The Murray Project" was, and here Neuhaus followed George Weigel, "a distinctively Roman Catholic way of affirming and living 'the American proposition.'" This aphorism stood simply for an effort to renew "the American design of a public order for alien citizens who will never be completely at home until they reach the heavenly *polis*" (248). Although Murray had pointed the way, his ideas needed approval from the church hierarchy. That made John Paul and Ratzinger crucial to "the Catholic Moment" and explained why Neuhaus ended with an appeal to authority. This was not the authoritarianism of the pre–Vatican II church or the one that spooked liberals such as Paul Blanshard. It was the authority of Christ and believers in submission to him through his church, a form of authority best expressed in the teaching of John Paul. This form of submission and understanding of political life in relation to eternal realities was the version of Christianity that "might renew the American experiment in liberal democracy" (280).

An American Pope

George Weigel was the junior member of the neoconservative triumvirate that included him, Novak, and Neuhaus. Born in 1951 in Baltimore and a product of Maryland Roman Catholic educational institutions (Saint Mary's University), Weigel labored in exile in Seattle before returning to the East Coast in 1986 as a fellow at the Woodrow Wilson International Center for Scholars. In Washington, Weigel moved into the think tank world devoted to religion and politics and eventually took up permanent residence at the Ethics and Public Policy Center, a neoconservative institution founded in 1976 to provide a forum for moral and religious reflection on policy debates. In that setting, Weigel connected with Neuhaus and Novak. In fact, Neuhaus's biographer, Randy Boyagoda, tells the story that Weigel was responsible in 1981 for smoothing over an acrimonious relationship between Neuhaus and Novak during the founding of the Institute on Religion and Democracy (IRD), an agency founded to monitor and counter the leftist proclivities of the Protestant mainline denominations. In a down-at-the-heels pizza joint, Neuhaus and Novak shared a meal that allowed them to let past disagreements go and work together on faith-based conservative enterprises such as IRD. Weigel's role in brokering this friendship, according to Boyagoda, situated the Baltimorean to "become Neuhaus' most important colleague" after 1980.[21] Indeed, in 1990, when Neuhaus converted to Roman Catholicism, Weigel was one of his sponsors, along with Avery Cardinal Dulles, at a Mass celebrated by New York City archbishop John O'Connor.

Although the junior member of this select group of Roman Catholic public intellectuals, Weigel did not imitate or depend on his senior colleagues for the contribution he made to debates about the church and American life. His first serious contribution to policy debates came with *Tranquillitas Ordinis: The Present Failure and Future Promise of American Catholic Thought on War and Peace* (1987). Though the title suggested a parochial book—and in some sense it was, since Weigel engaged a set of Roman Catholic figures and the U.S. bishops' letters on war—the publisher, Oxford University Press, suggested a wider readership. Andrew Sullivan, then a doctoral student at Harvard, reviewed the book for *New Republic* and called it "impressive" in its effort to "weave a coherent way out of the confusion" of Roman Catholic thought on war and peace.[22]

His second book appeared two years later, *Catholicism and the Renewal of American Democracy*. This work, a supplement to the sort of arguments that Neuhaus and Novak had been making throughout the 1980s about the dangers of secularization and the need for religion in public life, found a home with not a trade press but a Roman Catholic publisher—Paulist Press. An irony of the book, perhaps noticed only by students of U.S. Roman Catholic history, was that Isaac Hecker, one of the first voices of Americanism, condemned by Leo XIII, in 1899, established a publishing business that in 1913 blossomed as Paulist Press. Indeed, the paradox of Americanism haunted Weigel's book. Whereas nineteenth-century Americanists had wanted the church to adapt to political and social expectations of the United States, twentieth-century Roman Catholics such as Weigel argued for the United States to follow the church's lead on the importance of faith for American identity.

This call for leavening the "American experiment" with the Roman Catholic faith required clearing up some misunderstandings. One was the caricature of the church portrayed by the left and right within American Roman Catholicism. The *National Catholic Reporter* was representative of the left. A Kansas City–based newspaper founded in 1964, *NCR* was avowedly liberal and exhibited the emergence of the "new class" of intellectual elites in Roman Catholic circles. (Peter Berger's theories about intellectuals in modern society's class struggles were common tropes for Neuhaus, Novak, and Weigel.) The "great fear" that animated editors at *NCR* was the undoing of the Second Vatican Council by bishops, cardinals, and the pope. That council had liberated Roman Catholicism from its "rigidly authoritarian, depressingly clerical, rabidly anticommunist" past. In addition to defending Vatican II, *NCR* was in Weigel's estimate feminist, pro-gay, and hostile to the United States in the sense that the paper had "precious little use for America as a culture, society, or polity."[23]

The Roman Catholic right, represented by another newspaper, the *Wanderer*, kept faith with church teaching on women and sexuality but was also anti-American in spirit. A publication founded in the nineteenth century, the *Wanderer* defended the church's older ways and lamented the liberalizing effects of the Second Vatican Council. The paper's disagreement with America came in the form of concluding that modern liberal democracies were not congenial places for living out a pre–Vatican II piety. Readers and editors of the *Wanderer* generally agreed with the old estimate of Americanism as heresy and feared that Vatican II had created conditions to let Americanists run amuck.

Weigel positioned himself and like-minded Roman Catholics as the *tertium quid*, the moderate party between the extremes of the American church's right and left, in a manner reminiscent of Buckley's refusal to follow L. Brent Bozell into traditionalism or appreciate Garry Wills's sympathy for the left. This involved rendering a different estimate of both Roman Catholicism and the United States. He started with the nation and set up the Vernon Louis Parrington and Charles Beard economic interpretation of the American founding as his foil. According to Weigel, the founders were interested in a "commercial republic" but not exclusively so. He quoted historians who credited founders such as James Madison with creating political institutions centered on "the concept of public virtue." Even Europeans such as Jacques Maritain could see that the stereotype of "American materialism" was "no more than a curtain of silly gossip and slander." Instead, Maritain believed that "generosity, good will, [and] the sense of human fellowship" characterized the American people." Roman Catholics had little to fear from engaging in public life. Rather than soiling themselves with materialism or secularism, American politics afforded an opportunity to participate in debates about "a view of the human person that is derived from transcendent moral norms."[24]

But what about the papacy? How did its authority (or authoritarianism) fit with the U.S. political system? Here Weigel was ready with anecdotes about and quotes from John Paul II to show that the church had reached a point in which its elites knew the difference between *authoritative* and *authoritarian.* That distinction had prepared the church, as John Paul understood, to bring "the great tradition of Christianity" into a full dialogue with "the modern currents of thought." Weigel quoted the pope's 1987 remarks during a visit with President Ronald Reagan. Among the most admirable "values" of the United States was "freedom." "The concept of freedom is part of the very fabric of this nation as a political community of free people," John Paul said. "Freedom is a great gift, a great blessing of God." Consequently, Weigel saw in the pope what Neuhaus recognized in "the Catholic moment": namely, an opportunity for Roman Catholicism to teach that the "spiritual hollowness" that modern people sense thanks to the limits of liberal secularism could be filled by "opening one's self to being grasped by the truly authoritative, by the Gospel and by Him whom the Gospel proclaims as Lord and Savior."[25]

This was a reiteration of John Courtney Murray's effort to ground the American founding on notions compatible with Roman Catholic traditions, and Weigel was not bashful about claiming the Jesuit's mantle. In fact, Weigel started by invoking the enthusiasm and optimism of the nineteenth-century Americanists, especially Archbishop John Ireland, and their desire to "make America Catholic." Weigel agreed with Ireland that "there was no contradiction between being a Catholic and being an American." But the layman admired even more the archbishop's sense of mission, that a "Catholic imperative" to renew the American experiment and even modernity itself was the challenge for modern Roman Catholicism. The only reservation that Weigel had about Ireland's Americanism was that the renewal of American democracy in the late twentieth century was not exclusively a Roman Catholic imperative but also a task shared with mainline and evangelical Protestants. Even so, Weigel believed Roman Catholics could take the lead in this ecumenical effort, and no one was better suited to provide the platform for that leadership than Murray. For the Vatican II theologian recognized that "the American experiment" was pivotal for renewing modern society since it was a "laboratory for coming to grips with the problem of ordered freedom."[26] Murray saw that the modern world needed order to offset the chaos that had emerged after World War II. In Weigel's estimate, in Murray's conception of religious freedom, embraced at the Second Vatican Council, the church had found a way to take the lead in giving modernity purpose and meaning, or giving liberty order.

Unquestioned throughout Weigel's argument (and in Neuhaus's and Novak's writings as well) was the idea that the church's mission involved renewing democracy in the United States. In the long scope of Christian history, rare was any communion's identification with democracy (as opposed to monarchy). Sometimes churches did identify with nations, especially in the confessional era of European history when the newly emerging nation-states identified as Lutheran, Anglican, Calvinist, or Roman Catholic. But for Christians in fellowship with the bishop of Rome, national churches were always a problem because they compromised a higher loyalty to the religious and political unity of Christendom. That outlook was partly responsible for Leo XIII's condemnation of Americanism.

None of this history or Roman Catholic conviction deterred Weigel. "Somebody will take the lead in forming contemporary democratic culture, and in articulating a public philosophy capable of sustaining and enriching it," Weigel declared.[27] Mainline Protestants had abandoned the field, leaving the task to Roman Catholics. As much as Weigel drew inspiration from nineteenth-century Americanists, this was a different order of Americanism. The likes of John Ireland were largely concerned with assimilating an immigrant church in an anti-Catholic culture. Weigel showed that Ireland had succeeded. Roman Catholics in the United States had Americanized to the point of assuming leadership in the revitalization of a political system that had historically drawn much more on either Protestant or secular outlooks. It was akin to the Quebecois insisting that Francophone Canadians had the responsibility to renew their nation's traditions, heavily redacted through British and Protestant history, of loyalism and the trinity of peace, order, and good government. Stranger occurrences have happened in human history. But Weigel's proposal was a remarkable development in the history of Roman Catholic Americanism.

From President to Pope

In the 1950s, when Roman Catholic political conservatives hatched what became known as "the conservative movement," one of their chief ambitions was to commandeer a political party, one with a former reputation for harboring anti-Catholicism, and put an ideologically sound statesman in the White House. By the 1980s, perhaps with just such a man as president (i.e., Ronald Reagan), Roman Catholic political conservatives set their eye on the papacy. In the 1950s the United States needed a party and politicians who would restore the nation's constitutional and federal ideals. But after the moral excesses of the 1960s and the nation's drift into secularism, the United States needed to recover the spiritual ideals that made its political institutions possible. From one angle, then, the shift in goals from Buckley, Bozell, and Wills during the run-up to Barry Goldwater's presidential candidacy in 1964 to Neuhaus, Novak, and Weigel during John Paul II's tenure was considerable. The older Roman Catholics were political first with religion supplementing their conservatism. For the younger Roman Catholics religion drove their understandings of politics, economics, and foreign affairs. The older Roman Catholics had access to statesmen; the younger moved among the curia.

But for both sets of Roman Catholics, the United States was a Christian nation that the country's original believers, Protestants, had let go to seed. Buckley made his original foray as a pundit by complaining about the complacency of Yale's Protestant establishment's naive unwillingness to defend America's political traditions. So too Roman Catholic neoconservatives, especially Neuhaus and Weigel, who knew firsthand the leftward drift of mainline Protestantism through their work with the Institute on Religion and Democracy, looked to Roman Catholicism as the best hope for renewing Christian influence on public life. Evangelical Protestants were not a factor in American politics for Buckley's conservatives, though by the time that Neuhaus, Novak, and Weigel were gaining prominence in conservative circles, born-again believers were politically vigorous. These conservative Protestants, however, lacked both the institutions and habits of political reflection that Roman Catholicism in the United States possessed. For that reason, in 1994 Neuhaus would spearhead with Chuck Colson, a former aide to Richard Nixon, an ecumenical forum, "Evangelicals and Catholics Together," as a mechanism by which Protestants and Roman Catholics could confess a common faith and pursue a shared understanding of the good society. Still, for American Christians who wanted to have a larger platform from which to speak about public affairs, the Protestant stages looked small compared to Roman Catholic venues.

As strategic as Rome appeared in relation to either the mainline Protestants' headquarters on the Upper West Side or the evangelical base of suburban Chicago, Neuhaus, Novak, and Weigel had to make a lot of excuses for the church that held the promise of renewing American democracy. To be sure, they refused to sugarcoat the struggles of the American church after the Second Vatican Council. It was liturgically chaotic, doctrinally flimsy, and politically polarized. But these neoconservatives still believed Roman Catholicism could rescue the United States. That was a much more optimistic rendering than 1960s conservatives writing for *National Review* had produced.

In a series the magazine ran on the Second Vatican Council, Thomas Molnar, a philosopher who left Hungary to elude the Soviets, defended the church's conservatism and lamented the reformers at the council. "Let's face it," he wrote, "the ideologues of the *aggiornamento* are champions of the Church's fragmentation and dilution." They want "to destroy the delicate balance between monarchy, aristocracy, and democracy within the Church." For Molnar, updating the church and engaging the modern world was simply a means by which Rome could "meet its brothers of the world revolution halfway: in common worship of the UN and totalitarian world government." Will Herberg, who wrote regularly for *National Review*, was equally unimpressed by the Second Vatican Council. He believed that the church did not need *aggiornamento* but a "more intelligent and discriminating *Syllabus of Errors* for our time."[28] Looking to Rome as a buttress against modernity, however, was not how Buckley viewed the church. The conservative movement of the 1950s appropriated distinctly American discussions about constitutionalism, federalism, republicanism, and popular sovereignty. These notions were not inherently at odds with church teaching but sufficiently tainted after the French Revolution as to be foreign to Roman Catholic political theory.

That older dynamic of rivalry between modern politics and Rome's traditionalism was almost entirely missing from Neuhaus, Novak, and Weigel, for whom John Courtney Murray was the baseline for faith-based reflection about the United States. What united the older and younger Roman Catholic conservatives was an uncommonly positive estimate of the American experiment. The question was whether this evaluation had roots in authentically Roman Catholic soil.

8

AMERICANISM REDUX

To use or appropriate Roman Catholicism for the good of a nation, the United States in particular, was by almost any definition Americanism. That older Roman Catholic heresy had claimed that the American political system was not at odds with church teaching, even though the United States seemed to stand for most of the social and political realities that nineteenth-century popes had condemned. Americanists in the nineteenth century had argued that Vatican officials misread the United States, that the new nation was far friendlier to Roman Catholicism than Europeans imagined. Americanists also urged the church to update its polity in ways friendly to the nation's political sensibilities, a strategy that would make Roman Catholicism look less odd in the United States and give American bishops a freer hand in regulating church life. Americanists, in other words, looked for ways to adapt Roman Catholicism to life in a secular, constitutional republic.

The same was largely true for many post–World War II politically conservative Roman Catholics, from William F. Buckley, Jr., to Richard John

Neuhaus. These conservatives saw no tension between American politics and Roman Catholic faith. At the same time, they saw great continuity between Roman Catholic political reflection and the American form of government embodied in the founding. To be sure, twentieth-century Americanists stressed different features of country and church in the way they harmonized politics and religion. Unlike nineteenth-century Americanists who regarded liberal politics as largely beneficial for the church, twentieth-century Americanists argued that Roman Catholicism possessed what a secularized and increasingly decadent American society needed. Still, neither paleo- nor neo-Americanists debated whether the narratives of church and nation stood for differing ideals—Rome for history and tradition, the United States for modernity and freedom. Combining those symbols, no matter how great the differences, was not only possible but beneficial for both nation and church.

Not until the mid-1980s, however, did the efforts of political conservatives such as George Weigel, Richard John Neuhaus, and Michael Novak begin to come under scrutiny by Roman Catholics as a potentially dangerous case of Americanism (which may be another indication of how greatly the Second Vatican Council altered expectations and outlooks inside the church). Still, an important development that triggered a lively and ongoing debate about Americanism was the publication of Jay Dolan's *The American Catholic Experience* (1985). A historian at the University of Notre Dame, Dolan was a Democrat through and through, and he was determined to use the updating for which the Second Vatican Council called to write a history of American Roman Catholicism that highlighted its national and populist characteristics. By claiming the church is "first and foremost the people of God" rather than a hierarchical institution, the council stood Roman Catholic teaching "on its head."[1] Dolan did not say but implied that the "we-the-people" sentiment behind national ideals had now become a legitimate perspective by which to evaluate the church in the United States.

The historian's narrative of postconciliar developments in the United States was generally positive. In fact, the simultaneity of the Second Vatican Council, which "symbolized a break with tradition," and the election of John F. Kennedy as president showed that Roman Catholicism was finally "in tune with the times." Indeed, the council grappled with the question of adapting the church to modern society in ways that nineteenth-century

Americanists had. Pluralism in theology and devotion was the keynote of the "new Catholicism," and it also meant that the church in the United States, which possessed "a unique measure of cultural pluralism not present in other countries," was experiencing firsthand the transition from the old to the new. "A new spirit is alive in American Catholicism," Dolan concluded, "and the twenty-first century belongs to it."[2]

Dolan's catalog of intellectual currents in American Roman Catholicism did not include either the conservative movement of the 1960s or the neoconservative antisecularism of the 1980s. He celebrated the arrival of academic freedom at Roman Catholic universities and the cause of social justice advocated by many Roman Catholic activists. He also highlighted the leadership of Daniel and Philip Berrigan in the peace movement of the early 1970s. Dolan's neglect of the Roman Catholic right and attention to the church's political left wing may account for the discomfort that Richard John Neuhaus and George Weigel expressed over Dolan's own version of Americanism. Neuhaus rejected Dolan's construal of U.S. Roman Catholic history as a constant struggle between conservative and progressive forces, with the former being Roman and the latter American. Perhaps, Neuhaus wrote, " 'American' and 'Catholic' are not antinomies at all," at which point he invoked John Courtney Murray for an understanding of Roman Catholicism that was both "good Catholic" and "true American." Neuhaus believed that the Roman Catholicism that Dolan celebrated was not "very distinctively Catholic."[3] Weigel also wondered about the faith that informed Dolan's interpretation of the American church. In order to reclaim the republican heritage of the colonial church and break with the "flag-waving patriotism" of the "ghetto church," the "Jay Dolan Project" relied on "fundamental changes in *theological* outlook." In other words, Dolan's Americanist church was also a doctrinally liberal church.[4]

The irony was that the church's left and right at the very time of Neuhaus's "Catholic Moment" could each claim that the other side's faith was more American than Roman Catholic. The reason invariably was that partisans led with politics and forced their faith to follow. The resulting debate caught many Roman Catholics off guard, though it also reminded many of the historic tensions between the United States and Rome. For most of Europe's history prior to the French Revolution, divine right monarchy was the best form of government, and medieval and early modern Roman Catholic theologians and jurists supplied the rationale for such order. Indeed, even claims for papal supremacy in the late medieval era bore directly the fingerprints of divine right monarchy—the pope as *the* divine right monarch who ruled from an elevated position even above the emperor and kings.[5] Republicanism emerged in the American and French Revolutions as one hedge against rule by one. For European Roman Catholics, powerful centralized governments in the form of "throne and altar" arrangements were much more common than republicanism after 1800, especially in predominantly Roman Catholic nations such as Austria, France, and Spain. For church members in the United States, in contrast—with rare exceptions such as Brent Bozell—such hierarchical governments held little appeal. Neuhaus and Weigel were as much republican in their political preferences as Jay Dolan or even Garry Wills. Even so, each side viewed their antagonists' faith as insufficiently authentic thanks to political convictions derived from partisan debates within the U.S. government.

Consequently, just at the time when Roman Catholicism became a fixture on the political Right, another Americanist controversy emerged but with a ironic twist. Unlike the nineteenth-century debates in which U.S. bishops needed to heed the final determinations of the papacy and Vatican curia, in the late twentieth century American Roman Catholics on each side tried to enlist the papacy for their own version of faith-based politics. That appeal to Rome was a delicate one because it could either unsettle Roman Catholic assimilation to American political norms or undo the Second Vatican Council's reforms. Either way, practically no Roman Catholic citizen of the United States wanted to return to an understanding of the faith that pitted ancient and hierarchical Rome against modern and republican Washington, D.C.

Assimilation or Conformity

For most of the Roman Catholic experience in the United States prior to the 1960s, American clergy and laity had received clear instructions from the papacy about the dangers of the modern world—namely, freedom of thought, religious pluralism, and free markets (for starters). The Second Vatican Council communicated a markedly different attitude toward modernity. The bishops across a number of subjects attempted to find ways that the church could be open to the modern world and thereby extend Christian influence in societies afflicted by war, ideology, and secularization. On the specific matter of freedom of conscience or religious liberty, the council had embraced a view that seemed to condone the Roman Catholic experience in the United States. John Courtney Murray's views on religious liberty not only informed the bishops' deliberations in Rome but also became a signal to churchmen and laity in the United States that the older Vatican suspicions of Americanism—adapting the faith to liberal society—had lifted. Ironically, the Second Vatican Council unintentionally made the dilemmas of Americanism all the more prevalent since the lines between the church and the world were not erased but in the process of being redrawn. If the church became too much like a secularizing and globalizing world, could Roman Catholicism itself become worldly?

The danger of Americanism was an implicit theme of a book by Dorothy Dohen, *Nationalism and American Catholicism* (1967), which started as a doctoral dissertation written during the Second Vatican Council. In the preface, Joseph P. Fitzpatrick, a sociologist at Fordham University, invoked Murray by asserting that the "singular" task of the modern church was to clarify "the relation of the sacred to the secular in a nation in which they are separate." Fitzpatrick also understood Murray to mean that Roman Catholics in the United States were at a "unique advantage" in this task since they knew firsthand the "American experience" of relating faith and politics. It was an odd claim, since Fitzpatrick went on to introduce the danger of letting American norms set the direction for church life. He agreed with Dohen, the author, about the need to be ever "vigilant about the strange direction which social and political activities" can give to faith, as evidenced by the book's documentation of the nationalistic statements and endeavors of six leading U.S. bishops (i.e., the nation as "final arbiter of human affairs").[6] If anything, Dohen's book could well have functioned as a warning against Murray because the experience of the United States had more often than not led ecclesiastics to veer from church teaching.

Dohen's analysis of Americanist bishops and Roman Catholic patriotism in *Nationalism and American Catholicism* was at times more sociological than theological. She also indicated that the bishops' identification with American civil religion was at least ironic (because it owed so much to Protestantism and the Enlightenment), if not unfortunate. She had no trouble amassing evidence of Roman Catholic expressions of Christian nationalism. Archbishop John Ireland always made for good copy if not also a bit of embarrassment. He wrote: "We cannot but believe that a singular mission is assigned to America, glorious for itself and beneficent to the whole race, the mission of bringing about a new social and political order, based more than any other upon the common brotherhood of man, and more than any other securing to the multitude of the people social happiness and equality of rights." Dohen commented that despite an older innocence about the dangers of "temporal imperialism," Ireland's understanding was "simplistic."[7] She even wondered if he might have considered how a Canadian audience might hear such assertions.

Even so, Dohen said little about the Vatican's perceptions of such episcopal patriotism, Leo XIII's condemnation of Americanism, or the Second Vatican Council's loosening of restrictions and what they might mean for patriotism among the faithful. She tended to take the American bishops' word that they were not guilty of Americanism. But she did see what no doubt many nineteenth-century European clerics observed when they feared the direction of Roman Catholicism in the United States, namely, the "danger of minimizing the importance of certain dogmas." Dohen herself detected no "direct demonstration" of softening "transcendental beliefs." She conceded that "such a possibility remains open."[8]

Dohen even spotted signs of such liberalization in 1960s American politics. Supporters of Barry Goldwater in the 1964 election attached bumper stickers to their cars that read, "Keep God in America." Closer to home among Roman Catholics, Dohen cited a study that indicated members of her church accounted for more than half of the John Birch Society's membership. Certain church papers (in Brooklyn and Los Angeles) portrayed anyone who spoke of "internationalism as the very devil himself." Dohen also commented on Joseph McCarthy's Roman Catholic background and observed that "the spiritual descendents of the one-hundred-percent Americans . . . are likely to be lineal descendents of Catholic immigrants."[9]

Reviews of Dohen's book indicated no real interest in her subtext, which was to question the compatibility of Roman Catholicism with Americanism. In *America* magazine, Bruce F. Biever credited Dohen with prompting "men of faith" to ask if they had "paid too high a price for our cozy niche in the American way of life."[10] That remark might have applied as much to the comforts of suburban living as to unrestrained patriotism. University of Notre Dame historian Philip Gleason, in an academic review, criticized the vagueness of Dohen's categories such as nationalism and ideology. He also suggested that the bishops Dohen featured were not as wrongheaded as they appeared. Of course, bishops such as Carroll, England, and Hughes were "highly patriotic, admired American institutions, praised freedom and other American values, called for support of the country in wartime" but Gleason wondered if any of these attributes rose to the level of nationalism. In fact, he thought these instances of patriotism were "better understood as legitimate expressions of identification with American values and institutions."[11]

A student of nineteenth-century Roman Catholicism in the United States himself, Gleason also indicated that the historical context could justify the bishops' patriotism. "To expatiate on the virtues of Americanism to immigrant Catholics, many of whom resisted Americanization," Gleason cautioned, or to "enlarge on the compatibility of Catholicism and republican institutions, when many non-Catholics denied the two were at all reconcilable, should hardly be equated with undue nationalism." Gleason's analogy—excessive study can hurt young people's health but "admonitions to study hard" are not evidence of "destructive tendencies"—was a way of indicating how commonsensical Americanism might be.[12] What Gleason did not mention was whether patriotic admonitions in the context of nineteenth-century papal warnings about republicanism were appropriate then. Nor did he comment on whether 1960s Roman Catholics, long since assimilated to the United States, still needed such inducements to identify with the United States or what such loyalty might mean for Rome's historic approach to civil government.

As a student of German American Roman Catholics who resisted the assimilationist designs of Irish American bishops in the United States, Gleason was himself highly versed in the Americanist controversy even if he was interested more in its ethnic and sociological dimensions than its theology or ecclesiology. German Roman Catholic immigrants to the United States, as Gleason showed in *The Conservative Reformers* (1968), were caught between the exuberant patriotism of U.S. bishops and the political radicalism of secular German Americans.[13] An additional front in that three-way struggle was the relation of German American Roman Catholics to the papacy, though Gleason acknowledged that the conservative subjects he studied regarded Leo XIII's condemnation of Americanism as a vindication of their worries about church life in the United States.

Over time, the chief outlet for German Americans, the Central Verein, a mutual aid society, adopted an antisocialist posture in the Progressive era. In turn, its conservatism fueled the anticommunism that was so characteristic of twentieth-century Roman Catholicism in Europe and North America until the Second Vatican Council.

Then at the beginning of a gifted career as a leading interpreter of the Roman Catholic experience in the United States, Gleason worried openly about Roman Catholic identity in the aftermath of the Second Vatican Council. On the one hand, by the 1960s Roman Catholics were no longer outsiders in American society. They had "made it" as members of the middle class and had "overtaken Protestants" in measures of wealth and occupational status (still a little behind in college attendance). In short, according to Gleason, Roman Catholics were no longer outsiders but had been "thoroughly assimilated and Americanized." On the other hand was the double whammy of the council. Although many Americans in the church welcomed John XXIII's call for *aggiornamento*, the subsequent council "shook everything loose." "Authoritative teachers" who were supposed to determine what Roman Catholicism meant were now in "deep disagreement" about the very substance of the faith.[14]

Gleason called this the "crisis of Americanization," and his description of it in the postconciliar environment could have prompted comparison between the 1960s and the church's earlier Americanist crisis from the 1880s: "Far-reaching changes are needed to bring the Church into line with modern society and culture and to accommodate to the new mentality gaining ground among Catholics. But it is cruelly difficult to make such changes while at the same time preserving an underlying continuity with the past, preventing the loss of identity, and maintaining minimal cohesiveness with the Catholic population."[15]

In the nineteenth and early twentieth centuries, maintaining cohesiveness among U.S. Roman Catholics placed republicanism and democracy in a liberal society at odds with expectations for a Christendom-modeled society with the papacy at the top as the Vicar of Christ. By the 1960s the lessons learned from the papacy's loss of temporal power and the separation of church and state even in formerly Roman Catholic societies forced clergy and laity to adjust expectations for the church overseeing social and political affairs. Even so, papal authority in spiritual affairs was still crucial to Roman Catholic identity, and papal instruction on social affairs (i.e., the social teaching of the church) gave the impression that church members and clergy should still adhere to church teaching as a way, in Gleason's terms, of "maintaining minimal cohesiveness."[16] His perception, even informed by historical scholarship, was that U.S. Roman Catholics had been through the crisis of Americanization before but were no better prepared for postconciliar changes than their European peers.

Gleason's colleagues in the U.S. Roman Catholic guild of historians seemed no more ready to connect old and new versions of Americanism or the church's relationship to modern society. In his comprehensive and astute survey of Roman Catholicism in the United States, *American Catholics* (1981), James Hennesey included the controversy over Americanism in a chapter on the national church's "growing pains." He portrayed the debates as part of American Roman Catholics' "internal identity crisis." Their fellow citizens perceived Roman Catholics as "immigrant newcomers." In the face of strident nationalism, Roman Catholics needed to identify with their country and establish themselves as legitimately American. The timing was unfortunate for the American church because the nineteenth-century Americanist controversy coincided with the Vatican's resistance to all forms of "centrifugal action." The setting was also not propitious. Americanists, Hennesey implied, were caught up in European church politics and international conflicts (the Spanish-American War) over which U.S. Roman Catholics had no control. European bishops and cardinals had plenty of reasons to resent the United States, but Roman Catholics living in America were overwhelmingly a poor and minority people trying to make their way. After Leo XIII's encyclical, *Testem benevolentiae*, the controversy "died" but "scars remained." For the next fifty years Roman Catholics in America "slipped more or less peaceably into a half-century's theological hibernation."[17]

The Second Vatican Council, for Hennesey, was one prod to awaken U.S. Roman Catholics, but so were success, migration from the ghetto to the suburbs, and the political conflicts of the 1960s. In a postconciliar world, Roman Catholics everywhere were experiencing what church members had lived through when coming to and settling in the United States—a world in flux. Indeed, Hennesey described Roman Catholicism from the Council of Trent to the Second Vatican Council as characteristically "immutable." Now in the 1960s, the institution that stood impervious to history was mired in change—"dissent" and "diversity at the highest levels of the church."[18]

The one parallel with nineteenth-century Americanism that Hennesey detected was an interest in the Holy Spirit. What for Isaac Hecker had been a call for openness to spiritual insight outside church structures had become in the 1960s a Roman Catholic interest in charismatic and highly emotional forms of devotion (e.g., *Cursillo*). Despite the vast changes in U.S. Roman Catholicism and its part in global developments, Hennesey ended on an optimistic note, confident that Roman Catholics would not be assimilated but retain their own religious identity. He quoted Michael Novak, who was then writing for *Commonweal* and asserted that Roman Catholics were different from others because of their "sense of reality," "version of realism," "passion for justice," and "approach to suffering."[19] This theological vision had informed Roman Catholics on their arrival in the New World, guided the immigrant church, and would continue to inform them in the postconciliar world. It was a consoling conclusion, but Hennesey's implicit blessing on all forms of American Roman Catholicism did not prepare readers for the sorts of polarization inside the church that followed Vatican II.

Gerald Fogarty's rendering of U.S. Roman Catholicism through the lens of the American bishops' relationship to the Vatican ended on an equally positive note, even if his book gave plenty of reasons for being worried. He concluded *The Vatican and the American Hierarchy from 1870 to 1965* (1982) with the reassuring observation that the American church had "become a thriving branch of the Church universal." Fogarty marshaled numbers—dioceses, parishes, cardinals—to demonstrate U.S. Roman Catholicism's health. At the same time, his upbeat estimate seemed to draw as much strength from the nation where U.S. Roman Catholics lived as from the communion to which they belonged. The Catholic Church in the United States had evolved from "a Church in a missionary country," to one in "a little known republic," to one that "sends missionaries to foreign countries," in a nation that "holds the balance of power in the western world."[20] Fogarty knew that tensions still "existed and will probably continue to exist between the Vatican and the American church." But for Fogarty, they were now minor.

Those strains owed to the dual identity that American Roman Catholics endured. To their fellow citizens they needed to prove (as Al Smith and John F. Kennedy did) their bona fides as Americans. To do this the church had to Americanize in ways that sounded foreign to Europeans used to hierarchical politics, thus making their faith suspect. During the years when bishops such as John Ireland were blurring distinctions between the United States' aims and the church's divine mission, American bishops sounded foreign and even radical to Europeans. In 1899, when Leo XIII condemned Americanism, the United States represented the overthrow of a political order familiar to Europe and the church's hierarchy. To Europeans, the United States was truly a *novus ordo seclorum*. In addition, U.S. Roman Catholics needed to prove to Vatican officials and European clergy that they could shoulder the burden of participating in worldwide ministry rather than being the recipient of assistance (lay and clerical) from established Roman Catholic countries. Instead of a mission church, Americans needed to be a missionary-sending church. Fogarty's narrative indicated that the American church had gained a measure of autonomy as early as 1908, when Pius X removed it from the jurisdiction of the Congregation for the Propagation of the Faith and placed American Roman Catholics under the Sacred Consistorial Congregation. Yet within two decades, when Roman Catholics saw the first of their number run for president of the United States, they still experienced suspicions from fellow citizens that Roman Catholicism was at odds with the country's political ideals and from Vatican officials who seemed to follow the affairs of Mexico more closely than those of the United States.[21]

This is where the rising status of the United States made a significant difference for clergy and church members both in America and around the world. After World War II, by the time that John Courtney Murray was striving for intellectual coherence between Roman Catholic natural law traditions and the political ideals of the American founding, the United States had emerged in the eyes of European churchmen as a nation with "vibrant Catholicism" and sufficient resources to defend the church and the world "against the new threat of Communism." Attention to these historical contexts not only echoed Murray's call to examine the historical background that informed papal directives and the Roman Catholic experience in places such as the New World. Historicism also prompted Fogarty to discount theology as the most important factor in the Vatican's outlook on American developments. Church teachings were not a set of abstract truths but "the interface of ideas with historical and political

realities."²² Whether that rendering of the notion that "ideas have consequences" meant that much of the friction between the American church
and the Vatican was largely the result of an intellectual misunderstanding
of differing social contexts, Fogarty did not say. But his discounting of
ideas, while creating an opening for Roman Catholics to adapt to liberal
society, also put in jeopardy church dogma and the hierarchy that issued
and enforced it. Could Fogarty have meant to imply that the infallible
dogma of papal supremacy was simply the product of mid-nineteenth-
century political struggles on the Apennine peninsula?

Jay Dolan's assessment of the Americanist controversy in *The American Catholic Experience* said less about the conflict between faith and national identity than it did about Christians making adjustments to modern
society and culture. Here he appropriated Harvard University historian
William R. Hutchison's definition of modernism in his intellectual history
of liberal Protestantism—cultural adaptation, divine immanence in culture, and religiously based progressivism. Where the Vatican and Roman
Catholic conservatives held on to notions of truth as timeless, Americanists followed with the insights of historicism and saw truth emerging from
historical context. Liberals, Dolan wrote, "manifested sensitivity to the
idea of historical development," while Rome's neoscholastics were of "a
classical frame of mind." Americanism, then, was not so much a contest
over church and state or the proper ordering of society in relation to the
church but a "clash not only between opposing cultures but also between
conflicting worldviews."²³

This way of reading Americanism, sure enough, allowed Dolan to
maintain his republican-friendly reading of Roman Catholicism in the
United States without having to adjust his political preferences to papal
instruction. At the same time, he provided a window into the cultural conflict inherent in the nineteenth-century Americanist controversy when it
touched on the sensitive issue of devotion. Immigrants in the United States
experienced an upsurge in private devotional practices—prayer books,
devotional guides, sacred objects—to which Americanists objected. The
common Roman Catholic devotion was too enthusiastic or emotional, not
sufficiently refined and subdued. Traditional piety also cut Roman Catholics off from their Protestant neighbors even if it offered consolation.
"Throughout the era of the immigrant church," Dolan wrote, "the United
States was perceived by most Catholics as too Protestant and thus too

threatening." Roman Catholic devotion gave to ordinary church members "a system of meaning in a society which at the time was able to offer few viable alternatives."[24]

Although the democrat in Dolan forced him to regard popular piety sympathetically, he also recognized that "devotional Catholicism" facilitated the "Romanization" of the American church. After Leo XIII's condemnation of Americanism and the spread of Roman Catholic piety, "the spirit of independence articulated by Carroll, England, Hecker, Ireland, and others disappeared." That was then. By the time of Dolan's writing, the American spirit had begun to resurface. "There is no longer one way to do theology, to worship at Mass, to confess sin, or to pray," Dolan wrote. "There are various ways of being Catholic, and people are choosing the style that best suits them."[25]

In a 1993 essay on the historiography of Americanism, Philip Gleason summarized a vast literature among church historians about the Americanist heresy and its implications for cultural assimilation. The general consensus among both the older and younger historians was that the Americanist bishops made a positive contribution to the American church by paving the way for church members to leave the ghetto and join the mainstream. The younger historians were sometimes more likely than the older scholars to fault the Americanist bishops for their nationalist jingoism. Other historians, young and old, generally exonerated the Americanists of heresy. Leo XIII was largely correct, they argued, in his estimate of Americanism's dangers, but, according to the historiographical consensus, the U.S. bishops were mostly innocent of any serious breach of the faith. And when it came to the theological heresy of modernism, condemned by Pius X in 1907 and sometimes considered the inevitable outcome of Americanism, U.S. church historians regarded the Americanist bishops as innocent again. Naive might be the better conclusion since most historians judged the hierarchy's embrace of the United States and its political ideas to be unrelated to theology. The question that lingered was whether the church's past was providing guidance for contemporary Roman Catholics. Although older writers on Americanism, such as Robert D. Cross in *The Emergence of Liberal Catholicism in America* (1958) or Daniel Callahan in *The Mind of the Catholic Layman* (1963), had looked to the Americanist bishops for help in navigating post–World War II America (and even a Roman Catholic presidency), the younger historians had not offered substantial advice to the American church on how to negotiate its social surroundings. That guidance increasingly fell to lay participants with decidedly partisan views about the nation's political parties and the virtues of Ronald Reagan and Pope John Paul II.[26]

Americanists Some

When Gleason summarized the historiography of Americanist Roman Catholicism, he was aware of a contemporary version of Americanism. He called it an "Americanist turn," by which he referred to writers who had attempted to appropriate for the contemporary church what had been banned prior to the Second Vatican Council. Some authors used the nineteenth-century Americanists to call for democratic elements within church governance. Others from the left were critical of Americanism as a betrayal of Christian faithfulness and the cause of the church's failure to speak out prophetically against injustice. Gleason was also aware of the triumvirate of Weigel, Neuhaus, and Novak as promoters of an Americanist faith that was vague about the priority of loyalties to nation and church. Finally, Gleason acknowledged the presence of traditionalists who saw Americanism as a threat to Rome's teachings and practices.

Critics of postconciliar Americanism—the social justice and traditionalist wings of the American church—by necessity needed to sit in judgment, just as nineteenth-century popes had, not only of church members but also of American society and politics. One of the earliest critics from the ecclesiological right was Joseph A. Varacalli, a sociologist at the State University of New York, Nassau Community College. His first book, based on his Rutgers University dissertation, *Toward the Establishment of Liberal Catholicism in America* (1983), was an extended critique of the U.S. bishops' bicentennial program, "Liberty and Justice for All." Both Varacalli's analysis and the bishops' commemoration of the American founding reflected the assimilationist tendencies of 1970s Roman Catholicism. Varacalli dressed his traditionalist outlook in the garb of modern sociology and used his academic expertise to fault U.S. bishops for embracing left-wing politics. No matter the tension between a layperson challenging a successor to the apostles, Varacalli's point was to show that a liberalizing tendency had prevailed in the American church. By this the sociologist did not mean the progressive nature of the causes that had animated many voices in "Liberty and Justice for All." Instead, by liberalism Varacalli meant the triumph of modern social developments—bureaucratization, professionalism, and specialization—within the church such that the authority of bishops had faded into the background.[27]

The effects of these structural changes in the church also had consequences for church teaching. Varacalli argued that the American church's engagement with the wider society around it had opened the church to pluralism and compromised its witness to transcendent, unchanging truths. He observed that these tendencies were always part of the American church's experience—especially in its Americanizing forms. But after the Second Vatican Council, such liberalism had received the hierarchy's implicit approval and overwhelmed the American church. According to Varacalli, "Vatican II allowed and encouraged American Catholics—particularly of liberal stripe—to enter into theological dialogue with, and for practical purposes, to join the American Civil Religion."[28] (Varacalli followed Robert Bellah's definition of civil religion, which involved identifying common principles among the nation's believers for the sake of national unity and purpose.)

From the other side of Americanism's critics came David O'Brien's call for a "public Catholicism." A historian at Holy Cross College, O'Brien drew the assignment of narrating Roman Catholic political engagement for the bicentennial (1989) of John Carroll's appointment as bishop of Baltimore, a volume authorized by the U.S. bishops. In his concluding estimate of Roman Catholic history, which featured a mildly positive and brief estimate of Americanists' efforts to embody immutable truths within the vicissitudes of an American time and place, O'Brien identified three ways of being Roman Catholic in late twentieth-century America, all informed by the national context. One was an evangelical faith that stressed institutional devotion less than personal holiness—"what would Jesus do?"—in ordinary walks of life. A second approach was to keep faith with the immigrant style of being Roman Catholic, which took shape in parish-based community organizations for the sake of a "grassroots empowerment of poor people." Although O'Brien thought the social teaching implicit in this part of American Roman Catholicism had yet to find its proper "theological reflection," he conceded that the immigrant church was also defective thanks to parochial schools and sexual mores that isolated church members from the rest of society.[29]

The last way that Roman Catholicism found public expression in the United States was through a republican approach that had carried the day with the American church's bishops. Here the aim was to leaven a "public moral consensus" by defending human dignity and persons' rights. O'Brien thought all three approaches were deficient because they encouraged a separation between the church and the world. "Not until the layperson, seeking to live with integrity as a Christian and responsibly as a citizen"—from a Roman Catholic executive to a nun—"becomes the center of pastoral attention and theoretical reflection," O'Brien asserted, "will this dichotomy, so self-serving for the church and so counterproductive for its public mission, be overcome." The politics of the immigrant church appealed most to O'Brien. But in the end, American Roman Catholics needed to view the United States as "their own . . . land" for which they were responsible and so "enliven public life and restore a sense of public responsibility in American institutions."[30]

One way of reading O'Brien was to conclude that the republican brand of American Roman Catholicism had accomplished theological vindication (through John Courtney Murray, at least) but that the immigrant approach was still in need of doctrinal foundations. O'Brien failed to mention David Schindler in his overview of Roman Catholic history, but about the time that *Public Catholicism* was being published, the professor of theology at the University of Notre Dame was emerging as a fierce critic of Murray and the Americanists on theological and philosophical grounds. (Schindler eventually moved from Notre Dame to the Catholic University of America, where he taught and administered the Pontifical John Paul II Institute on Marriage and the Family.)

During the mid- to late 1980s, Schindler began to push back against the Americanist circle of Novak, Neuhaus, and Weigel. If the neoconservative triumvirate gained credibility for its associations with cardinals in the United States and friendliness with John Paul II and his enforcer at the Congregation for the Doctrine of the Faith, Joseph Ratzinger, Schindler had his own points of access to ecclesiastical nobility. He became editor of the American edition of *Communio*, a theological journal established by some of the leading theologians at the Second Vatican Council, including

Hans Urs von Balthasar, Henri de Lubac, Louis Bouyer, and Ratzinger. Prior to the council, these theologians had functioned more or less as dissenters from the neo-Thomism that dominated Roman Catholic intellectual life. But by the 1970s they worried that the church was misappropriating the council and so constituted their own Christian brand of neoconservatism—the idea popularized by Irving Kristol that a neoconservative is a liberal mugged by reality. Part of Schindler's task as a member of the *Communio* school was to wake American Roman Catholics up to the weaknesses implicit in embracing the United States as an outworking of fundamental Christian truths.

In the fall of 1987 Schindler wrote one of his first explicit critiques of George Weigel's Americanism. In a warm-up for his 1989 book, *Catholicism and the Renewal of American Democracy*, Weigel had asked whether the United States was basically bourgeois (and thus materialistic and acquisitive). He answered no. Schindler took the opposite view and relied on insights of the *Communio* school. For the average reader unfamiliar with recent Roman Catholic theology, Schindler's prose was heavy going. He appealed to two intellectual authorities, Ratzinger and Christopher Dawson. From the former, Schindler appropriated insights into the nature of the human person (self) derived from trinitarian theology and Christological dogma. Accordingly, to be truly human ontologically was to be receptive of God and others (interiority), to give back, which is "prior to seeking and taking," and to experience all aspects of life in such relation to God and others (integration). From Dawson, Schindler drew the conclusion that instead of being properly introverted according to a Christian understanding of the self, America was extroverted in the sense that the culture it nurtured relied on people whose activities were external or outward-directed.[31] Whether Schindler knew it or not, he had raised the bar for the United States considerably higher than where Leo XIII had placed it when he condemned Americanism.

Schindler referred often to Dawson to understand the history of the West and the decline of Christian civilization. But to point out America's flaws, the Notre Dame theologian needed help. To Weigel's assertion that Americans displayed remarkable generosity, Schindler countered that this was "exactly the achievement-extroversion-oriented sort of generosity" that failed to meet Ratzinger's standard of the human person. To Weigel's additional observation that Americans were an overwhelmingly religious people, Schindler objected that levels of church attendance said "exactly nothing" about the degree to which such religious observance marks "the incarnational (i.e., transforming and integrative) quality of that relation in the range of activities taken up by these persons." In other words, Weigel's evidence of America's receptivity to Roman Catholicism was actually "manifestations of secularization." What made this conclusion airtight was the U.S. record on abortion. The understanding of legal rights that legalized "the killing of [the] unborn" rested on "an ontology of extroversion." Abortion, then, was not an exception to the rule of American life but deeply connected to a flawed culture. Schindler understood that he was raising the stakes for evaluating the United States, that he may have even sounded "utopian." But every society needed a standard: "does recognition of the inevitability of human selfishness-sinfulness forbid us to work for an onto-logic—an order—of generosity in a culture," or must we follow Weigel's pattern and "leave an onto-logic—order—of selfishness-sinfulness in place?"[32] Schindler's answer was clear, and it registered a substantial rebuke to Americanism in all its forms.

That rejection of Roman Catholic efforts to accommodate the United States was particularly evident when Schindler discussed John Courtney Murray. A few years after his critique of Weigel, Schindler took aim at Murray and the inconsistency in the American Jesuit's defense of religious freedom. Here was the classic antagonism between philosophically coherent arguments and pragmatic social arrangements. Schindler believed that Murray's defense of the First Amendment—a peace offering in return for pluralistic coexistence—was in fact a betrayal of first principle. "One cannot give *meaning* to the religious clauses of the First Amendment," he stipulated, "without *in fact* favoring some set of particular religious convictions." As such, because the American founding spelled out neither the religious nor the philosophical basis for the liberties it proposed to secure, it was a "con game."[33]

Schindler needed to perform some fancy footwork to accomplish his own critique because Murray had been part of the Second Vatican Council not only in body but also in spirit. The bishops had sought to embrace a form of liberalism that was procedural (American constitutionalism) rather than ideological (French laicism). To do this Schindler took readers into the arcane texts of *ressourcement* theology and contrasted Murray's neoscholasticism and its dualism (grace added to nature) with Henri de Lubac's integralism (grace as the context for nature). Schindler also appealed to the Vatican, this time directly to John Paul II, in whose encyclicals the American theologian found a "christologically centered humanism" that also happened to affirm de Lubac's insights. He called for a "truly 'Catholic moment' in America" that challenged "regnant liberalism" in the United States, one that did not merely accommodate the public order in the way Murray and Richard John Neuhaus had.[34] Whether Schindler intended it or not, his critique of Murray's Americanism involved appropriating a host of theological voices—primarily twentieth-century European—that were foreign to Roman Catholics in the United States.

Schindler knew that his own rejection of liberalism could come across as an endorsement of theocracy. Even so, he complained that liberalism had nothing to offer to "any non-Western (or non-liberalized) religion—with respect to any country where a traditional (or non-dualistic) worldview still predominates." Liberalism would inevitably destroy political orders where religious orthodoxy—Islam, Judaism, African religion—supplied the foundation for civil authority. What Schindler failed to address was whether his own (or John Paul's or de Lubac's) integralism would secure a place for Roman Catholics in an Islamic or Jewish state. Schindler's theory prevented him from recognizing the reality of pluralism that liberalism attempted to resolve. Consequently, when he affirmed that an "integration" of the secular and sacred was nonetheless fully compatible with religious freedom and did not require a confessional state, Schindler pulled back from the consistency he demanded from Murray. The *Communio* theologian insisted that Christology as the basis for life together in society and the church's platform for converting the state was still compatible with religious freedom. The reason was that following Christ was not fundamentally coercive but loving.[35] That sounded good, maybe even modern. But if Schindler faulted Murray's brief for liberalism as inevitably leading to secularism, why was Schindler himself immune from the charge that his Christian humanism logically led to Christendom?

Schindler was by no means responsible for sowing seeds of suspicion about Murray and the version of Americanism he proposed and the Second Vatican Council seemingly approved. Discomfort with the Americanness of the U.S. church arguably owed most to Roman Catholic ambivalence about the nation and its policies, domestic and international. Once on the margins looking in at the American mainstream, Roman Catholics after

1950 had become partners in national life precisely at a time when the United States was experiencing the challenges of global hegemony. The dangers of so identifying with the United States became particularly evident, though, when some Roman Catholics, such as Weigel, Neuhaus, and Novak, produced apologies for the nation and its unique capacities in ways that for the historically minded resembled Eusebius's praise of Constantine.

For Thomas Storck, who taught for a time at Christendom College, a traditionalist institution that took its inspiration from L. Brent Bozell and *Triumph* magazine, Americanism of the kind proposed by Novak and others had ceased to be Christian. For Storck, the idea of America as a proposition, as the historically unprecedented nation that incarnated freedom and bestowed its blessings on the rest of the world, was a "kind of idolatry," even a heresy. So bloated had Americanism become that Storck felt compelled to issue a Tertullian-inspired either-or: "Although the Great Seal of the United States proclaims officially . . . the New Order of the Ages, only the one Church of God can claim that title, for only the Incarnation of Jesus Christ and the introduction of saving grace into human history have essentially changed anything."[36] Storck's rejection of Americanism would not have persuaded the dogmatically timid. But when Michael Sean Winters reviewed David Schindler for the *New Republic*, he indicated that even mainstream Roman Catholics were worried that Americanism would erode Roman Catholic identity: "The neo-conservative Catholics seem not to understand the distinction between engagement with the world and complicity with the world. For this reason, they have lost the greatest advantage that faith confers upon the faithful in any society: a genuinely critical standpoint."[37]

It came in a different form and context, but the idea that the salt of the church had lost its saltiness by assimilating the American environment was not much removed from the fear that had prompted popes a century earlier to condemn Americanism.

Americanism with an Edge

Winters may have thought neoconservatives such as Weigel had lost their prophetic voice by tying American and Roman Catholic ways so strongly, but Neuhaus surprised many in the church and policy circles when he devoted the November 1996 issue of *First Things* to "The End of Democracy." It included pieces by Neuhaus's conservative intellectual associates, including Hadley Arkes, a political scientist at Amherst College; Robert H. Bork, a former federal judge and then a scholar at American Enterprise Institute; Charles (Chuck) Colson of Prison Fellowship; Robert P. George, a legal scholar at Princeton University; and Russell Hittinger, a professor of law and religion at the University of Tulsa. (All of the contributors, except for Colson, were or became Roman Catholic.) Each essayist took exception to the Supreme Court's hegemony in American jurisprudence, with abortion rights functioning as the chief irritation. The justices had usurped the power of federal and state legislatures, and the Supreme Court had achieved power outsized from its original constitutional provisions, known in grade school as checks and balances. That complaint echoed, for those with ears to hear, the older objections of Clarence Manion and William F. Buckley, Jr., about the way that the federal government had outgrown the provisions of the American founding.

Most of the articles registered points that were standard fare in Neuhaus's magazine, but what caught the eye of many and crossed the line of still others was the editor's asking out loud in his introductory essay whether the U.S. government had become illegitimate. "Democratic politics means that 'the people' deliberate and decide" how we ought to order our life together, Neuhaus explained. In the American system, "the people do that through debate, elections, and representative political institutions." Neuhaus then asked, "Is that true today? Has it been true for, say, the last fifty years?" His answer was no. "It is not the judiciary that deliberates and answers the really important questions entailed in the question, How ought we to order our life together?" He went on to invoke the Declaration of Independence and the precedent set for resistance to tyrannous governments that were guilty of a "long train of abuses and usurpations." Neuhaus did not rely on the subtext but put his point into the text: "The government of the United States of America no longer governs by the consent of the governed.. . . . The courts have not, and perhaps cannot, restrain themselves, and it may be that in the present regime no other effective restraints are available. If so, we are witnessing the end of democracy." The political problem also had a religious dimension, one that frequently attended discussions of Americanism or assimilation. " 'God and country' is a motto that has in the past come easily," Neuhaus wrote, to almost all Americans. The danger of the contemporary situation was that Christians were moving to a point where "God and country" had morphed into "God or country?"[38]

The irony of the *First Things* symposium was that the chief orchestrators of the latest iteration of Americanism were precisely the ones who questioned the United States in ways that not even the most supreme of popes had dared to imagine. "The End of Democracy" was also sufficiently provocative to attract journalistic attention in the wider world of the American church. For instance, David S. Toolan, a priest, wrote a longish essay for *America* magazine indicating that most readers did not know about Neuhaus or his comrades. Toolan identified the *First Things* editor, along with Weigel and Novak, as the most prominent neoconservatives who had challenged the American church's progressive establishment and certain parts of the Second Vatican Council's theology to move American Roman Catholicism "to the right." Toolan credited these conservatives with speaking in a way that engaged non-Catholics, for avoiding nostalgia for the church of the First Vatican Council, and for catching the millennial optimism of John Paul II.[39] Their least appealing quality—here Toolan voiced *America*'s editorial outlook—was a full-throated embrace of market capitalism that was at odds with significant parts of Roman Catholic social teaching. Capitalism's exaltation of individualism, for example, was in conflict with Roman Catholic emphases on social solidarity.

Toolan, who wrote while the fallout from "The End of Democracy" was still settling, included reactions mainly from political and cultural conservatives before adding his own cautionary advice to Roman Catholic readers about American public life. Neuhaus's radical critique of the Supreme Court may have cost him members of his editorial board—among them Peter Berger and Gertrude Himmelfarb—but Toolan's verdict was that *First Thing*'s editor had crossed the line. Neuhaus had failed to take into account two realities that should inform Roman Catholic estimates of the nation's affairs. The first was pluralism: "Beware of appearing to hold a monopoly on the truth or exclusive possession of the moral high ground." The second was Roman Catholicism's recent arrival in the American mainstream: Roman Catholics still possessed a vision of the "ideal society [derived] from the Gospels and tradition" that had removed them from discussions about religious freedom and democracy. Toolan concluded, "We neglect this *arriviste* status at our peril."[40]

Peril was precisely what Neuhaus encountered among some Jewish American reactions to "The End of Democracy." At *Commentary* magazine the range of responses was civil, pragmatic, and somewhat partisan. What should conservatives do about the courts, and did the Republican Party present a useful outlet for Americans with conservative convictions? Those questions were distinct from Neuhaus's Roman Catholicism. Even William F. Buckley avoided discussing religion. He wrote instead about strategies for a GOP congressional majority. One exception to the in-house debate at *Commentary* was Walter Berns's response, which raised directly and abruptly the place of Jews in a political order supposed to be fundamentally Christian in origin. The constitutional scholar at the American Enterprise Institute recalled a conference at which he had asked Russell Kirk, after presenting a case for a Christian commonwealth, what the intellectual hero of conservatives would "do with us Jews." Kirk replied that he did not mean to exclude Jews. Berns countered that the founders provided a better framework than a Christian commonwealth by separating church and state. Berns did not think that Neuhaus had made the same mistake as Kirk. Neuhaus was simply wrong not about desiring a Christian commonwealth but about the American founding. Gaining independence from King George and establishing a new order for the ages was not based on traditional morality informed by religion. Instead, the founders recognized "the rights of man" and then gave them "constitutional protection." Neuhaus was correct, Berns believed, to complain about the Supreme Court but wrong to justify that opposition with a reading of the founding that tilted Christian.[41]

In the pages of the *New Republic*, the reaction to "The End of Democracy" was even more fevered. There Jacob Heilbrunn was the first to invoke the word "theocon" in reference to Neuhaus and in so doing raised the specter of anti-Semitism. Heilbrunn contrasted the views of Leo Strauss on the founding, which emphasized the rights of man, with Roman Catholic conservatives, who looked to Thomas Aquinas. It was a strange reading of the conservative movement because Heilbrunn paid attention to an obscure ethics professor at Mount Saint Mary's University, Germain Grisez, and ignored entirely John Courtney Murray, who had been the true inspiration for politically conservative Roman Catholics. Even so, Heilbrunn was on to the same point that Berns had raised with Kirk: if you read too much Christianity into the nation's origins, what

happens to non-Christians? Heilbrunn was enough a student of the political Right to remember Brent Bozell and the frustration that sometimes afflicted believers who became impatient with America's religious diversity
and abandonment of Christendom. Heilbrunn regarded Neuhaus and fellow Roman Catholics as "radicals and subversives." "They see America in
1990 as the abolitionists saw it in 1860—as a state that is violating God's
law and must be resisted."[42] To be on the side of antislavery was a compli-
ment, even if backhanded. To be a theocon was only negative.

Reactions to Heilbrunn from both Michael Novak and Robert George
registered the degree to which the label "theocon" stung. George claimed
that the natural law tradition was no more Christian than it was Jewish
or secular, which was fair but hardly did justice to Rome's attachment to
natural law even as Protestants and secularists had abandoned it. Novak,
who did not support "The End of Democracy," defended Neuhaus. The
First Things editor was no anti-Semite and was in fact a progressive by
most measures of 1960s politics. Novak also objected to Heilbrunn's
characterization of Thomism as "un-American." That made Heilbrunn's
article the "loopiest and most bigoted anti-Catholic piece" Novak had
read "in years." Heilbrunn responded and failed to concede ground. The
effort to read the United States and the nation's founding as chiefly the
outgrowth of the Christian West posed "a threat to the neutrality embodied in the First Amendment and, hence, to Jews (as well as secularists)."[43]

Whether Schindler, Storck, and other critics of the Roman Catholic
Americanists noticed or not, Neuhaus and his critics occupied the same
ground. Of course, within the church their understanding of Roman Catholicism's relationship to American democracy and liberalism diverged,
with Neuhaus and others arguing for harmony, while Schindler and
company came down on the side of conflict. Outside the church in the
mainstream of American society, however, Roman Catholics as diverse
as Neuhaus and Schindler looked un-American thanks to the way faith
shaped their politics. To be sure, that reaction could be yet another instance of one of the United States' large prejudices—anti-Catholicism. But
just as important to notice is that the liberal society to emerge from the
American founding posed a tension for all serious believers who resided
in the United States. It may not have involved the same conflict inherent
in Tertullian's famous query, "What hath Jerusalem to do with Athens?"
That tension did include a rivalry between religious fidelity and patriotic

loyalty. Ethnic Protestants, Muslims, and Jews throughout American history had experienced a version of what Roman Catholics faced in setting up churches and living out their faith. The temptation to assimilate or adopt a separatist posture has always beleaguered religious groups and institutions in the United States.

For Roman Catholics, however, thanks to the historic political and social power of their bishops and pope, the tension was particularly acute. From Buckley, Bozell, and Garry Wills to Novak, Neuhaus, and Weigel, Christians in fellowship with the bishop of Rome confronted a series of options for being a church member within the United States. The election of a Roman Catholic president and a historic gathering of bishops only added to the dilemmas of church members whose bishops had opposed liberalism (in most forms) for the better part of the modern era. If a generation of American church members even after the updating of the Second Vatican Council were still wondering about Rome's relationship to Washington, D.C., the American church's own fraught relationship both to the Vatican and the United States gave reassurance that they were not alone.

Conclusion

Freedom and Roman Catholicism in Postconciliar America

As much as Richard John Neuhaus upset his own editorial board at *First Things* by wondering in print about "the end" of American democracy, by the first decade of the next century he was back to his old self thanks largely to President George W. Bush. According to Neuhaus's biographer, Randy Boyagoda, the editor-priest lost some of his reputation as a flamethrower when Karl Rove set up a breakfast meeting during the spring of 1998 between Neuhaus and Bush, then the governor of Texas but with interest in running for president. After returning to New York City, Neuhaus wrote a letter to Bush in which he complimented the governor for his "politics of hope" and the promise of a "revival of moral responsibility." Neuhaus also encouraged Bush to aim for moral clarity on abortion. Bush replied with thanks for the *First Things* editor's "enlightenment on the main issue that matters in the long run of our country, the need for a cultural shift."[1]

When Bush eventually defeated Vice President Al Gore (with help from the Supreme Court, of all things), Neuhaus breathed a sigh of relief even while recognizing a deeply divided electorate:

> Bush beat Gore 54–43 with people who have incomes of $100,000 or more. But he had a larger advantage, 56–41, among married people with children. Among people who go to church once a week, Bush won 57–40, and among the 14 percent who attend church more than once a week, Bush obliterated Gore 63–36. . . . People who say they never go to church backed Gore 61–32, as did 70 percent of those who support the unlimited abortion license and the same percentage of those who identify themselves as gay, lesbian, or bisexual. To modify a motto from the 1992 election, It's sex, stupid.

Nor could Neuhaus resist noting that Bush's opponents, who complained about judicial overreach, now knew how it felt to bemoan the high court's prerogatives. "It was especially nice to have sundry pundits recalling what we have been saying about the judicial usurpation of politics," he wrote, "and suggesting that this journal is owed apologies."[2]

Even if Neuhaus returned from intellectual exile during the Bush 43 presidency, he was still cautious about the United States. After the attack on New York City and Washington, D.C., on September 11, 2001, when Bush declared that "freedom and fear, justice and cruelty, have always been at war" and Americans knew "that God is not neutral between them," Neuhaus defended the president's words. "America has once again given public expression to the belief," as Abraham Lincoln stated, "that we are 'one nation under God.'" Neuhaus added that this status involved both divine protection and judgment. Confidence in the former was faith, awareness of the latter was humility. The United States enjoyed this relationship with God because "He is the Father of the common humanity of which we are part."[3] Neuhaus's exegesis of "under God" left room for American greatness even as it shunned jingoism.

At the same time, the Bush presidency afforded opportunity, thanks to the cultural contests implicit in the nation's partisan politics, for Neuhaus to return to the theme, once championed by Protestants, that America was a Christian nation. For instance, in a series of observations on whether Jewish Americans might feel threatened by the resurgence of religion during the Bush years, Neuhaus tacked toward national greatness. "America is something quite new in world history," Neuhaus wrote, and Christian influences on the nation were partly responsible. "There is here a context of security and mutual trust that makes possible a genuine encounter between Jews and Christians, and between Judaism and Christianity" because "America is, as it always has been, an incorrigibly, confusedly, and conflictedly a Christian society." Even so, Neuhaus conceded that the nation could undermine serious Roman Catholicism. Since America's bicentennial, Roman Catholics had become "just like everybody else." The reason was a trend among Roman Catholics to emphasize "being American Catholics rather than . . . Catholic Americans," with emphasis on the adjective modifying the noun. When it came to David Gelertner's proposal that Americanism itself was the fourth biblical religion (along with Judaism, Roman Catholicism, and Protestantism), Neuhaus cried foul. This was a form of idolatry. As worthwhile as reflections on America's place in divine providence were, for Christians, "Christ and his body the Church is our first community, prior in time and prior in allegiance."[4]

Neuhaus's execution of this high-wire act—balancing faith and nationalism—was insufficient for Damon Linker, one of Neuhaus's colleagues at *First Things*. Linker had started at the magazine in 2001 as associate editor after training in political science (Ph.D. from Michigan State University), and then different stints—teaching at Brigham Young University and speechwriting for New York City mayor Rudolph W. Giuliani. By 2005, when Linker began to write a book about *First Things'* influence, Neuhaus found out and expressed "cause for concern" to colleagues.[5] Those anxieties turned out to be plausible when in 2006 Linker came out with *The Theocons: Secular America under Siege*. He explained the book was about a small group of "theoconservative intellectuals," chiefly Neuhaus but also Michael Novak and George Weigel, who were responsible for an "unprecedented rise in public religiosity" in the United States. Linker wrote with the zeal of a prophet tasked with warning Americans about the threat these writers posed to America's "tradition of secular politics." For three decades these intellectuals had "analyzed" and "assaulted" "every conceivable aspect of secular liberalism." The success of the book depended on readers using Linker to defend "themselves against their self-declared enemies."[6]

As breathless as Linker's preface seemed, he clearly had not been reading the Roman Catholic critics of Neuhaus's Americanism. Rather than posing a threat to secular America, Neuhaus's critics had argued that the *First Things* editor and his colleagues were damaging the faith. As Ross Douthat pointed out in an exchange for the *New Republic* soon after the book's publication, Linker had implicitly ruled as illegitimate "the attempt to link the American Founding to the Catholic natural-law tradition," which was at the heart of Neuhaus's work. If that were the case, then Linker also invalidated the well-regarded work of John Courtney Murray, as well as the reforms of Roman Catholicism at the Second Vatican Council. And if all of those pieces were at issue in Linker's assessment, Douthat added, then "orthodox Catholicism is essentially incompatible with the American liberal order." Furthermore, it meant that Neuhaus was wrong to tell U.S. Roman Catholics that "there's no great tension between Rome and the United States."[7]

Between Rome and the American Republic

Had the synthesis of modern politics and conservative Roman Catholicism, neo-Americanism, finally in the first decade of the new century become unsustainable? Answers to that question also need to include Roman Catholics beyond the pages of *First Things*. Whether they followed Neuhaus or not, the U.S. bishops in 2012 began to celebrate, even if defensively, American freedoms with a so-called Fortnight for Freedom. This annual program became a vehicle of protest as well as a voice of neo-Americanism. Its design was to call attention to governmental restrictions on services provided by Roman Catholic humanitarian agencies, such as the Affordable Care Act's requirement that Roman Catholic institutions provide health insurance that covered contraception, sterilization, and abortion-inducing drugs. Although President Obama's health insurance plan had caused the most hardships, the bishops also worried about federal laws that prevented churches from harboring "undocumented aliens" and that forced Roman Catholic foster care and adoption agencies to place children with same-sex couples. The Fortnight designated the days between June 21 and July 4 as a time to emphasize "our Christian and American heritage of liberty" in special periods of "prayer, study, catechesis, and public action."[8]

To assist parishes and families, the bishops also provided resources such as inserts placed inside worship bulletins. One of these aids reproduced the Second Vatican Council's statement on religious liberty. Another provided prayers to Mary as "patroness of our country" with this petition:

> O GOD OUR CREATOR, from your provident hand we have received our right to life, liberty, and the pursuit of happiness. You have called us as your people and given us the right and the duty to worship you, the only true God, and your Son, Jesus Christ. . . . Grant, we pray, O heavenly Father, a clear and united voice to all your sons and daughters gathered in your Church in this decisive hour in the history of our nation, so that, with every trial withstood and every danger overcome—for the sake of our children, our grandchildren, and all who come after us—this great land will always be "one nation, under God, indivisible, with liberty and justice for all."[9]

The bishops' call for liberty even constructed a narrative of American freedom that placed Roman Catholicism not on the margins as the church had been, at least until John F. Kennedy's election, but at the center. Freedom, they argued, was the United States' "special inheritance" and part of the nation's mission to the world. The bishops invoked James Gibbon, one of the leading nineteenth-century Americanists, who in 1887 told an audience in Rome that the American church had prospered thanks to the "civil liberty we enjoy in our enlightened republic." They also included Gibbons's remark that "in the genial atmosphere of liberty [the church] blossoms like a rose." Gibbons's successors did not add that the magisterium had disputed the U.S. bishop's estimate. But they did quote Pope Benedict XVI, who affirmed religious liberty as "the most cherished of American freedoms."[10]

The bishops' esteem for liberty placed Roman Catholicism squarely in developments that ran from the Protestant Reformation through the Enlightenment to modern politics. The colony of Maryland became an experiment in religious toleration but little removed from William Penn's Pennsylvania. To Roman Catholics belonged Maryland's 1649 Act Concerning Religion, "the first law in our nation's history to protect an individual's right to freedom of conscience." Protestants back in England may have sabotaged Maryland's tolerant society, but soon American statesmen such as Washington and Jefferson had picked up the mantle of "the most sacred of all property," freedom of conscience. The bishops also featured the first American archbishop, John Carroll, and his support for liberty, along with a quote from the Roman Catholic chief justice of the Supreme Court, John Roberts. The denouement of the bishops' narrative was a quotation from Martin Luther King's letter from the Birmingham jail: "I would agree with Saint Augustine that 'An unjust law is no law at all.' . . . To put it in the terms of Saint Thomas Aquinas, an unjust law is a human law that is not rooted in eternal law and natural law."

This confluence of Roman Catholicism with the advance of freedom allowed the bishops to appeal to two English martyrs, Thomas More and John Fisher, without having to explain that they were victims of the Protestant intolerance or that such antagonism between Protestants and Roman Catholics was responsible for a long history of anti-Catholicism in the United States. Such untidy details would have sapped the bishops' enthusiasm: "We are Catholics. We are Americans. We are proud to be both, grateful for the gift of faith which is ours as Christian disciples, and grateful for the gift of liberty which is ours as American citizens. To be Catholic and American should mean not having to choose one over the other. Our allegiances are distinct, but they need not be contradictory, and should instead be complementary." Perhaps not as indigenous and whole-some as mom, baseball, and apple pie, but Roman Catholicism, from the bishops' perspective, was fully American.

However excessive the bishops' embrace of Americanism, those who followed Pope Francis's visit to the United States in the fall of 2015 would have been hard-pressed to distinguish the sentiments of the American prel-ates from their superior in the Vatican. At the time of his trip, Francis was the fourth pope in Christian history to travel to the United States. The first, Paul VI, visited in 1965, which coincided with the Second Vatican Council's embrace of modern society. John Paul II was the most peripatetic of popes. He traveled to the United States officially five times, in 1979, 1987, 1993, 1995, and 1999 (plus two stopovers in Alaska en route to other lands). His successor, Benedict XVI, in 2008 also paid his respects. On each occasion, said pope took the opportunity to address geopolitics and conduct church business (meeting with national curia, officiating at Mass, or giving a homily). Paul VI used his trip to call on delegates to the United Nations to make peace a priority. John Paul II was less outspoken about politics, but during his 1987 visit he became the first pope to visit the White House and implicitly bless President Ronald Reagan's admin-istration. Benedict XVI followed a similar script and performed religious duties alongside a formal visit with President George W. Bush at the White House.

From one angle Pope Francis's trip looked conventional except for the pontiff's own reputation as one part radical, one part populist. By the time of his visit Francis had gained a reputation as a renegade, a reformer, a pope who spoke off the cuff and sometimes contradicted Rome's traditional teaching. Three weeks before his arrival, the *Washington Post* ran a story that featured eight of Francis's most liberal assertions, including "even atheists can go to heaven." Another story in the *Post* highlighted seven policies on which Francis was at odds with Republican leaders in Congress, such as his support for the Iranian nuclear agreement, immigration reform, and climate change policy. Reporters at the *Post* speculated as well that President Barack Obama might benefit from being associated with the pope. In one story, a theologian said, "If Obama said some of the things that Francis says, he'd be labeled a Trotsky-ite."[11]

Nevertheless, for all of Francis's advance billing as a radical, the pope dissented nary a word from the U.S. bishops' praise for America. In his address to Congress on September 24, Francis highlighted the accomplishments of Abraham Lincoln, Martin Luther King, Dorothy Day, and Thomas Merton to underscore themes of his own papacy—calling attention to the plight of labor and the poor, the inhumanity of violence, the dangers of nativism, and environmental wastefulness. Even so, the Declaration of Independence's famous words—"all men are created equal"— were on the side of serving and promoting the "good of the human person and based on respect for his or her dignity." Indeed, he closed by signaling his own agreement with "the richness of [America's] cultural heritage," a spirit that he hoped would "continue to develop and grow, so that as many young people as possible can inherit and dwell in a land which has inspired so many people to dream."[12]

These remarks were similar to ones Francis spoke on the steps of Philadelphia's Independence Hall a week later. The "ringing words" of the Declaration "continue to inspire us today, even as they have inspired peoples throughout the world to fight for the freedom to live in accordance with human dignity." Francis ended by reminding Americans to be grateful "for the many blessings and freedoms [they] enjoyed."[13]

When President Obama welcomed the pope to the White House, he repaid Francis's praise and linked Roman Catholicism to the nation's ideals and mission. The president thanked the pope for reminding Americans that "the Lord's" most powerful message was "mercy," for leading in better relations with Cuba, for affirming and defending religious liberty, and for teaching about care for the environment. President Obama conceded that the moral standard set by Francis could generate discomfort in light of the gap between ideals and practice. But this was actually a "blessing": "You shake our conscience from slumber; you call on us to rejoice in Good News, and give us confidence that we can come together in humility and service, and pursue a world that is more loving, more just, and more free. Here at home and around the world, may our generation heed your call to 'never remain on the sidelines of this march of living hope.'"[14]

Even granting that Francis and Obama were going through the motions of heads-of-state protocol, their statements showed not the slightest hint of the older antagonisms that had been an obstacle to John F. Kennedy fifty-five years earlier or that had inspired Pius X's *Syllabus of Errors*. Unlike an older calculus of church-state relations that pitted Rome's tradition-bound, hierarchical faith against American rationality and equality, by 2015 the ideals of the federal government's chief executive and the successor to Saint Peter were so similar that anyone born after 1964 could not have imagined a time when some Americans feared a Roman Catholic president. Pope Francis himself blessed the nation's and church's troubled pasts by turning memory into an occasion for uplift. "A people which remembers does not repeat past errors," he said. "It looks with confidence to the challenges of the present and the future."[15]

Episcopate Corrected

One of the unintended consequences of the hierarchy's embrace of liberty was that it also freed the laity to criticize the bishops. Soon after the first announcement for the Fortnight for Freedom, *Commonweal* magazine sponsored a forum to evaluate the program. If critics of Neuhaus such as Damon Linker found Americanist Roman Catholics too Christian for America's good, Roman Catholic journalists and professors judged the bishops too American. In a magazine designed to give voice to laity, that the editors invited no contributions from clergy was not surprising. What was unusual was the magazine's treatment of church teaching as if it were a policy proposal from the American Enterprise Institute.

That approach characterized the legal scholars who contributed to the forum and took exception to the way the bishops framed religious liberty. For instance, the Brookings Institution's William Galston faulted the bishops for formulating moral compromise too broadly when, in an echo of the *First Things* symposium, "The End of Democracy," the bishops declared that citizens had a responsibility to disobey unjust laws. Galston countered that every time an American pays taxes for a policy or activity she considers unjust, she violates her conscience. "Are we obligated to stop paying taxes?" Galston asked. The bishops had failed to exhibit "principled casuistry." Michael P. Moreland, dean of Villanova University's law school, thought the bishops had missed a chance to distinguish the freedoms of institutions (Roman Catholic hospitals and adoption services) from civil rights. So too Douglas Laycock from the University of Virginia's law school concluded that the bishops had confused their own morality with the attributes of an unjust law. "The bishops are of course free to demand that government and secular social-service agencies exclude gays and lesbians and unmarried straight couples from adopting children or providing foster care," Laycock observed. "But that is not an argument for religious liberty; it is an argument for regulating secular life."[16]

If Fortnight for Freedom failed to balance on the scales of legal reasoning, *Commonweal*'s contributors also faulted the bishops for departing from Roman Catholic standards. The only theologian to write, Cathleen Kaveny from the University of Notre Dame, noticed that the bishops did not place restrictions on religious liberty the way the Second Vatican Council had. "Vatican II's *Declaration on Religious Freedom* recognizes that there are 'due limits' on the exercise of religious freedom, including the need to promote a 'just public order,' and preserve the 'equality of the citizens before the law.' " Kaveny added that "for years, Catholic moralists and lawyers have railed against the assertion of rights claims without any consideration of relational responsibilities." Not only had the bishops apparently ignored those qualifications, but they had also forgotten entirely the Vatican's earlier critique of Americanism, as Mark Silk, a scholar at Trinity College and the one non-Catholic in the forum, pointed out. The bishops' appeal to Archbishop Gibbon ignored that Rome responded by anathematizing him "as heretical." Silk added that it took American bishops almost two generations before they could "find their tongues on the subject."[17]

The most pointed set of reflections came from Peter Steinfels, a Fordham University professor formerly of the *New York Times*, who situated the bishops' statement in the context of the church's internal struggles. The "current explosion of episcopal fervor for religious freedom," Steinfels asserted, stemmed from the "bishops' belated realization of their diminished hold over Catholic opinion and Catholic institutions—and in the implausible belief that this diminishment would not be the case if only the clergy had been more assertive in enforcing Catholic teachings, largely about sexuality and gender."[18] Steinfels did not offer direct proof of that speculative verdict. But the *Commonweal* forum itself was testimony to the bishops' loss of stature. The magazine's Roman Catholic editors had subjected the spiritual counsel of the apostles' successors to respectful but pointed criticism. In addition to challenging the bishops, *Commonweal* also used the expertise of lawyers, theologians, and journalists who apparently knew more about law and policy than the episcopate.

In an earlier era, the one of a predominantly immigrant church, the bishops constituted the smartest persons in the diocese. With the coming of education, affluence, and professional expertise, the bishops' main claim to authority stemmed from their spiritual status. Technically, church office was supposed to outrank secular professional credentials. What bishops declared was on the order of a sacred pronouncement. But when it came to utterances about law, policy, or national government in a modern, middle-class church, the bishops, as the *Commonweal* forum indicated, were simply stating opinions that could be balanced with the insights of professionals trained in such matters. The irony was that for the laity and policy experts, the bishops seemed to follow national ideals more than theological norms. Not to be missed, as well, was how the laity's critique of the bishops was as much a function of Americanism's triumph in the church as a call to greater religious fidelity. Prior to Vatican II, the laity did not have room, let alone the training, to challenge the bishops.

If the *Commonweal* forum revealed how Americanism was altering church life, the controversy that *New York Times* columnist Ross Douthat instigated with criticisms of Pope Francis was further evidence that adjusting Roman Catholicism to modernity was still unsettled even five decades after Vatican II. Soon after Francis's visit to the United States, Douthat, an outspokenly conservative and Roman Catholic op-ed writer, devoted a Sunday column to the idea that the pope was behind "a plot to change" the faith. The specific ploy was marriage and the question of whether divorced and remarried Roman Catholics were eligible for communion. Synods of bishops had met for two successive years in Rome to consider proposals that would make the church less restrictive. Although the questions at stake went deep into the fine print of canon law and church teaching, the matter was pressing in the American context for conservatives such as Douthat. He, like those before him, from Buckley to Neuhaus, believed that Christian norms were important for social stability in the West. For Douthat specifically marriage and child rearing were incubators of social capital since families performed services that other agencies, state or private, could not. What made Douthat's column particularly provocative was his assertion that Francis was "clearly looking for a mechanism that would let him exercise his powers without undercutting his authority."[19]

Within a week, a group of Roman Catholic scholars, led by John O'Malley, a Jesuit priest and prolific historian at Georgetown University who had written important books on the Council of Trent and the Second Vatican Council (for starters), wrote an open letter to the *Times* that did not answer Douthat's charges but threatened with an unusual appeal both to church power and journalistic ethics: "Aside from the fact that Mr. Douthat has no professional qualifications for writing on the subject, the problem with his article and other recent statements is his view of Catholicism as unapologetically subject to a politically partisan narrative that has very little to do with what Catholicism really is. Moreover, accusing other members of the Catholic church of heresy, sometimes subtly, sometimes openly, is serious business that can have serious consequences for those so accused. This is not what we expect of the *New York Times*."[20] The authors ignored marriage and Douthat's apparent disrespect for papal authority, and they failed to offer a correct understanding of Roman Catholicism. Instead, the letter ironically agreed with the columnist. The teachings of the church and departure from them (heresy) were serious, and readers of the *Times* did not need to see discussions of such narrowly ecclesiastical matters in the nation's secular newspaper of record. Instead of appealing to sacred office or church power, the letter invoked expertise. Douthat was not trained to write about Roman Catholicism the way the signers of the letter were. Surely the editors of the *Times*, as moderns, could recognize that academic training carried more weight than a columnist's opinions. The letter's authors avoided the category of genre, which would have given Douthat more expertise at writing op-ed columns than theologians crafting correspondence or judging the merits of journalism.

Yet the most important aspect of this contretemps was the window it opened once again on the awkward relations between modern society's structures, from journalism to academic specialization, and Rome's older defense of hierarchy and deference. A layperson had openly challenged the successor to Saint Peter in the pages of the nation's leading newspaper and did so not as a guest contributor but as a full-time staff member. Leading Roman Catholic academics, naturally inclined to think for themselves, took umbrage that a journalist had challenged the pope. They also questioned the integrity of a publication that their peers likely regarded as the gold standard for news and opinion. Neither side showed any obvious concern for episcopal authority. Rather than let bishops settle the matter, the exchange between Douthat and his foes demonstrated that the older, established channels for explaining and defending the faith—bishops and priests—were no match for the minds and outlets available to lay Roman Catholics with advanced degrees, academic expertise, and access to the mass media.

Americanism Still a Heresy?

As much as the debates in *Commonweal* and the *Times* revealed that Roman Catholics were not of the same mind about the church's relationship to modern society, those disputes were mild compared to a revival of antiliberalism from Roman Catholic intellectuals. In fact, recent critiques of modernity's twin political ideas—liberty and democracy—have gone beyond any of the arguments leveled against Neuhaus or his Americanist colleagues (Novak and Weigel). Even more surprising, they have found a home in the pages of Neuhaus's journal, *First Things*.

First came Brad Gregory's widely debated *Unintended Reformation* (2012), a book that traced the woes of modern secular society (with its materialism, hedonism, pluralism, and unbelief) back to the disruptive effects of Protestantism. According to Gregory, a historian at the

University of Notre Dame, Martin Luther did not hope for a world of cheap goods available at Walmart or easy access to pornography, but he did challenge Christendom's order that led to the modern West's decadence. Next in the line of modern-day Savonarolas was Rod Dreher's *The Benedict Option* (2016). An opinion writer who went from mainline Protestantism to Roman Catholicism and then to Eastern Orthodoxy, Dreher registered a sweeping complaint against the morally relativistic West by appropriating Alasdair MacIntyre, a widely read Roman Catholic philosopher at the University of Notre Dame. Just as MacIntyre had argued in *After Virtue* that modern Christians needed to learn from Benedict of Nursia's withdrawal from Roman society in order to save civilization, so Dreher asserted that twenty-first-century believers (of all stripes) needed to form intentional associations to transmit faith and morality to the next generation. Adding to these critiques of modern liberal society was Patrick Deneen's *Why Liberalism Failed*. The political philosopher at the University of Notre Dame echoed Gregory's and Dreher's laments about modern liberal society but extended the critique to argue that, contrary to John Courtney Murray, the founding of the United States was fatally flawed. The reason was that the Founders drew Lockean and Hobbesian notions of human nature. Politics so conceived inevitably generated "pathologies" at once holding true to liberalism's fundamental claims but also betraying promises of liberty and equality. Instead of working out a compromise with religious traditions, liberalism was a threat to them.

In the midst of this assault on the modern West came an unexpected and remarkable debate over the power of nineteenth-century popes and the legitimacy of abducting children. It started with a review in *First Things* of Edgardo Mortara's previously unpublished memoirs, *Kidnapped by the Vatican?* Mortara was a Jewish boy from Bologna who became a ward of Pius IX when his family's Italian servant believed the boy's life was in danger and baptized him (canon law made provisions for such baptisms). Church law required that Christians rear a baptized child, and since Mortara's parents would not convert, papal police took the six-year-old Edgardo, who then received a parochial education and eventually entered the priesthood. The incident gained international attention, and Pius IX's refusal to give Edgardo up or soften church law was one factor in the loss of the Papal States and Italy's subsequent unification in 1871.

As troubling as Mortara's case might be to modern sensibilities, the reviewer in *First Things*, Romanus Cessario, a professor of theology at a Boston seminary, used the publication to defend the church's understanding of baptism and Pius IX's obedience. Church teaching "bound Pius to give Mortara a Catholic upbringing that his parents could not," Cessario explained. What is more, Pius's decision actually reflected a truth that Christians share with Jews, namely, a "higher loyalty that they honor in ways that seem incomprehensible to the world." Cessario's logic led him to pit church and synagogue against a secular outlook that denies "these higher loyalties."[21]

Negative reactions were fierce and swift. Matthew Franck wrote at the *Weekly Standard* that Pius was "grievously" wrong even on Roman Catholic grounds. Robert George, a prominent legal scholar at Princeton and a force among conservative Roman Catholics, wrote on his Facebook page, "The taking of the child by force from his parents and family was an abomination and defending it is an embarrassment." If political and Roman Catholic conservatives were embarrassed, liberal voices in the church were outraged. Michael Sean Winters opened his commentary on the review by calling for Cessario's firing: "Not permitted to retire early. Not permitted to resign. He should be sacked and sacked publicly." At *Commonweal*, a voice for the progressive laity among U.S. Roman Catholics, Kevin J. Madigan observed that Cessario (and his editors) were "still captive to the assumptions, rejected authoritatively by executive decrees of Vatican II and by several popes."[22]

Indeed, Cessario's review and its responses revealed just how vastly different were the church's attitudes to politics between the 1860s and 1960s. Pius may have understood Roman Catholic teaching on human nature, church authority, and politics to allow for papal unilateralism in the case of a Jewish boy. But in the Second Vatican Council's adjustments, the older understanding of church-state relations, in which liberalism belonged to *The Syllabus of Errors*, had become as objectionable as liberal politics used to be. R. R. Reno's explanation of his decision as editor of *First Things* to publish the review tried to skirt the issue of the church's old authoritarianism versus the Second Vatican Council's modern adjustments by saying that the question was really one of a person's obedience to "God's eternal decrees." Few readers accepted Reno's excuse except those most hostile to liberalism's degeneracy.[23]

Arguably, the most poignant perspective on the Mortara controversy came from Nathan Shields at *Mosaic* magazine, an online Jewish publication. A composer by day, Shields could not help but wonder about the timing of a review that praised a pope's actions precisely when the church had distanced itself from the anti-Semitism that had haunted Christendom's political theology and the Vatican's defense of it. Pius IX's "sweeping and uncompromising opposition to the heresies of modernity" may have appealed to radical traditionalists on the far right of Roman Catholicism, but it was odd fare for a journal that under Neuhaus had been such an important vehicle for appropriating John Courtney Murray's justification for the American founding. Shields observed that for decades "the most prominent Catholic intellectual in America was William F. Buckley," whose brand of "Christian individualism" looked as "liberal as a Toyota Prius." In contrast, a "philosophically consistent Catholic anti-liberalism" had emerged not simply to protest liberalism's flaws but also to expose a rift among Roman Catholics—namely, those comfortable with modernity and those who thought the church was at its best when antimodern. That divide had, Shields went on to observe, made the critics of liberalism (and defenders of Pius IX) oblivious to the historic plight of Jews in Roman Catholic societies. An exception to this was Neuhaus himself, who was a "noted philo-Semite" and "believed the values of the Church to be in principle reconcilable with the ideals of the American founding." In a follow-up piece in which Shields responded to defenders of Pius IX, he predicted that future harmonizations of Roman Catholicism and liberal modernity would be unsteady because of the "irreconcilable claims of tradition and modernity, the competing demands of fidelity to the past and accommodation with the present."[24]

That point about a basic antagonism between Roman Catholicism and modern politics received confirmation indirectly from Adrian Vermeule, a distinguished professor of constitutional law at Harvard University. A former clerk for Supreme Court justice Antonin Scalia and a recent convert from Anglicanism to Roman Catholicism, Vermeule confirmed Shields's point in a piece on the dangers of secular liberalism published in the British journal *Catholic Herald*. The Harvard professor had already added to what Reno, the editor of *First Things*, called "rethinking" John Courtney Murray and "the congeniality of the American project to Catholicism." Only two months before his piece in *Catholic Herald*, Vermeule had written that intolerance was "essential" to liberalism and that the Roman Catholic Church was "liberalism's principal target and antagonist." Now, coincident with the review of Mortara's memoir, came Vermeule's verdict that whether or not they should take prisoners, Roman Catholics could not make peace with liberalism: "There is no reason to think that a stable, long-term rapprochement between Catholicism and the liberal state is realistically feasible, whether or not it would be desirable. . . . The 'tradition' of liberalism, really an anti-tradition, is founded on that substantive creed and cannot coherently even be identified, let alone followed, without entering into those anti-traditionalist ideas and sympathetically interpreting and applying them."[25] If they had been written seventy years earlier, Paul Blanshard undoubtedly would have cited Vermeule's words to prove Roman Catholicism's threat to the United States.

The Fleeting "Catholic Moment"?

When John F. Kennedy became president of the United States, the stigma of Roman Catholicism lifted. No matter what Kennedy's own convictions and practice were, practically no one in the church, from bishops and cardinals to priests and laity, took exception. American church members generally agreed that church and state should be separate and were likely comfortable, as Kennedy claimed to be, with refusing to receive government support for parochial schools. After the seemingly seismic accommodations to modernity at the Second Vatican Council, American Roman Catholics continued the process of adaptation, now with the magisterium's blessing. From William F. Buckley, Jr.'s coterie of journalists who constructed a version of national greatness for an emergent conservative movement to John Courtney Murray and his effort to link the American founding to natural law, clergy and laity were confident that Rome and Washington, D.C., were fundamentally compatible. As historian R. Scott Appleby put it, the outlook that flourished after World War II regarded "the American experiment as exemplary, even revelatory" of the truth about society and government. These Roman Catholics saw "no contradiction between what John Courtney Murray called 'the American proposition' . . . and their Catholic faith." "Even the original Americanists," Appleby added, "did not go this far."[26]

These dramatic changes during the 1960s may suggest that the politically conservative Roman Catholic figures featured in this book were little more than sticks floating in a much larger stream of ecclesiastical and social circumstances that no single figure or publication could manage. In contrast to Martin Luther King, Jr., who dominated the civil rights movement, the activities and arguments of William F. Buckley, Jr., or Richard John Neuhaus on behalf of neo-Americanist Roman Catholicism seem minor. Nevertheless, because of Rome's long-standing resistance to modernity and because of the United States' inveterate anti-Catholicism, to champion American norms as Buckley, Neuhaus, and their colleagues did was indeed historic. To be sure, many Roman Catholics before these conservatives had praised the United States, but few had trafficked so comfortably with secular liberals and Protestants or had managed to construct a political movement that reoriented one of the country's major political parties.

At the same time, neo-Americanists drew a map for Roman Catholics to harness serious religious conviction to secular civil polity. In addition, they inspired a body of literature in a number of academic fields that challenged the direction the country had taken since the New Deal.[27] So influential was the Americanism of conservative Roman Catholics that they convinced evangelical Protestants to abandon historic anti-Catholic prejudices, learn from Roman Catholic scholars, and cooperate on specific fronts of the culture wars.[28] Meanwhile, neo-Americanism arguably shifted perceptions of Roman Catholicism so that few citizens object to the presence of a majority of Roman Catholic justices on the Supreme Court. Perhaps, most remarkable of all, these conservatives gained the ear and even seemed to win the approval of the papacy itself when John Paul II and Benedict XVI cooperated with Neuhaus's organization and colleagues. (According to George Weigel, John Paul II asked him to write a biography of the pope, which duly appeared as *Witness to Hope* [HarperCollins, 1999]. Also, in 1988 Neuhaus hosted Joseph Cardinal Ratzinger, who became Benedict XVI, for the Institute on Religion and Public Life's annual Erasmus Lecture.) In the same way that James Chappel has recently argued for a set of European Roman Catholic intellectuals who wrestled with fascism and communism to forge a "modern Catholicism," so too figures such as Buckley and Neuhaus were able "to show that there is no necessary contradiction between Catholicism and modernity."

The political form that neo-Americanism took, unlike Europe's Christian Democratic parties, was Republicanism and movement conservatism.[29]

Yet critics of neo-Americanism, from early skirmishes between Buckley and the Jesuit editors of *America* to recent critiques of political liberalism from Roman Catholic scholars, display a level of discomfort with neo-Americanists' blending of faith and politics that reflects historic antagonisms between modern politics and the Vatican's defense of tradition. Just as a certain equilibrium has always characterized church life on the ground in the United States, so also the specter of ultramontanism haunts any Roman Catholic who pretends to know church history and uses it to object to crises in modern society.

For instance, Massimo Faggioli, a historian at Villanova University, is critical of neo-Americanism for being more nationalist than Roman Catholic. That 52 percent of U.S. Roman Catholics voted for Donald Trump in the 2016 presidential election was proof for him that neo-Americanism was prone to easy and tawdry deployments of the slogan "Make America Great Again." How Faggioli's defense of Vatican II matched his call for Roman Catholics to adhere to Pope Francis's "social-political message" of "mercy, social justice, and inclusion of the poor" was not a tension he noted or a question he answered.[30] A secular republic, after all, needing to conform to papal teaching—whether progressive or traditional—is not liberal. Had not Vatican II given Roman Catholics in the United States freedom to vote for their preferred candidate or to adopt their own political philosophy? Or do critics of neo-Americanism, such as Faggioli, implicitly support a church-state relationship where popes and Vatican officials instruct church members and politicians on economics and politics?

Whatever the reason for discontent with neo-Americanism, the College of the Holy Cross church historian David J. O'Brien, whose empathy for Americanism surfaced in his bicentennial history of the U.S. church (see chapter 8), may provide the best perspective on figures such as Buckley and Neuhaus. For O'Brien, neo-Americanism was an outcome made possible by Vatican II. Although more sympathetic to the American church's left than to political conservatives, O'Brien acknowledged that neo-Americanism was a welcome result of Rome's reckoning with modernity. Still, he complained that historians of Roman Catholicism had yet to acknowledge its importance. "Americanism was the crucial question" for Roman Catholics in the United States after Vatican II, and "it remains the missing page." This "critical" outlook had implications, according to O'Brien, for both church and society.[31] It should, he argued, resurrect the history of the church in the United States, forge a theology that showcases the experience of the laity, and recognize the roles that laity and clergy play in church life.

Whether Buckley or Neuhaus would have agreed with O'Brien on specifics is debatable. Still, when the Holy Cross historian wrote about the need to balance catholicity with Americanism in ways that embraced "the reflections of Lincoln, the dedication of democratic reformers, and the vision of Martin Luther King," O'Brien implicitly approved of what the neo-Americanists had done. However much they overestimated the U.S. role in history or esteemed the Republican Party as the best vehicle for fulfilling the nation's purpose, neo-Americanists endeavored to ground the eternal truths of their faith in the concrete realities of U.S. domestic and foreign policy. In an importance sense, they were merely heeding Vatican II's call for a modern faith.

NOTES

Preface

1. Jon Butler, "Born-Again America? A Critique of the New 'Evangelical Thesis' in Recent American Historiography" (paper presented at the American Society of Church History, Washington, D.C., December 29, 1992), 2.

2. D. G. Hart, *A Secular Faith: Why Christianity Favors the Separation of Church and State* (Chicago: Ivan R. Dee, 2006); D. G. Hart, *From Billy Graham to Sarah Palin: Evangelicals and the Betrayal of American Conservatism* (Grand Rapids, Mich.: Eerdmans, 2011).

Introduction

1. "Editorial Comments by the Nation's Press on Victory for Kennedy," *New York Times*, November 11, 1960, 24; Arnoldo Cortesi, "Vatican Calls Kennedy Election Proof of American Democracy," *New York Times*, November 10, 1960, 1.

2. Mark S. Massa, *Catholics and American Culture: Fulton Sheen, Dorothy Day, and the Notre Dame Football Team* (New York: Crossroad, 1999), 130; Charles R. Morris, *American Catholic: The Saints and Sinners Who Built America's Most Powerful Church* (New York: Vintage Books, 1997), 280; Martin E. Marty, *Modern American Religion*, vol. 3, *Under God, Indivisible, 1941–1960* (Chicago: University of Chicago Press, 1996), 4; Jay P. Dolan, *In Search of an American Catholicism: A History of Religion and Culture in Tension* (New York: Oxford University Press, 2002), 192; Daniel Boorstin, "Editor's Preface" to John Tracy Ellis, *Catholicism*, 2nd rev. ed. (1956; Chicago: University of Chicago Press, 1969), ix.

3. Kennedy and Sorenson quoted in Massa, *Catholics and American Culture*, 129.

4. "City of God and Man," *Time*, December 12, 1960, 65.

5. Ibid., 70.

6. Liberalism here chiefly refers to the political arrangements of the U.S. founding, which included constitutional republicanism, separation of powers, federalism, separation of church and state, and popular sovereignty.

7. John T. Noonan, Jr., *The Lustre of Our Country: The American Experience of Religious Freedom* (Berkeley: University of California Press, 1998), 27.

8. John T. McGreevy, *Catholicism and American Freedom: A History* (New York: W. W. Norton, 2003), 166.

9. Harold E. Fey, "Can Catholicism Win America?," *Christian Century*, November 29, 1944, 1380.

10. Harold E. Fey, "The Center of Catholic Power," *Christian Century*, January 17, 1945, 76.

11. R. Scott Appleby, "The Triumph of Americanism: Common Ground for U.S. Catholics in the Twentieth Century," in *Being Right: Conservative Catholics in America*, ed. Mary Jo Weaver and R. Scott Appleby (Bloomington: Indiana University Press, 1995), 39; Massa, *Catholics and American Culture*, 10; Gary Wills, *The Future of the Catholic Church with Pope Francis* (New York: Viking, 2015), 124.

12. For an overview of Schlafly's political career, see Donald T. Critchlow, *Phyllis Schlafly and Grassroots Conservatism: A Woman's Crusade* (Princeton, N.J.: Princeton University Press, 2005).

13. William F. Buckley, Jr., *God and Man at Yale: The Superstitions of "Academic Freedom"* (1951; Washington, D.C.: Regnery, 2002), 3, 42, lxiii. The quotation from Seymour is on p. 3.

14. Critchlow, *Phyllis Schlafly*, 42–43.

15. On Rome's inveterate conservatism, see Russell Hittinger, "Introduction to Modern Catholicism," in *Teachings of Modern Christianity*, vol. 1, *On Law, Politics, and Human Nature*, ed. John Witte, Jr., and Frank S. Alexander (New York: Columbia University Press, 2006), chap. 1.

16. Sam Haselby, *The Origins of American Religious Nationalism* (New York: Oxford University Press, 2016), 232, 61, 228.

17. Robert P. Jones, *The End of White Christian America* (New York: Simon & Schuster, 2016).

18. Thomas J. Sugrue, "The Catholic Encounter with the 1960s," in *Catholics in the American Century: Recasting Narratives of U.S. History*, ed. R. Scott Appleby and Kathleen Sprows Cummings (Ithaca, NY: Cornell University Press, 2012), 73, 74.

19. James Chappel, *Catholic Modern: The Challenge of Totalitarianism and the Remaking of the Church* (Cambridge, Mass.: Harvard University Press, 2018), 9.

1. Belonging to an Ancient Church in a Modern Republic

1. Charles C. Marshall, "An Open Letter to the Honorable Alfred E. Smith," *Atlantic Monthly*, September 1927, http://www.theatlantic.com/magazine/archive/1927/04/an-open-letter-to-the-honorable-alfred-e-smith/306523/.

2. *The Syllabus of Errors* (1864), Papal Encyclicals Online, https://www.papalencyclicals.net/pius09/p9syll.htm.

3. Quoted in Gerald P. Fogarty, "Reflections on the Centennial of *Testem Benevolentiae*," *U.S. Catholic Historian* 17, no. 1 (Winter 1999): 2.

4. A valuable brief overview of the controversy comes from Philip Gleason, "'Americanism' in American Catholic Discourse," in *Speaking of Diversity: Language and Ethnicity in Twentieth-Century America* (Baltimore: Johns Hopkins University Press, 1992), chap. 10. The best detailed account is Gerald P. Fogarty, *The Vatican and the American Hierarchy from 1870 to 1965* (Stuttgart: Hiersemann, 1982).

5. *Longinqua* reproduced at http://w2.vatican.va/content/leo-xiii/en/encyclicals/docu ments/hf_l-xiii_enc_06011895_longinqua.html, accessed December 16, 2019.

6. *Testem benevolentiae*, quoted in Fogarty, *Vatican*, 178.

7. Fogarty, *Vatican*, 179.

8. See Peter D'Agostino, *Rome in America: Transnational Catholic Ideology from the Risorgimento to Fascism* (Chapel Hill: University of North Carolina Press, 2004).

9. *In amplimissimo* reproduced at http://www.papalencyclicals.net/Leo13/l13inamp. htm, accessed December 16, 2019.

10. Fogarty, *Vatican*, 189.

11. James Cardinal Gibbons, "Will the American Republic Endure?," in *A Retrospect of Fifty Years*, vol. 2 (Baltimore: John Murphy, 1916), 213.

12. Charles R. Morris, *American Catholic: The Saints and Sinners Who Built America's Most Powerful Church* (New York: Vintage Books, 1998), 128–29.

13. All quotations from Gerald P. Fogarty, "Public Patriotism and Private Politics: The Tradition of American Catholicism," *U.S. Catholic Historian* 4, no. 1 (1984): 23, 28.

14. Quotations from Robert A. Slayton, *Empire Statesman: The Rise and Redemption of Al Smith* (New York: Free Press, 2007), 33.

15. Al Smith quoted in Thomas J. Shelley, " 'What the Hell Is an Encyclical?': Governor Alfred E. Smith, Charles C. Marshall, Esq., and Father Francis P. Duffy," *U.S. Catholic Historian* 15, no. 2 (April 1997): 91.

16. Ibid.

17. Ibid., 93, 95.

18. Smith, "Catholic Power and Patriot: Governor Smith Replies," *Atlantic Monthly*, May 1927, http://www.theatlantic.com/magazine/archive/1927/05/catholic-and-patriot/306522/.

19. Ibid.

20. Allan J. Lichtman, *Prejudice and Old Politics: The Presidential Election of 1928* (Chapel Hill: University of North Carolina Press, 1979), 232.

21. Patrick W. Carey, *American Catholic Religious Thought: The Shaping of a Theological and Social Tradition* (Milwaukee: Marquette University Press, 2004), 88.

22. Quoted in Fogarty, "Public Patriotism," 37.

23. For explanations of the rise of post–World War II anti-Catholicism, see Philip Gleason, *Contending with Modernity: Catholic Higher Education in the Twentieth Century* (New York: Oxford University Press, 1995), chap. 12; John T. McGreevy, *Catholicism and American Freedom: A History* (New York: W. W. Norton, 2003), chap. 6.

24. McGreevy, *Catholicism and American Freedom*, 167, 168.

25. Paul Blanshard, *American Freedom and Catholic Power* (Boston: Beacon, 1949), 292, 313, 323.

26. Ibid., 102.

27. Marshall, "Open Letter."

28. John Courtney Murray, "Leo XIII and Pius XII: Government and the Order of Religion," in *John Courtney Murray: Religious Liberty, Catholic Struggles with Pluralism*, ed. J. Leon Hooper (Louisville, Ky.: Westminster / John Knox Press, 1993), 79, 83, 88.

29. McGreevy, *Catholicism and American Freedom*, 208.

30. Morris, *American Catholic*, 277.

2. Public Duty, Private Faith

1. Paul Blanshard, *American Freedom and Catholic Power* (Boston: Beacon, 1951), 257.

2. Quoted in Gerald P. Fogarty, *The Vatican and the American Hierarchy from 1870 to 1965* (Wilmington, Del.: Michael Glazier, 1985), 365.

3. Quoted in Joseph A. Komonchak, " 'The Crisis in Church-State Relationships in the U.S.A.': A Recently Discovered Text by John Courtney Murray," *Review of Politics* 61, no. 4 (Fall 1999): 713.

4. Robert Dallek, *An Unfinished Life: John F. Kennedy, 1917–1963* (New York: Back Bay Books, 2004), 70.

5. Thomas Reeves, *A Question of Character: A Life of John F. Kennedy* (New York: Free Press, 1991), 31.

6. Dallek, *Unfinished Life*, 30, 45; Gary Scott Smith, *Faith and the Presidency: From George Washington to George W. Bush* (New York: Oxford University Press, 2009), 260.

7. Quoted in Dallek, *Unfinished Life*, 59.

8. Ibid., 59, 86–87.

9. All quotations from Smith, *Faith and the Presidency*, 261.

10. Shaun Casey, *The Making of a Catholic President: Kennedy vs. Nixon 1960* (New York: Oxford University Press, 2009), 3–5.

11. Ibid., 17, 20; Lawrence H. Fuchs, *John F. Kennedy and American Catholicism* (New York: Meredith Press, 1967), 165, 166.

12. Quoted in W. J. Rorabaugh, *The Real Making of the President: Kennedy, Nixon, and the 1960 Election* (Lawrence: University of Kansas Press, 2009), 49.

13. Ibid., 52–53.

14. Theodore H. White, *The Making of the President* (London: Cape, 1960), 107, 108.

15. Quoted in Casey, *Making of a Catholic President*, 125.

16. Ibid., 134.

17. Ibid., 142.

18. Ibid., 166.

19. Quoted in Rorabaugh, *Real Making of the President*, 144.

20. The full text is available at https://www.jfklibrary.org/Asset-Viewer/ALL6YEBJME KYGMCntnSCvg.aspx, accessed December 18, 2019. All quotations of the speech are from this source.

21. The King speech is available at https://www.archives.gov/files/press/exhibits/dream-speech.pdf, accessed December 18, 2019.

22. Quotations from Casey, *Making of a Catholic President*, 171–74.

23. The Kennedy-Nixon debates are available at http://debates.org/index.php?page=october-13-1960-debate-transcript, accessed December 18, 2019.

24. The full text of President Kennedy's inaugural address is at https://www.jfklibrary. org/Asset-Viewer/BqXIEM9F4024ntFl7SVAjA.aspx, accessed December 18, 2019.

25. "City upon a Hill Speech" (January 9, 1961), John F. Kennedy Presidential Library and Museum, https://www.jfklibrary.org/learn/about-jfk/historic-speeches/the-city-upon-a-hill-speech, accessed February 8, 2020.

26. Richard M. Gamble, *In Search of the City on a Hill: The Making and Unmaking of an American Myth* (New York: Continuum Books, 2012), 133.

27. Quoted in William Manchester, *Death of a President—November 20–November 25, 1963* (New York: Harper & Row, 1967), 559.

28. Ibid., 582, 586.

29. *American Heritage* magazine, *Four Days: The Historical Record of the Death of President Kennedy* (New York: American Heritage, 1964), 142.

30. Robert N. Bellah, "Civil Religion in America," *Daedalus* 96, no. 1 (Winter 1967): 5.

31. Fuchs, *John F. Kennedy*, 163, 164–65.

32. Mark S. Massa, "A Catholic for President? John F. Kennedy and the 'Secular' Theology of the Houston Speech, 1960," *Journal of Church and State* 39, no. 2 (Spring 1997): 312, 316.

3. Americanism for the Global Church

1. Quoted in Carol Glatz, "'So Dastardly a Crime': Pope Paul VI's Reaction 50 Years Ago," Catholic News Service blog, November 18, 2013, https://cnsblog.wordpress.com/2013/11/18/so-dastardly-a-crime-pope-paul-vis-reaction-50-years-ago.

2. Lawrence McAndrews, *What They Wished For: American Catholics and American Presidents, 1960–2004* (Athens: University of Georgia Press, 2013), 20.

3. The text of John XXIII's speech is available at http://www.vatican2voice.org/91docs/opening_speech.htm, accessed December 23, 2019.

4. Quoted in McAndrews, *What They Wished For*, 24–25.

5. The antipope is the term for illegitimate claimants to the papal throne during the Western Schism (1378–1417), when Europe's loyalty was divided between the Avignon and Roman papacies.

6. Quoted in "Religion: I Choose John," *Time*, November 10, 1958.

7. *Mater et magistra*, paragraphs 34, 37, and 79, available at http://w2.vatican.va/content/john-xxiii/en/encyclicals/documents/hf_j-xxiii_enc_15051961_mater.html, accessed December 23, 2019.

8. Ibid., paragraph 127.

9. *Pacem in terris*, paragraph 11, available at http://w2.vatican.va/content/john-xxiii/en/encyclicals/documents/hf_j-xxiii_enc_11041963_pacem.html, accessed December 19, 2019. Subsequent references to paragraph numbers appear parenthetically within the text.

10. Quotations from Leslie Griffin, "Pope John XXIII (1881–1963)," in *The Teachings of Modern Christianity on Law, Politics, and Human Nature*, ed. John Witte, Jr., and Frank S. Alexander (New York: Columbia University Press, 2006), 162, 163.

11. Quoted in Barry Hudock, *Struggle, Condemnation, Vindication: John Courtney Murray's Journey toward Vatican II* (Collegeville, Minn.: Liturgical Press, 2015), 15.

12. Pope Leo XIII, *Longinqua* (1895), paragraph 6, available at http://w2.vatican.va/content/leo-xiii/en/encyclicals/documents/hf_l-xiii_enc_06011895_longinqua.html, accessed December 23, 2019.

13. Quoted in Hudock, *Struggle*, 37.

14. Ibid., 73, 74, 75, 80.

15. Ibid., 82.

16. Ibid., 86.

17. Ibid., 98.

18. Ibid., 104.

19. "To Be Catholic and American," *Time*, December 12, 1960, http://content.time.com/time/magazine/article/0,9171,871923,00.html.

20. Robert McAfee Brown, *Observer in Rome: A Protestant Report on the Vatican Council* (Garden City, N.Y.: Doubleday, 1964), 174.

21. Leslie Griffin, "Commentary on *Dignitatis humanae* Declaration on Religious Freedom," in *Modern Catholic Social Teaching: Commentaries and Interpretations*, ed. Kenneth R. Himes (Washington, D.C.: Georgetown University Press, 2005), 248; italics in the original.

22. Quoted in Hudock, *Struggle*, 117.

23. Ibid., 119.

24. Ibid., 133.

25. John Courtney Murray, "The Problem of Religious Freedom," in *Religious Liberty: Catholic Struggles with Pluralism*, ed. J. Leon Hooper (Louisville, Ky.: Westminster / John Knox Press, 1993), 183.

26. Quoted in Hudock, 134.

27. Murray, "Problem of Religious Freedom," 187–88.

28. Quoted in Hudock, *Struggle*, 134.

29. Quoted in Griffin, "Commentary on *Dignitatis humanae*," 249.

30. Griffin was quoting theologian Mary Hobgood. See ibid., 254.

31. *Dignitas humanae*, paragraph 1, available at http://www.vatican.va/archive/hist_councils/ii_vatican_council/documents/vat-ii_decl_19651207_dignitatis-humanae_en.html, accessed December 22, 2019. Subsequent references to paragraph numbers appear parenthetically within the text.

32. Griffin, "Commentary on *Dignitas humanae*," 255, makes this point.

33. Gerald P. Fogarty, *The Vatican and the American Hierarchy from 1870 to 1965* (Stuttgart: Hiersemann, 1982), 399.

34. Ibid., 247.

35. Hudock, *Struggle*, 146.

36. Fogarty, *Vatican and the American Hierarchy*, 401, quotation on 403.

37. *Pacem in terris*, paragraph 65; Griffin, "Commentary on *Dignitatis humanae*," 254.

4. Liberal Catholics, American Conservatives

1. Garry Wills, *Bare Ruined Choirs: Doubt, Prophecy, and Radical Religion* (Garden City, N.Y.: Doubleday, 1972), 64, 65.

2. Ibid., 70, 71.

3. Ibid., 53.

4. Ibid., 54.

5. Quoted in Garry Wills, *Politics and Catholic Freedom* (Chicago: Regnery, 1964), 6.

6. From *National Review*, "Magazine's Credenda," quoted in John B. Judis, *William F. Buckley, Jr.: Patron Saint of the Conservatives* (New York: Simon & Schuster, 1991), 133.

7. Quoted in Judis, *William F. Buckley*, 46, 47.

8. Ibid., 58.

9. William F. Buckley, Jr., *God and Man at Yale: The Superstitions of Academic Freedom* (Chicago: Regnery, 1951), 3.

10. Ibid., 122.

11. Ibid., 194, 195.

12. Quoted in George H. Nash, "*God and Man at Yale* Revisited," in *Faith, Freedom, and Higher Education: Historical Analysis and Contemporary Reflections*, ed. P. C. Kemeny (Eugene, Ore.: Pickwick, 2013), 82.

13. McGeorge Bundy, "The Attack at Yale," *Atlantic Monthly*, November 1951, http://www.theatlantic.com/magazine/archive/1951/11/the-attack-on-yale/306724/.

14. Judis, *William F. Buckley*, 96.

15. Ibid., 97–98.

16. This interpretation follows Donald Crosby, *God, Church, and Flag: Senator Joseph R. McCarthy and the Catholic Church, 1950–1957* (Chapel Hill: University of North Carolina Press, 1978).

17. William F. Buckley, Jr., and L. Brent Bozell, *McCarthy and His Enemies: The Record and Its Meaning* (Chicago: Regnery, 1954), 331.

18. Quoted in Judis, *William F. Buckley*, 110.

19. Ibid., 166.

20. Buckley, "Disruptions and Achievements of Vatican II," *Nearer My God: An Autobiography of Faith* (Garden City, N.Y.: Doubleday, 1997), 97.

21. *Mater et magistra*, paragraph 20, available at http://w2.vatican.va/content/john-xxiii/en/encyclicals/documents/hf_j-xxiii_enc_15051961_mater.html, accessed December 23, 2019.

22. Quoted in Wills, *Politics and Catholic Freedom*, 3.

23. Ibid., 4.

24. Ibid., 4, 5, 14, 16.

25. Will Herberg, "The Limits of Papal Authority," *National Review*, August 24, 1964, 731.

26. Ibid., 732.

27. Murray Kempton, "Issues of Catholic Freedom," *National Review*, September 22, 1964, 829, 830, 831.

28. Buckley, "Our Mission Statement," *National Review*, November 19, 1955, http://www.nationalreview.com/article/223549/our-mission-statement-william-f-buckley-jr.

29. Garry Wills, *Confessions of a Conservative* (Garden City, N.Y.: Doubleday, 1979), 62.

30. Ibid., 63.

31. *Lumen gentium*, paragraph 22, available at http://www.vatican.va/archive/hist_coun cils/ii_vatican_council/documents/vat-ii_const_19641121_lumen-gentium_en.html, accessed December 23, 2019.

32. John O'Malley, *What Happened at Vatican II?* (Cambridge, Mass.: Harvard University Press, 2010), 301, 302, 303.

33. *Lumen gentium*, paragraph 22.

34. Ibid., paragraph 37.

5. The Extremities of Defending Liberty

1. Rick Perlstein, *Before the Storm: Barry Goldwater and the Unmaking of the American Consensus* (New York: Hill & Wang, 2001), 389.

2. Ibid., 413.

3. Ibid., 377, 378, 391.

4. Quoted in Mark D. Popowski, *The Rise and Fall of "Triumph": The History of a Radical Catholic Magazine, 1966–1976* (Lanham, Md.: Lexington Books, 2012), 3.

5. The best guide to the intellectual contours of 1950s conservatism is George H. Nash, *The Conservative Intellectual Movement in America, since 1945* (New York: Basic Books, 1976).

6. Quoted in Perlstein, *Before the Storm*, 13.

7. Barry Goldwater, *The Conscience of a Conservative* (Shepherdsville, Ky.: Victor, 1960), 14, 17, 20–22.

8. Ibid., 28, 29, 31, 32, 47, 48.

9. Ibid., 34, 37.

10. Quoted in John B. Judis, *William F. Buckley, Jr.: Patron Saint of the Conservatives* (New York: Simon & Schuster, 1991), 138–39.

11. Goldwater, *Conscience*, 122.

12. Quotations from Perlstein, *Before the Storm*, 94, 95.

13. Bozell, "National Trends," *National Review*, December 5, 1959, 515.

14. Bozell, "Goldwater's Leadership: An Assessment," *National Review*, August 13, 1960, 75.

15. Clarence Manion, *Lessons in Liberty: A Study of God in Government* (South Bend, Ind.: University of Notre Dame Press, 1939), 3, 4.

16. Ibid., 6–7.

17. Ibid., 14–15; italics in original.

18. Ibid., 21, 23, 25.

19. Ibid., 193, 196.

20. Clarence Manion, *The Conservative American: His Fight for National Independence and Constitutional Government* (New York: Devin-Adair, 1964), 6–9; italics in original.

21. Ibid., 27.

22. Ibid., 44.

23. See Duane Tananbaum, *The Bricker Amendment Controversy: A Test of Eisenhower's Political Leadership* (Ithaca, N.Y.: Cornell University Press, 1988), 46ff.

24. Manion, *Conservative American*, 116.

25. Ibid., 104.

26. Ibid., 129, 134.

27. Ibid., 129, 193, 198, 202.

28. Perlstein, *Before the Storm*, 105.

29. "The Sharon Statement," https://www.yaf.org/news/the-sharon-statement, accessed December 29, 2019.

30. Gregory L. Schneider, *Cadres for Conservatism: Young Americans for Freedom and the Rise of the Contemporary Right* (New York: New York University Press, 1999), 35.

31. Quoted ibid., 36.

32. Brent Bozell, "Challenge to Conservatives, II," *National Review*, January 14, 1961, 12.

33. Quoted in Judis, *William F. Buckley*, 198.

34. Buckley, "Soft on Communism," *National Review*, October 20, 1964, 905; William Rusher, "Crossroads for the GOP," *National Review*, February 12, 1963, 109–12.

35. Russell Kirk, "The Mind of Barry Goldwater," *National Review*, August 27, 1963, 149, 150.

36. Quoted in Judis, *William F. Buckley*, 222.

37. Ibid., 224.

38. Ibid., 230.

39. Ibid., 232.

6. The Limits of Americanism

1. Andrew Hartman, *A War for the Soul of America: A History of the Culture Wars* (Chicago: University of Chicago Press, 2015), 5.

2. Ibid., 14.

3. Quotations from George H. Nash, *The Conservative Intellectual Movement in America, since 1945* (New York: Basic Books, 1976), 281.

4. Quoted in Mark D. Popowski, *The Rise and Fall of Triumph: The History of a Radical Roman Catholic Magazine, 1966–1976* (Lanham, Md.: Lexington Books, 2012), 46.

5. L. Brent Bozell, Jr., *The Warren Revolution: Reflections on the Consensus Society* (New Rochelle, N.Y.: Arlington House, 1966), 22, 23.

6. Ibid., 25, 28, 29, 30, italics in original.

7. Ibid., 75, 77, italics in original.

8. Ibid., 78, 79.

9. See Daniel Kelly, *Living on Fire: The Life of L. Brent Bozell, Jr.* (Wilmington, Del.: ISI Books, 2014), 101–2, for a summary of the reception of *The Warren Court*.

10. L. Brent Bozell, Jr., "The Strange Drift of Liberal Catholicism," *National Review*, August 12, 1961, 85.

11. L. Brent Bozell, Jr., "Who Is Accommodating to What?," *National Review*, May 4, 1965, 377.

12. John B. Judis, *William F. Buckley, Jr.: Patron Saint of the Conservatives* (New York: Simon & Schuster, 1991), 319.

13. *The Best of Triumph* (Port Royal, Va.: Christendom Press, 2004), xx; Judis, *William F. Buckley*, 319.

14. L. Brent Bozell, Jr., "Death of the Constitution," in *Best of Triumph*, 385, 386.

15. Ibid., 389, 390, 391.

16. Warren H. Carroll, "The History of History," in *Best of Triumph*, 512, 517, 520.

17. W. H. Marshner, "Politique D'Abord," in *Best of Triumph*, 544, 545.

18. L. Brent Bozell, Jr., "*Humanae Vitae*, Part One: Thou Shalt Love Life," in *Best of Triumph*, 224.

19. Ibid., 230, 233.

20. Quoted in Popowski, *Rise and Fall of Triumph*, 115.

21. Ibid., 35, 36.

22. Ibid., 36.

23. Garry Wills, "Catholics and Population," *National Review*, July 27, 1965, 645, 646.

24. Ibid., 647.

25. Quotations from Patrick Allitt, "Catholic Conservative Intellectuals and the Politics of Sexuality," in *Church Polity and American Politics: Issues in Contemporary American Catholicism*, ed. Mary C. Segers (New York: Garland, 1990), 201, 200.

26. Garry Wills, *Lead Time: A Journalist's Education* (Garden City, N.Y.: Doubleday, 1983), ix.

27. Garry Wills, *The Second Civil War: Arming for Armageddon* (New York: New American Library, 1968), 166, 168.

28. Patrick Allitt, *Catholic Intellectuals and Conservative Politics in America, 1950–1985* (Ithaca, N.Y.: Cornell University Press, 1993), 266.

29. Garry Wills, *Nixon Agonistes: The Crisis of the Self-Made Man* (Boston: Houghton Mifflin, 1970), ix, 583.

30. Ibid., 581–82, 587, 588.

31. Ibid., 548–49.

32. Ibid., 550, 551, 553, 554, 556.

33. Frank S. Meyer, "Attack on Middle America," *National Review*, October 20, 1970, 1112, 1113.

34. Ibid.

35. Wills, *Nixon Agonistes*, 40.

36. Judis, *William F. Buckley*, 324, 325.

37. Wills, *Bare Ruined Choirs: Doubt, Prophecy, and Radical Religion* (Garden City, N.Y.: Doubleday, 1972), 9, 260.

38. Ibid., 246.

39. Ibid., 246, 247, 248.

40. Garry Wills, *Confessions of a Conservative* (Garden City, N.Y.: Doubleday, 1979), 213, 214; Carl T. Bogus, *Buckley: William F. Buckley Jr. and the Rise of American Conservatism* (New York: Bloomsbury, 2011), 325. In *Confessions*, 47, Wills relates his first awkward encounter with Kirk (along with Frank Meyer) and was never able to overcome that first impression.

41. Dietrich von Hildebrand, "The Case for the Latin Mass," in *Best of Triumph*, 65.

42. Editors, "Soul, Brother," in *Best of Triumph*, 343, 348.

43. L. Brent Bozell, Jr., "Khesahn? What's That?," in *Best of Triumph*, 420, 417.

44. Quoted in Judis, *William F. Buckley*, 340.

45. Ibid., 325–26.

46. Meyer, "Attack on Middle America," 1113.

7. Americanism Revived

1. Quoted in John B. Judis, *William F. Buckley, Jr.: Patron Saint of the Conservatives* (New York: Simon & Schuster, 1991), 361.

2. Ibid., 384.

3. Timothy A. Byrnes, *Catholic Bishops in American Politics* (Princeton, N.J.: Princeton University Press, 1991), 75ff, provides detail on the 1976 presidential campaign.

4. George Nash, *The Conservative Intellectual Movement in America, since 1945* (New York: Basic Books, 1976), 312.

5. Ibid.

6. Quoted in Patrick Allitt, *Catholic Intellectuals and Conservative Politics in America, 1950–1985* (Ithaca, N.Y.: Cornell University Press, 1993), 255.

7. Quoted in Damon Linker, *The Theocons: Secular America under Siege* (New York: Anchor Books, 2007), 30.

8. Michael Novak, "The Grand Inquisitor, Born Again," *National Review*, September 14, 1979, 1158, 1159.

9. Ibid., 1159.

10. Michael Novak, "Extremism as a Virtue," *National Review*, November 9, 1979, 1427; "Saints and Self-Interest," *National Review*, April 18, 1980, 476.

11. Michael Novak, "The Failure of 'Christian Politics,'" *National Review*, May 16, 1980, 603.

12. Michael Novak, "A Closed Church, Again," *National Review*, February 5, 1982, 113; "The Pope's Brilliant Encyclical," *National Review*, October 16, 1981, 1210; "Thinking about Equality," *National Review*, October 12, 1979, 1317.

13. Michael Novak, "The Bishops Speak Out," *National Review*, June 10, 1983, 681.

14. Richard John Neuhaus, "What the Synod Wrought," *National Review*, February 14, 1986, 29, 34.

15. Richard John Neuhaus, "Democratic Morality," *National Review*, July 18, 1986, 47; "God Save the Vulnerable Court," *National Review*, August 15, 1986, 40; "Policy by Pathology," *National Review*, December 5, 1986, 46.

16. Richard John Neuhaus, "Parochial Patriots," *National Review*, June 20, 1986, 46; "A Death Much Exaggerated," *National Review*, August 28, 1987, 44; "Testifying to Transcendence," *National Review*, September 12, 1986, 46.

17. Richard John Neuhaus, "Picking Fights by Proxy," *National Review*, October 10, 1986, 48.

18. Richard John Neuhaus, "Will It Liberate? Questions about Liberation Theology," *National Review*, March 13, 1987, 48; "*Tranquillitas ordinis*: The Present Failure and Future Promise of American Catholic Thought on War and Peace," *National Review*, April 10, 1987, 44.

19. Richard John Neuhaus, "The Catholic Moment," *National Review*, November 7, 1986, 46.

20. Richard John Neuhaus, *The Catholic Moment: The Paradox of the Church in the Postmodern World* (San Francisco: Harper & Row, 1987), 41–42. Subsequent references to page numbers appear parenthetically within the text.

21. Randy Boyagoda, *Richard John Neuhaus: A Life in the Public Square* (New York: Image, 2015), 224.

22. Andrew Sullivan, "Cross Purposes," *New Republic*, June 1, 1987, 33.

23. George Weigel, *Catholicism and the Renewal of American Democracy* (New York: Paulist Press, 1989), 47n1, 51, 69.

24. Ibid., 17, 19, 26.

25. Ibid., 43, 41, 44.

26. Ibid., 1, 98.

27. Ibid., 12.

28. Thomas Molnar, "The Ideology of *Aggiornamento*," *National Review*, May 4, 1965, 366; Will Herberg, "Open Season on the Church?," *National Review*, May 4, 1965, 364.

8. Americanism Redux

1. Jay Dolan, *The American Catholic Experience: A History from Colonial Times to the Present* (Garden City, N.Y.: Doubleday, 1984), 9.

2. Ibid., 424, 453, 454.

3. Richard John Neuhaus, *The Catholic Moment: The Paradox of the Church in the Postmodern World* (San Francisco: Harper & Row, 1987), 240, 247.

4. George Weigel, "Telling the American Catholic Story," *First Things*, November 1990, 48.

5. Francis Oakley gives an impressive account of the sacral monarchy origins of papal supremacy in *The Mortgage of the Past: Reshaping the Ancient Political Inheritance (1050–1300)* (New Haven, Conn.: Yale University Press, 2012).

6. Joseph P. Fitzpatrick, preface to *Nationalism and American Catholicism*, by Dorothy Dohen (New York: Sheed & Ward, 1967), ix, 6.

7. Dohen, *Nationalism and American Catholicism*, 58, 109.

8. Ibid., 183, 187.

9. Ibid., 8, 47, 48.

10. Bruce F. Biever, "Nationalism and American Catholicism," *America*, March 18, 1967, 67.

11. Philip Gleason, "Contemporary Catholicism and American History," *Review of Politics* 30, no. 1 (January 1968): 113.

12. Ibid.

13. Philip Gleason, *The Conservative Reformers: German-American Catholics and the Social Order* (Notre Dame, Ind.: University of Notre Dame Press, 1968).

14. Philip Gleason, "Catholicism and Cultural Change in the 1960s," *Review of Politics* 34, no. 4 (October 1972): 95, 94.

15. Philip Gleason, "Crisis of Americanization," in *Contemporary Catholicism in the United States*, ed. Philip Gleason (Notre Dame, Ind.: University of Notre Dame Press, 1969), 28.

16. Ibid.

17. James Hennesey, *American Catholics: A History of the Roman Catholic Community in the United States* (New York: Oxford University Press, 1981), 196, 198, 203.

18. Ibid., 314.

19. Ibid., 331.

20. Gerald Fogarty, *The Vatican and the American Hierarchy from 1870 to 1965* (Wilmington, Del.: Michael Glazier, 1985), 402, 403.

21. Ibid., 204, 235.

22. Ibid., xviii, xvii.

23. Dolan, *American Catholic Experience*, 310, 316.

24. Ibid., 236–39.

25. Ibid., 319.

26. Philip Gleason, "The New Americanism in Catholic Historiography," *U.S. Catholic Historian* 11, no. 3 (July 1993): 1–18.

27. Joseph A. Varacalli, *Toward the Establishment of Liberal Catholicism in America* (Lanham, Md.: University Press of America, 1983), 10.

28. Ibid., 151.

29. David O'Brien, *Public Catholicism* (New York: Macmillan, 1989), 244, 247.

30. Ibid., 251, 252.

31. David Schindler, "Is America Bourgeois?," *Communio* 14 (Fall 1987): 270, 273.

32. Ibid., 276, 282, 283, 288.

33. David Schindler, "Religious Freedom, Truth, and American Liberalism: Another Look at John Courtney Murray," *Communio* 21 (Winter 1994): 711.

34. Ibid., 704, 740.

35. Ibid., 720, 739.

36. Thomas Storck, "American Idolatry," *Fidelity*, May 1990, 8.

37. Michael Sean Winters, "Balthasar's Feast," *New Republic*, August 30, 1999, 40.

38. "The End of Democracy? The Judicial Usurpation of Politics," *First Things*, November 1996, https://www.firstthings.com/article/1996/11/the-end-of-democracy-the-judicial-usurpation-of-politics.

39. David S. Toolan, "The 'Catholic Moment' under Siege," *America*, March 1, 1997, 3, 4.
40. Ibid., 9.
41. Gertrude Himmelfarb, "On the Future of Conservatism," *Commentary*, February 1997, https://www.commentarymagazine.com/articles/on-the-future-of-conservatism/.
42. Jacob Heilbrunn, "Neocon v. Theocon," *New Republic*, December 30, 1996, 24.
43. Michael Novak et al., "Neocon v. Theocon: An Exchange," *New Republic*, February 3, 1997, 28.

Conclusion

1. Quoted in Randy Boyagoda, *Richard John Neuhaus: A Life in the Public Square* (New York: Image, 2015), 339–40.
2. Richard John Neuhaus, "The Two Politics of the Election 2000," *First Things*, February 2001, https://www.firstthings.com/article/2001/02/the-two-politics-of-election.
3. The Editors, "In a Time of War," *First Things*, December 2001, https://www.firstthings.com/article/2001/12/in-a-time-of-war.
4. See the following articles by Richard John Neuhaus in *First Things*: "Dechristianizing America," June 2006, https://www.firstthings.com/article/2006/06/dechristianizing-america; "The 45 Years That Might Have Been," December 2005, https://www.firstthings.com/article/2005/12/the-years-that-might-have-been; "America as a Religion," April 2005, https://www.firstthings.com/article/2005/04/america-as-a-religion.
5. Quoted in Boyagoda, *Richard John Neuhaus*, 363.
6. Damon Linker, *Theocons: Secular America under Siege* (New York: Doubleday, 2006), xiii–xiv.
7. Ross Douthat and Damon Linker, "American Catholicism," *New Republic*, October 9, 2006, https://newrepublic.com/article/61657/american-catholicism.
8. United States Conference of Catholic Bishops (USCCB), "Our First, Most Cherished Liberty: A Statement on Religious Liberty," http://www.usccb.org/issues-and-action/religious-liberty/our-first-most-cherished-liberty.cfm, accessed January 8, 2020.
9. USCCB, "Mary Immaculate Patroness of Our Country, Pray for Us," 2012, http://www.usccb.org/issues-and-action/religious-liberty/upload/Immaculate-Conception-English.pdf.
10. USCCB, "Our First, Most Cherished Liberty." All quotations in this section are from this document.
11. Anthony Faiola, "8 of Pope Francis' Most Liberal Statements," *Washington Post*, September 7, 2015, https://www.washingtonpost.com/news/worldviews/wp/2015/09/07/what-has-pope-francis-actually-accomplished-heres-a-look-at-7-of-his-most-notable-actions; James Hohmann and Elise Viebeck, "The Daily 202: Pope Francis Visit Puts Republicans on the Defensive," *Washington Post*, September 21, 2015, https://www.washingtonpost.com/news/powerpost/wp/2015/09/21/the-daily-202-pope-francis-visit-puts-republicans-on-the-defensive; Candida Moss quoted in Greg Jaffe and Juliet Eilperin, "In Pope Francis's Visit, White House Sees a Chance to Transcend Politics," *Washington Post*, September 17, 2015, https://www.washingtonpost.com/politics/in-pope-franciss-visit-white-house-sees-a-chance-to-transcend-politics/2015/09/17/af60fbf4-5d60-11e5-8e9e-dce8a2a2a679_story.html/.
12. Chris Cillizza, "Pope Francis' Speech to Congress," September 24, 2015, https://www.washingtonpost.com/news/the-fix/wp/2015/09/24/pope-franciss-speech-to-congress-annotated/?utm_term=.921a9f13f1f4.
13. "Pope Francis' Remarks at Independence Hall," September 26, 2015, https://www.nytimes.com/2015/09/26/us/pope-francis-remarks-at-independence-hall.html.

14. "Remarks by President Obama and His Holiness Pope Francis at Arrival Ceremony," September 23, 2015, https://www.whitehouse.gov/the-press-office/2015/09/23/remarks-president-obama-and-his-holiness-pope-francis-arrival-ceremony.

15. "Pope Francis' Remarks at Independence Hall."

16. William Galston, "The Bishops and Religious Liberty," *Commonweal*, May 30, 2012, https://www.commonwealmagazine.org/bishops-religious-liberty.

17. Ibid.

18. Ibid.

19. Ross Douthat, "The Plot to Change Catholicism," *New York Times*, October 17, 2015, https://www.nytimes.com/2015/10/18/opinion/sunday/the-plot-to-change-catholicism.html.

20. "To the Editor of the New York Times," reprinted at *(DT) Daily Theology*, October 26, 2015, https://dailytheology.org/2015/10/26/to-the-editor-of-the-new-york-times/.

21. Romanus Cessario, "*Non Possumus*," *First Things*, February 2018, https://www.first things.com/article/2018/02/non-possumus.

22. Matthew Franck, "A Needless Quarrel: On Edgardo Mortara and First Things," *Weekly Standard*, January 18, 2018, https://www.weeklystandard.com/matthew-j-franck/ a-needless-quarrel-on-edgardo-mortara-and-first-things; Robert George quoted in Rod Dreher, "The Edgardo Mortara Case," *American Conservative*, January 9, 2018, http://www. theamericanconservative.com/dreher/the-edgardo-mortara-case; Michael Sean Winters, "Fr. Cessario's Edgardo Mortara Essay Is Inexcusable," *National Catholic Reporter*, January 19, 2018, https://www.ncronline.org/news/people/distinctly-catholic/fr-cessarios-edgardo-mortara-essay-inexcusable; Kevin J. Madigan, "We Cannot Accept This: A Response to Romanus Cessario's 'Non Possumus,'" *Commonweal*, January 25, 2018, https://www.commonwealmaga zine.org/we-cannot-accept.

23. R. R. Reno, "Judaism, Christianity, and *First Things*," *First Things*, January 12, 2018, https://www.firstthings.com/web-exclusives/2018/01/judaism-christianity-and-first-things.

24. Nathan Shields, "The Church's Once-Notorious Seizure of a Jewish Child Is Back. Why?," *Mosaic*, March 5, 2018, https://mosaicmagazine.com/essay/history-ideas/2018/03/the-churchs-once-notorious-seizure-of-a-jewish-child-is-back-why/; Nathan Shields, "Should Religious People Affirm the Modern Liberal Order, or Reject It?," *Mosaic*, March 26, 2018, https:// mosaicmagazine.com/response/history-ideas/2018/03/should-religious-people-affirm-the-modern-liberal-order-or-reject-it/.

25. "Letters," *First Things*, January 2018, https://www.firstthings.com/article/2018/01/ letters; Adrian Vermeule, "A Christian Strategy," *First Things*, November 2017, https://www. firstthings.com/article/2017/11/a-christian-strategy; Adrian Vermeule, "As Secular Liberalism Attacks the Church, Catholics Can't Afford to Be Nostalgic," *Catholic Herald*, January 5, 2018.

26. R. Scott Appleby, "The Triumph of Americanism: Common Ground for U.S. Catholics in the Twentieth Century," in *Being Right: Conservative Catholics in America*, ed. Mary Jo Weaver and R. Scott Appleby (Bloomington: University of Indiana Press, 1995), 40.

27. On intellectual conservatism and its links to politics, see George H. Nash, *The Conservative Intellectual Movement in America* (Wilmington, Del.: ISI Books, 2006); Patrick Allitt, *Catholic Intellectuals and Conservative Politics in America, 1950–1985* (Ithaca, N.Y.: Cornell University Press, 1993); Patrick Allitt, *The Conservatives: Ideas and Personalities throughout American History* (New Haven, Conn.: Yale University Press, 2009), chaps. 6–10.

28. See, for instance, James Davison Hunter, *Culture Wars: The Struggle to Define America* (New York: Basic Books, 1991); Mark A. Noll and Carolyn Nystrom, *Is the Reformation Over? An Evangelical Assessment of Contemporary Roman Catholicism* (Grand Rapids, Mich.: Baker Books, 2005).

29. James Chappel, *Catholic Modern: The Challenge of Totalitarianism and the Remaking of the Church* (Cambridge, Mass.: Harvard University Press, 2018), 257.

30. Massimo Faggioli, "The Church in the Trump Era: Catholicism or Americanism?," *La Croix International*, November 14, 2016, https://international.la-croix.com/news/the-church-in-the-trump-era-catholicism-or-americanism/4200.

31. David J. O'Brien, "Catholic Americanism: Past, Present, Future," in *Weaving the American Catholic Tapestry: Essays in Honor of William L. Portier*, ed. Derek C. Hatch and Timothy R. Gabrielli (Eugene, Ore.: Pickwick, 2017), 107.

BIBLIOGRAPHIC ESSAY

This book should fall squarely in the secondary literature on the history of religion and politics or church-state relations in the United States. Perhaps because Roman Catholicism possesses a version of exceptionalism almost as pronounced as the American expression, very often the history of Protestants and their denominations have framed discussions about church-state relations to the exclusion of Rome and its American structures. An older set of contributions to the subject of religion and public life involved the place of Christianity in a secular society such as the United States. Some of those inquiries included Stephen L. Carter, *The Culture of Disbelief: How American Law and Politics Trivialize Religious Devotion* (New York: Anchor Books, 1993); Richard John Neuhaus, *The Naked Public Square: Religion and Democracy in America* (Grand Rapids, Mich.: Eerdmans, 1984); Garry Wills, *Under God: Religion and American Politics* (New York: Simon & Schuster, 1990); Glenn E. Tinder, *The Political Meaning of Christianity: An Interpretation* (Baton Rouge: Louisiana State University Press, 1989); Isaac Kramnick and R. Laurence Moore,

244 *Bibliographic Essay*

The Godless Constitution: The Case against Religious Correctness (New York: W. W. Norton, 1996); Mark A. Noll, George M. Marsden, and Nathan O. Hatch, *The Search for Christian America* (1983; Colorado Springs, Colo.: Helmers & Howard, 1989); Frank Lambert, *Religion in American Politics: A Short History* (Princeton, N.J.: Princeton University Press, 2010); Philip Hamburger, *Separation of Church and State* (Cambridge, Mass.: Harvard University Press, 2002); Steven Green, *The Second Disestablishment: Church and State in Nineteenth-Century America* (New York: Oxford University Press, 2010); and Mark A. Noll and Luke E. Harlow, eds., *Religion and American Politics: From the Colonial Period to the Present* (1992; New York: Oxford University Press, 2007).

Once the religious Right (and especially evangelical Protestants) became such a sizable portion of the Republican Party's base, much of the historical literature shifted to explanations of how evangelicals gained such clout. Books that reveal that side of religion-and-politics discussions include Randall Balmer, *Thy Kingdom Come: How the Religious Right Distorts the Faith and Threatens America: An Evangelical's Lament* (New York: Basic Books, 2006); Darren Dochuk, *From Bible Belt to Sunbelt: Plain-Folk Religion, Grassroots Politics, and the Rise of Evangelical Conservatism* (New York: W. W. Norton, 2010); Daniel K. Williams, *God's Own Party: The Making of the Christian Right* (New York: Oxford University Press, 2010); John Fea, *Was America Founded as a Christian Nation? A Historical Introduction* (Louisville, Ky.: Westminster/John Knox, 2011); D. G. Hart, *From Billy Graham to Sarah Palin: Evangelicals and the Betrayal of American Conservatism* (Grand Rapids, Mich.: Eerdmans, 2011); and R. Marie Griffith, *Moral Combat: How Sex Divided American Christians and Fractured American Politics* (New York: Basic Books, 2017).

Meanwhile, the broad and extensive literature about church-state relations with Roman Catholics in the United States in view remained a separate arena for investigation and interpretation. The following paragraphs that either put Roman Catholics and political conservatism since World War II into a broader perspective or examine this history's specific features only include secondary sources. But those curious should also keep in mind and consult the vast number of scholarly articles published in *U.S. Catholic Historian*, the journal that began in 1983 under the auspices of the United States Catholic Historical Society. The American Catholic Historical Association started in 1919 and publishes articles on the global church in a variety of times and places. Its journal, the *Catholic Histori-cal Review*, is also a storehouse of mature scholarship in Roman Catholic history in the United States. In addition to those periodicals, this book has relied heavily on the magazines that politically conservative Roman Catholics founded, including *National Review, First Things, Triumph, Modern Age, Intercollegiate Studies Review,* and *University Bookman.* For the reception of Roman Catholic conservative writings and arguments by members of the American church, *Commonweal, America,* and *Theological Studies* are valuable.

For broader assessments of Roman Catholics in the United States, several surveys are reliable: John Tracy Ellis, *American Catholicism* (Chicago: University of Chicago Press, 1956); James J. Hennesey, American Catholics: *A History of the Roman Catholic Community in the United States* (New York: Oxford University Press, 1981); Jay P. Dolan, *The American Catholic Experience: A History from Colonial Times to the Present* (Garden City, N.Y.: Doubleday, 1985); and Charles Morris, *American Catholic: The Saints and Sinners Who Built America's Most Powerful Church* (New York: Vintage, 1998).

The Americanist controversy is one of the most important topics for understanding the relationship of Roman Catholicism to the United States and its political traditions (including especially religious liberty). The place to start is with Gerald P. Fogarty and his two books, *The Vatican and the Americanist Crisis: Denis J. O'Connell, American Agent in Rome* (Rome: Miscellanea Historiae Pontificiae, 1974), and *The Vatican and the American Hierarchy from 1870 to 1965* (Stuttgart: Anton Hiersemann, 1982). Other important works include Thomas T. McAvoy, *The Great Crisis in American Catholic History, 1895–1900* (Chicago: Regnery, 1957); Robert D. Cross, *The Emergence of Liberal Catholicism in America* (Cambridge, Mass.: Harvard University Press, 1958); and Andrew Greeley, *The Catholic Experience: An Interpretation of the History of American Catholicism* (Garden City, N.Y.: Doubleday, 1967). For studies of important figures in the American church during the controversy, readers should consult Robert Emmett Curran, *Michael Augustine Corrigan and the Shaping of Conservative Catholicism in America, 1878–1902* (New York: Arno, 1978); Patrick Carey, *An Immigrant Bishop: John England's Adaptation of Irish Catholicism to American Republicanism* (New York: U.S. Catholic Historical Society, 1982); David F. Sweeney, *The Life of*

John Lancaster Spalding, First Bishop of Peoria, 1840–1916 (New York: Herder & Herder, 1965); Marvin R. O'Connell, *John Ireland and the American Catholic Church* (St. Paul: Minnesota Historical Society, 1988); and John Farina, *An American Experience of God: The Spirituality of Isaac Hecker* (New York: Paulist Press, 1981).

Related to the actual features of the United States that troubled Vatican officials is the national character of the church that took root. Here readers should consult the following: Peter D'Agostino, *Rome in America: Transnational Catholic Ideology from the Risorgimento to Fascism* (Chapel Hill: University of North Carolina Press, 2004); R. Scott Appleby and Kathleen Sprows Cummings, eds., *Catholics in the American Century: Recasting Narratives of U.S. History* (Ithaca, N.Y.: Cornell University Press, 2012); John McGreevy, *Catholicism and American Freedom: A History* (New York: W. W. Norton, 2004); Mark S. Massa, *Catholics and American Culture: Fulton Sheen, Dorothy Day, and the Notre Dame Football Team* (New York: Crossroad, 1999); Philip Gleason, ed., *Contemporary Catholicism in the United States* (Notre Dame, Ind.: University of Notre Dame Press, 1969); Philip Gleason, *Keeping the Faith: American Catholicism Past and Present* (Notre Dame, Ind.: University of Notre Dame Press, 1987); Andrew M. Greeley, *American Catholic: A Social Portrait* (New York: Basic Books, 1977); and John T. Noonan, Jr., *The Lustre of Our Country: The American Experience of Religious Freedom* (Berkeley: University of California Press, 1998).

An important factor in the national identity of Roman Catholicism in the United States was anti-Catholicism. For insightful perspectives on anti-Catholic prejudice in the United States, see John Higham, *Strangers in the Land: Patterns of American Nativism, 1860–1925* (New Brunswick, N.J.: Rutgers University Press, 1955); Mark S. Massa, *Anti-Catholicism in America: The Last Acceptable Prejudice* (New York: Crossroad, 2005); Philip Jenkins, *The New Anti-Catholicism: The Last Acceptable Prejudice* (New York: Oxford University Press); and Justin Nordstrom, *Danger on the Doorstep: Anti-Catholicism in American Print Culture* (Bloomington: Indiana University Press, 2003).

On the specific ties between Roman Catholics and political conservatism after World War II, the following are essential reading: George H. Nash, *The Conservative Intellectual Movement in America, since 1945* (New York: Basic Books, 1979); Patrick Allitt, *Catholic Intellectuals and*

Conservative Politics in America, 1950–1985 (Ithaca, N.Y.: Cornell University Press, 1985), which set the standard for evaluating many of the figures covered in this book. Other useful works on Roman Catholics and American conservatism include Patrick Allitt, *The Conservatives: Ideas and Personalities throughout American History* (New Haven, Conn.: Yale University Press, 2009); Ronald Lora, *Conservative Minds in America* (New York: Rand McNally, 1917); Donald T. Critchlow, *Phyllis Schlafly and Grassroots Conservatism: A Woman's Crusade* (Princeton, N.J.: Princeton University Press, 2005); Rick Perlstein, *Before the Storm: Barry Goldwater and the Unmaking of the American Consensus* (New York: Hill & Wang, 2009); Kim Phillips-Fein, *Invisible Hands: The Making of the Conservative Movement from the New Deal to Reagan* (New York: W. W. Norton, 2009); and Sam Tanenhaus, *The Death of Conservatism: A Movement and Its Consequences* (New York: Random House, 2010).

William F. Buckley, Jr., and Russell Kirk are among the Roman Catholic political conservatives to receive the most attention. The most useful guides include John B. Judis, *William F. Buckley, Jr.: Patron Saint of the Conservatives* (New York: Simon & Schuster, 1988); Carl T. Bogus, *Buckley: William F. Buckley Jr. and the Rise of American Conservatism* (New York: Bloomsbury, 2011); Jeremy Lott, *William F. Buckley* (Nashville: Thomas Nelson, 2010); Alvin S. Felzenberg, *A Man and His Presidents: The Political Odyssey of William F. Buckley Jr.* (New Haven, Conn.: Yale University Press, 2017); Bradley J. Birzer, *Russell Kirk: American Conservatism* (Lexington: The University Press of Kentucky, 2015); W. Wesley McDonald, *Russell Kirk and the Age of Ideology* (Columbia: Missouri University Press, 2004); and James E. Person, *Russell Kirk: A Critical Biography of a Conservative Mind* (Lanham, Md.: Madison Books, 1999).

Brent Bozell has also received limited attention in Daniel Kelly, *Living on Fire: The Life of Brent Bozell, Jr.* (Wilmington, Del.: ISI Books, 2014); and Mark D. Popowski, *The Rise and Fall of* Triumph: *The History of a Radical Catholic Magazine, 1966–1976* (Lanham, Md.: Lexington Books, 2012).

Because of Buckley's and Bozell's work for Senator Joseph McCarthy, anticommunism's contribution to political conservatism is another path of investigation. Particularly useful here are Donald Crosby, *God, Church, and Flag: Senator Joseph R. McCarthy and the Catholic Church,*

1950–1957 (Chapel Hill: University of North Carolina Press, 1978); Thomas C. Reeves, *The Life and Times of Joe McCarthy: A Biography* (New York: Stein & Day, 1982); and for earlier currents, Alan Brinkley, *Voices of Protest: Huey Long, Father Coughlin, and the Great Depression* (New York: Alfred A. Knopf, 1982).

Treatments of the figures surrounding *First Things* have been less numerous, but the following provide insight: Randy Boyagoda, *Richard John Neuhaus: A Life in the Public Square* (New York: Image, 2015); Damon Linker, *The Theocons: Secular America under Siege* (New York: Knopf/Doubleday, 2007); and Todd Scribner, *A Partisan Church: American Catholicism and the Rise of Neo-Conservative Catholics* (Washington, D.C.: Catholic University of America Press, 2015).

The theological inspiration for practically every patriotic American Roman Catholic after the Second Vatican Council was the Jesuit priest John Courtney Murray. Discussions of his contributions to the American church can be found in J. Leon Hooper, ed., *John Courtney Murray: Religious Liberty, Catholic Struggles with Pluralism* (Louisville, Ky.: Westminster / John Knox Press, 1993); Thomas T. Love, *John Courtney Murray: Contemporary Church State Theory* (New York: Doubleday, 1965); Donald E. Pelotte, *John Courtney Murray: Theologian in Conflict* (New York: Paulist Press, 1976); Barry Hudock, *Struggle, Condemnation, Vindication: John Courtney Murray's Journey toward Vatican II* (Collegeville, Minn.: Liturgical Press, 2015); Keith J. Pavlischek, *John Courtney Murray and the Dilemma of Religious Toleration* (Kirksville, Mo.: Truman State University Press, 1994); and John Witte, Jr., and Frank S. Alexander, eds., *The Teachings of Modern Roman Catholicism on Law, Politics, and Human Nature* (New York: Columbia University Press, 2007).

The experience of Roman Catholics who ran for political office—particularly the president of the United States—yields another perspective on the church's relationship to American polity. The biographies of Alfred E. Smith and John F. Kennedy are especially revealing and include Robert A. Slayton, *Empire Statesman: The Rise and Redemption of Al Smith* (New York: Free Press, 2007); Allan J. Lichtman, *Prejudice and Old Politics: The Presidential Election of 1928* (Chapel Hill: University of North Carolina Press, 1979); Robert Dallek, *An Unfinished Life: John F. Kennedy, 1917–1963* (New York: Back Bay Books, 2004); Thomas C. Reeves, *A Question of Character: A Life of John F. Kennedy* (New York:

Free Press, 1991); Lawrence H. Fuchs, *John F. Kennedy and American Catholicism* (New York: Meredith Press, 1967); Shaun Casey, *The Making of a Catholic President: Kennedy vs. Nixon 1960* (New York: Oxford University Press, 2009); W. J. Rorabaugh, *The Real Making of the President: Kennedy, Nixon, and the 1960 Election* (Lawrence: University of Kansas Press, 2009); and Gary Scott Smith, *Faith and the Presidency: From George Washington to George W. Bush* (New York: Oxford University Press, 2009).

A related consideration to the presidency is the place of Roman Catholics within the American electorate. Here the literature is vast, but these titles are helpful for beginning to make sense of the issues: Lawrence McAndrews, *What They Wished For: American Catholics and American Presidents, 1960–2004* (Athens: University of Georgia Press, 2013); John McGreevy, *Parish Boundaries: The Catholic Encounter with Race in the Urban North* (Chicago: University of Chicago Press, 1997); Gerald Gamm, *Urban Exodus: Why the Jews Left Boston and the Catholics Stayed* (Cambridge, Mass.: Harvard University Press, 1999); Mary Lethert Wingerd, *Claiming the City: Politics, Faith, and the Power of Place in St. Paul* (Ithaca, N.Y.: Cornell University Press, 2001); Evelyn Savidge Sterne, *Ballots and Bibles: Ethnic Politics and the Catholic Church in Providence* (Ithaca, N.Y.: Cornell University Press, 2004); Joshua M. Zeitz, *White Ethnic New York: Jews, Catholics, and the Shaping of Postwar Politics* (Chapel Hill: University of North Carolina Press, 2007); Mary Jo Weaver, ed., *What's Left? Liberal American Catholics* (Bloomington: Indiana University Press, 1999); and Mary Jo Weaver and R. Scott Appleby, eds., *Being Right: Conservative Catholics in America* (Bloomington: Indiana University Press, 1995).

One final set of considerations about political conservatism and Roman Catholicism in the United States concerns modernity, liberalism, and the Vatican's responses and adaptations to changes in the West since 1500. On the meaning of the major councils from Trent to Vatican II, the following are essential: John W. O'Malley, *Trent: What Happened at the Council?* (Cambridge, Mass.: Belknap/Harvard University Press, 2013); John W. O'Malley, *Vatican I: The Council and the Making of the Ultramontane Church* (Cambridge, Mass.: Belknap/Harvard University Press, 2018); John W. O'Malley, *What Happened at Vatican II* (Cambridge, Mass.: Belknap/Harvard University Press, 2010); Raymond F. Bulman and Frederick J. Parrella, eds., *From Trent to Vatican II: Historical and Theological Investigations* (New York: Oxford University Press, 2006); and Adrian Hastings, ed., *Modern Catholicism: Vatican II and After* (New York: Oxford University Press, 1990).

On the sometimes adversarial relationship between the church's hierarchy and modern political developments (especially liberalism and personal freedoms), readers should use R. Bruce Douglas and David Hollenbach, eds., *Catholicism and Liberalism: Contributions to American Public Policy* (Cambridge: Cambridge University Press, 1994); John Witte, Jr., and Frank S. Alexander, eds., *The Teachings of Modern Christianity on Law, Politics, and Human Nature* (New York: Columbia University Press, 2006); David Hempton and Hugh McLeod, eds., *Secularization and Religious Innovation in the North Atlantic World* (New York: Oxford University Press, 2017); Michael J. Lacey and Francis Oakley, eds., *The Crisis of Authority in Catholic Modernity* (New York: Oxford University Press, 2011); Francis Oakley, *The Conciliarist Tradition: Constitutionalism in the Catholic Church, 1300–1870* (New York: Oxford University Press, 2003); Leslie Woodcock Tentler, ed., *The Church Confronts Modernity: Catholicism since 1950 in the United States, Ireland, and Quebec* (Washington, D.C.: Catholic University of America Press, 2007); Leslie Woodcock Tentler, *Catholics and Contraception: An American History* (Ithaca, N.Y.: Cornell University Press, 2004); John Pollard, *The Papacy in the Age of Totalitarianism, 1914–1958* (Oxford: Oxford University Press, 2014); and James Chappel, *Catholic Modern: The Challenge of Totalitarianism and the Remaking of the Church* (Cambridge, Mass.: Harvard University Press, 2018).

Lest readers unfamiliar with Roman Catholic history take away the impression that the church's hierarchy was reactionary throughout the entire modern era, the church's teaching about society, including modern developments, should be kept in mind. The following are useful compendiums or summaries of the major elements in Roman Catholic social thought: Kenneth R. Himes, ed., *Modern Catholic Social Teaching: Commentaries and Interpretations* (Washington, D.C.: Georgetown University Press, 2005); David J. O'Brien and Thomas A. Shannon, eds., *Catholic Social Thought: The Documentary Heritage* (Maryknoll, N.Y.: Orbis Books, 2005); George Weigel and Robert Royal, eds., *A Century of Catholic Social Thought: Essays on "Rerum Novarum" and Nine Other Key*

Documents (Washington, D.C.: Ethics and Public Policy Center, 1991); Charles E. Curran, *Catholic Social Teaching, 1891–Present: A Historical, Theological, and Ethical Analysis* (Washington, D.C.: Georgetown University Press, 2002); J. S. Boswell, F. P. McHugh, and J. Verstraeten, eds., *Catholic Social Thought: Twilight or Renaissance?* (Leuven: Leuven University Press, 2002); and Michael J. Schuck, *That They May Be One: The Social Teaching of the Papal Encyclicals, 1740–1989* (Washington, D.C.: Georgetown University Press, 1991).

INDEX

abortion, 144, 147–48, 151, 161, 170, 201, 204, 209
Adams, John, 174
aggiornamento, 90, 143, 147, 183, 191
Allitt, Patrick, 7, 152
America, as Christian nation, 10–11, 27, 182, 210
America First Committee, 127
America (magazine), 90, 95, 101–5, 107, 142, 226
American Church (Roman Catholic)
    adaptation of, 224
    and American greatness, 162
    assimilation into America, 2, 36–37, 57–58, 171, 173
    as church of immigrants, 25–26, 28
    conservatism of, 113
    dual identity of, 193–94
    and liberalism, 224

patriotism of, 27–29, 31, 55, 86
political conservatism, of, 121
in public office, 18–19, 146
as a threat to America, 36–37
upward mobility of, 35, 40
American Constitution, 83, 85, 121, 124–25, 127, 131, 139–42, 145–46, 159
American Enterprise Institute, 13, 163, 166
American exceptionalism, xi, 28, 59, 64, 123–24, 128–29, 147
Americanism, as heresy, 5, 14, 23, 71, 87, 196
American War of Independence, 21
anti-Catholicism, 16, 35, 73, 214, 225
anticommunism, 91, 100, 102, 129, 131–32, 164, 167
anti-Semitism, 223
antiwar movement, 163–64

Appleby, R. Scott, 6, 224
Arkes, Hadley, 204
assimilation, 2, 28, 34, 36–37, 40,
    57–58, 173, 196, 197
Augustine, 157, 214

Balthasar, Hans Urs von, 200
Baroody, Bill, 133–34
Bay of Pigs invasion, 58
Bea, Augustin Cardinal, 78, 79, 82
Beard, Charles, 179
Beecher, Lyman, 52
Bellah, Robert, 63, 198
Bell, Daniel, 13
Benedict XIV, Pope, 103
Benedict XV, Pope, 29
Benedict XVI, Pope, 77, 213, 214, 225
Benedict of Nursia, 221
Berger, Peter, 165, 171, 178, 205
Berns, Walter, 206
Berrigan, Daniel, 155, 156, 163, 186
Berrigan, Phillip, 155, 156, 186
Biever, Bruce F., 189
Bill of Rights, 55, 136, 141
Blanshard, Brand, 93
Blanshard, Paul, 5, 9, 16, 35–38, 40, 41,
    52, 55, 56, 62, 73, 93, 95, 100, 224
Boas, George, 35
Bogus, Carl T., 157
Boniface VIII, Pope, 104–5
Bork, Robert H., 204
Bouyer, Louis, 200
Boyagoda, Randy, 177, 209
Bozell, L. Brent, 13, 16, 95–97, 116,
    133, 203
    anticommunism of, 149
    break from Americanism, 138, 148,
        159
    break with Buckley, 143–44, 179
    childhood and education, 114–15
    on contraception, 150, 151
    as ghostwriter for Goldwater, 114,
        116–21
    in Spain, 138–39
    traditionalism of, 157–59, 179

and *Triumph* magazine, 143–45,
    146–49
Bricker Amendment, 116, 127
Brown, Robert McAfee, 78, 163
Brown v. Board of Education (1954),
    118–19
Buchanan, Patrick J., 114
Buckley, William F., Jr., 7, 8–9, 11, 12,
    13–14, 70, 89–90
    on abortion, 151
    Americanism of, 15, 99, 184–85, 225
    anticommunism of, 95–97, 100
    avoided discussing religion, 206
    childhood and education, 90–92
    on faith and politics, 16
    on federal government, 204
    friendliness of, 91
    on future of conservatism, 160–61
    and Goldwater campaign, 132–34
    individualism of, 223
    on Nixon, 160
    on Pope John XXIII, 99–100, 102,
        109
    on race relations, 119
    sparring with Wills, 155
    split with Bozell, 143–44, 179
    on Yale, 8–9, 11, 91–95, 97, 172, 182
Bundy, McGeorge, 62, 94–95
Burke, Edmund, 153, 157
Burnham, James, 97–98
Bush, George W., 209–10, 215

Cahensly, Peter Paul, 23
Callahan, Daniel, 196
capitalism, 69–70, 98–99, 153,
    165–67, 205
capital punishment, 170
Carey, George, 142
Carroll, John, 190, 196, 198, 213
Carroll, Warren H., 146
Carter, Jimmy, 161, 167
"Catholic Moment," 177, 186, 202
"Catonsville Nine," 176
Cavalli, Fiorello, 73
Cessario, Romanus, 222

"Challenge of Peace" (U.S. Catholic Bishops), 168
Chambers, Whittaker, 97–98, 170
Chappel, James, 13–14, 225
Chesterton, G. K., 154
Christendom, 138, 148–49, 191, 202–3, 207, 221
Christiansen, Drew, 72
church and state
  in *Declaration of Religious Freedom*, 83–85
  Kennedy on, 47, 49, 53–54, 64
  Murray on, 4, 38–40, 73–75, 80–81, 82
  Roman Catholics on, 37–38, 191, 222
  Second Vatican Council on, 148
  Warren court on, 141
Cicognani, Amleto, 41–42
"city upon a hill" rhetoric, 59–61, 87
civil religion, 27, 59–61, 63–64, 118–19, 188, 198
civil rights movement, 40, 54–55, 58, 163
classical liberalism, 154, 167
Clergy and Laity Concerned about Vietnam, 163, 164
clericalization, 167
Coffin, Henry Sloane, 94
Cold War, 58, 107–8, 168
Colson, Charles (Chuck), 182, 204
Commentary (magazine), 206
Commonweal (magazine), 142, 144, 216–18, 220, 222
communism, 13, 14, 15, 96, 97, 107, 119–20, 126, 128–29, 136, 143, 173
conciliarism, 29, 77, 110
Congar, Yves, 77, 173
Congregation for the Doctrine of the Faith, 171, 176, 199
Congregation for the Propagation of the Faith, 194
Connell, Francis J., 39, 42, 74
Conscience of a Conservative (Goldwater), 114, 116–20, 125, 133
constitutionalism, 42–43, 140, 164, 201

constitutional liberalism, 38–39
contraception, 58, 147, 150–51
Coughlin, Charles, 34
Council of Trent, 173, 192
Criswell, W. A., 53
Critchlow, Donald, 9
Cross, Robert D., 196
Cuban Missile Crisis, 58, 66
culture wars, 59
Cuomo, Mario, 170
Cushing, Richard Cardinal, 46, 47, 61–62, 63, 68

Dallek, Robert, 45
Davis, Thomas N., 101–2
Dawson, Christopher, 200
Day, Dorothy, 34, 215
Declaration of Independence, 124–25, 146, 204, 215
Declaration of Religious Freedom, 83–87
democratic capitalism, 166–67
democratic morality, 169
Deneen, Patrick, 221
de Smedt, Joseph M., 80
devotional Catholicism, 195–96
Dewey, John, 35, 118
Diamond, Martin, 142
Dohen, Dorothy, 187–90
Dolan, Jay P., 2, 185–87, 195–97
Douthat, Ross, 212, 218–20
Dreher, Rod, 221
Duffy, Francis P., 30–31, 38
Dulles, Avery Cardinal, 177
Dunne, George H., 143
Dupanloup, Félix, 22, 73
Dwight, Timothy, 10

Edwards, Lee, 144
Eighteenth Amendment, 140
Eisenhower, Dwight, 46, 52, 98, 116, 128, 132, 153, 158
Ellis, John Tracy, 2
England, John, 190, 196
"error has no rights," 72, 78, 83, 87
Ethics and Public Policy Center, 177

ethnicity, 40, 165
evangelical Protestants, 50–52, 182, 225
"Evangelicals and Catholics Together," 182
Evans, M. Stanton, 131, 137
Extraordinary Synod (1985), 169, 175

Faggioli, Massimo, 226
Falwell, Jerry, 172
family planning, 148, 150–51
family values, 169–70
Farley, John Murphy, 31
Fenton, Joseph, 39, 77, 79, 82
Ferdinand VII, King, 139
Feulner, Edwin J., 144
Fey, Harold E., 6
Fifteenth Amendment, 118
First Amendment, 201
First Things (magazine), 7, 12, 204–7,
    209, 217, 220–22
First Vatican Council, 22, 110
Fisher, John, 214
Fitzpatrick, Joseph P., 188
Fogarty, Gerald P., 24, 27, 85, 87, 193–95
Ford, Gerald, 161
Fortnight for Freedom, 212–13, 216–17
Fourteenth Amendment, 141, 142
Francis, Pope, 6, 16, 214–16, 218–19, 226
Franck, Matthew, 222
Franco, Francisco, 138
freedom of conscience, 5, 70–71, 83, 213
French Revolution, 21, 85, 123, 183, 186
Friedman, Milton, 145, 154
Fuchs, Lawrence H., 63
"fusionism" 98–99

Galasius I, Pope, 3
Galston, William, 217
Gamble, Richard M., 60
Gelertner, David, 211
George, Robert P., 204, 207, 222
German Americans, 190–91
German National Socialism, 36
ghetto parishes, 40
Gibbons, James Cardinal, 26, 27, 29,
    213, 217
Glazer, Nathan, 13

Gleason, Philip, 189–92, 196–97
global overpopulation, 150–51
Goldwater, Barry, 8, 9, 15, 112–14, 158
    as conservative model, 127–28
    presidential campaign (1960), 116–17,
        120–21, 122
    presidential campaign (1964), 130–34,
        136, 145, 154, 182, 189
Graham, Billy, 50–51
Greater Houston Ministerial Association,
    53–56, 60
Gregory, Brad, 220–21
Griffin, Leslie, 83, 87
Grisez, Germain, 206
Griswold, A. Whitney, 94
Guttmacher, Alan, 151

Hannan, Philip, 61, 62–63, 168
Hart, Jeffrey, 137
Hartman, Andrew, 136
Haselby, Sam, 10
Hayes, Patrick Joseph, 31
Hays, Richard, 46
Hecker, Isaac, 23, 24, 178, 193, 196
Heilbrunn, Jacob, 206
Hennesey, James, 192–93
Herberg, Will, 107–8, 183
Heritage Foundation, 144
Heschel, Abraham Joshua, 163
Hildebrand, Dietrich von, 157
Himmelfarb, Gertrude, 205
Hiss, Alger, 127
Hofstadter, Richard, 114
Holy Spirit, 193
homosexuality, 169
Hudock, Barry, 76
Hughes, John, 190
human dignity, 71–72, 83
humanitarianism, 123
human rights, 70–71, 72, 83–84, 123
Humphrey, Hubert, 48–50
Hutchison, William R., 195

immigrants in the United States
    piety of, 195–96
    work ethic, 165

individualism, 93, 154, 205
Institute on Religion and Democracy, 177, 182
Institute on Religion and Public Life, 164, 225
Intercollegiate Studies Institute, 131, 144
internationalism, 130, 189
Ireland, John, 26, 32, 180, 189, 194, 196

Jaffa, Harry, 113, 154
Jefferson, Thomas, 168, 213
Jews, 69, 223
John Birch Society, 132–33, 189
John Paul II, Pope, 16, 167, 169, 174, 177, 197, 199, 214, 225
Johnson, Lyndon Baines, 50, 52, 113
Johnson, Paul, 175
John XXIII, Pope, 23, 58, 66–73, 75, 76, 78, 79, 81, 86, 173
    death of, 80
    on modernity, 15, 109
    on nuclear arms, 148
    Wills on, 105–6
Jones, Robert P., 11
Judis, John B., 91, 99, 134, 144, 145
just war theory, 168

Kaveny, Cathleen, 217
Keane, John J., 26
Kefauver, Estes, 47
Kelly, Daniel, 142
Kempton, Murray, 108
Kendall, Willmoore, 92, 144
Kennedy, Jacqueline, 2, 62
Kennedy, John F., 32, 102
    anticommunism of, 121
    assassination of, 65, 80
    childhood and education, 43–46
    civil religion of, 59–61, 63–64
    faith of, 54–56, 121, 173
    funeral of, 61–63
    Neuhaus on, 173
    presidency of, 57–61
    Presidential campaign, 43, 48–57, 76
    presidential election of, 1–5, 15, 185
    on separation of church and state, 14, 64

speech to the Greater Houston Ministerial Association, 53–56
    visit with Pope Paul VI, 67
    wealth of, 43–44, 48–49
King, Martin Luther, Jr., 54–55, 152, 164, 214, 215, 225, 227
Kirk, Russell, 97, 99, 132, 133, 144
Kitchel, Dennison, 133
Kristol, Irving, 13, 162, 200

laity, challenging Roman Catholic hierarchy, 218–20
Langan, John, 72
Latin Mass, 99, 145, 157
Lawrence, E. Michael, 144
Laycock, Douglas, 217
Leonard, John, 159
Leo XIII, Pope, 4, 19–20, 26, 69, 73, 81, 105
    anti-liberalism of, 42
    on church and state, 37–39
    condemnation of Americanism, 4, 5, 6, 23–24, 27, 37, 176, 178, 181, 189, 190, 194, 200
    Murray on, 39
liberal Protestantism, 195
liberation theology, 171, 175–76
libertarianism, 98
Lichtman, Allan J., 33
Liebman, Marvin, 130
limited government, 117, 129, 136
Lincoln, Abraham, 113, 210, 215, 227
Linker, Damon, 211–12, 216
localism, 118
Locke, John, 152, 168, 221
Lubac, Henri de, 74, 77, 200, 201–2
Luce, Henry, 97
Lucerne Memorial, 23
Lumen gentium, 109–10, 148
Lutheran Church, Missouri Synod, 163, 170
Luther, Martin, 221

McBrien, Richard, 174
McCarthy, Joseph, 96, 97, 115, 189
McClellan, James, 142

Macdonald, Dwight, 95, 97, 102
McGovern, George, 158
McGreevy, John T., 5, 38, 39
MacIntyre, Alasdair, 221
Madigan, Kevin J., 222
Madison, James, 168, 179
Mainline Protestantism, 10, 161,
    170, 181
Manchester, William, 62
Manion, Clarence, 115–17, 120,
    122–31, 204
Mao Zedong, 155
Maritain, Jacques, 82, 179
marriage, Roman Catholic Church on, 219
Marshall, Charles C., 19–20, 21,
    30–32, 37
Marshner, W. H., 147
Marty, Martin E., 2
Marxism, 96, 143, 168, 176
Massa, Mark S., 2, 7, 64
"Mater si, magistra no," 100, 110,
    120, 173
Mathias, Charles, 144
Merton, Thomas, 215
Methodists, on John F. Kennedy, 47
Meyer, Albert Cardinal, 82
Meyer, Frank S., 98–99, 154–55, 159
Milione, E. Victor, 144
Millar, Morehouse, 33
Miller, William E., 112
modernism, 31, 156, 196
Molnar, Thomas, 183
Montesquieu, 168
Mooney, Edward, 34
Moreland, Michael P., 217
More, Thomas, 214
Mormons, 25, 47
Morris, Charles R., 2, 28, 40
Mortara, Edgardo, 221–24
Moynihan, Daniel Patrick, 169
Murray, John Courtney, 4–6, 8, 38–40,
    54, 72–77, 79–83, 183
    advice to Kennedy campaign, 53, 54
    on American founding, 42–43, 221,
        223, 224

Americanism of, 148, 186
on natural law, 15, 16
Neuhaus on, 176–77
on religious liberty, 180, 188
Schindler on, 201–2
on separation of church and state,
    38–40
silencing of, 86, 109
under suspicion, 9
and Second Vatican Council, 80, 173
Weigel on, 180

Nash, George H., 7, 162
National Association of Evangelicals, 51
National Catholic Reporter, 178–79
National Catholic War Council, 29
National Catholic Welfare Conference,
    29, 34, 41–42
National Conference of Citizens for
    Religious Freedom, 52
National Council of Churches, 170
National Review (magazine), 7, 12, 13,
    89, 97–101, 144
    American Catholicism of, 99, 101
    Bozell in, 142
    and Goldwater campaign, 133–34,
        165–66
    Neuhaus columns in, 168–69
    on Nixon, 158
    Novak columns in, 165–66
natural law, 15, 16, 76, 149, 194, 212
negative liberty, 86
neo-Americanism, xi, 16, 185, 212, 226
neoconservatism, 162, 182–83, 186,
    199–200, 203
Neuhaus, Richard John, 7, 12, 16,
    162–65, 168–77, 225
    Americanism of, 99, 172–77, 182–83,
        184–85, 197, 203, 210–11
    contribution to *National Review*,
        168–69
    on Dolan, 186
    on end of democracy, 204–7, 209
    and George W. Bush, 209
    as theocon, 206–7, 211

New Deal, 34, 89, 101, 115, 118, 122,
    124–26, 128, 137, 139–40, 153–54
New Journalism, 152, 154
New Left, 136–37
Newman, John Henry, 88
New York Times, 171, 219
Niebuhr, Reinhold, 35, 72
Nixon, Richard M., 56–57, 120, 132,
    148, 152–53, 158, 160
Noonan, John T., Jr., 4–5
Novak, Michael, 13, 16, 162–63,
    165–68, 171, 193, 207
    Americanism of, 182–83, 197, 203
    contribution to *National Review*,
        165–66
    as theocon, 211
nuclear arms, 58, 66–67, 148, 168
Nutter, Warren, 154

Obama, Barack, 212, 215–16
O'Brien, David J., 198–99, 226–27
Ockenga, Harold J., 52
O'Connell, William Cardinal, 4, 28
O'Connor, John Cardinal, 170–71, 177
O'Connor, Martin J., 41
O'Malley, John, 110, 219
Ottaviani, Alfredo Cardinal, 74–75, 76,
    77–78, 79, 80
Oxnam, G. Bromiley, 47

pacifism, 168
papacy
    authority, 102–7, 109, 179–80
    as divine right monarch, 187
    hostility to modern world, 25
    infallibility of, 22, 35, 103, 107, 221
    opposed to political liberalism, 4, 21,
        71
    supremacy, 37, 110–11
    temporal power of, 25, 35, 191
    see also under individual popes
papal encyclicals
    Humanae vitae, 147–48, 150, 161
    Immortale dei, 107
    In amplimissimo, 26–27

Longinqua, 23
Mater et magistra, 58, 69–70, 89,
    99–100, 103, 119, 130
Pacem in terris, 66–67, 69, 70–72, 83,
    87, 105
Rerum novarum, 23, 69
Testem benevolentiae, 23–25, 26–27,
    192
Papal States, 21, 25, 35, 103, 221
parochial schools, 26, 36, 224
Parrington, Vernon Louis, 179
Paul VI, Pope, 65, 67, 74, 80, 82,
    148, 214
Pavan, Pietro, 80, 81, 82, 87
Peale, Norman Vincent, 51
Perkins, Frances, 30
Perlstein, Rick, 131
Pius IX, Pope, 13, 21–22, 38, 56, 221–23
Pius X, Pope, 31, 42–43, 79, 105, 194,
    196, 216
Pius XI, Pope, 29, 68, 105, 150
Pius XII, Pope, 66, 68, 75–76, 81, 85,
    89, 131
pluralism, 202, 205
Poling, Clark, 51
Poling, Daniel, 51
political liberalism, 5, 42, 71, 85, 86, 89,
    123, 145, 226
positive liberty, 86
Powell, Adam Clayton, Jr., 1
progressive education, 118
Protestant establishment, 8, 9, 19, 170,
    172, 182
Protestants and Other Americans United
    for the Separation of Church and
    State, 51
"public Catholicism," 198–99
Puritans, 59–60

race relations, 118–19, 151–52, 157–58, 164
Rahner, Karl, 77, 173
Rand, Ayn, 154
Ratzinger, Joseph Cardinal, 77, 171, 173,
    174–75, 176, 177, 199–200, 225.
    See also Benedict XVI, Pope

Rayburn, Sam, 53
Reagan, Ronald, 95, 134, 172, 180,
    181–82, 197, 214
Reeves, Thomas, 44
religious freedom, 5, 22
    Second Vatican Council on, 77–87,
        111
religious Right, 169, 172–73
Reno, R. R., 222, 223
Roberts, John, 214
Rockefeller, Nelson, 122, 132, 158
Roe v. Wade (1973), 148, 151
Roman Catholic Church
    adaptation to modern society, 43, 73,
        174–75, 223
    anticommunism of, 40, 96, 108
    antimodernism of, 14, 40, 108–9
    authoritarianism of, 93
    authority of, 174–75
    as buttress against modernity, 183, 185
    and Cold War, 13
    diversity of, 192–93
    immigrant churches, 11, 93–94,
        199, 218
    left and right, 95–96, 109
    see also American Church (Roman
        Catholic)
Roman Catholic traditionalism, 143,
    149, 157–59, 197, 223
Roosevelt, Franklin Delano, 34, 124–26,
    127, 140, 153–54
Roosevelt, Franklin Delano, Jr., 49, 50
Roszak, Theodore, 137
Rusher, William, 132, 133, 158
Ryan, John A., 4–5, 33, 40, 89

Schindler, David, 199–203, 207
Schlafly, Phyllis, 7–8, 9, 11
Schlamm, Willi, 97
Schlesinger, Arthur, Jr., 2, 62
Schneider, Gregory L., 131
Second Great Awakening, 10
Second Vatican Council (1962–65), 12,
    14, 66, 67–68, 71, 77
    "American contribution" to, 85
    and Americanism, 15, 198, 226–27

    Bozell on, 143
    on church-state relations, 148
    Dolan on, 185
    and Extraordinary Synod (1985), 169
    Hennesey on, 192
    liturgial revisions of, 61
    Neuhaus on, 173–74
    openness to modernity, 14, 43, 99,
        109–10, 157, 187–88, 222
    on religious freedom, 77–85, 111,
        213, 217
    undoing of, 178–79
    Wills on, 88–89, 156
Secretariat for Christian Unity, 78, 80
sectarian liberalism, 38
secularization, 65, 162, 165, 178, 185, 201
self-interest, 166–67
separation of church and state. *See*
    church and state
September 11, 2001 terrorist attacks, 210
Seymour, Charles, 8–9, 93
"Sharon Statement," 131–32
Shields, Nathan, 223
Silk, Michael, 217
Smith, Adam, 168
Smith, Al, 14, 18–21, 30–33, 37, 38,
    104, 193
    presidential campaign, 33, 48, 49,
        52–53
    working-class background, 43–44, 99
Smith, William J., 102
social contract, 145, 152
socialism, 69–70, 126, 166, 170, 171
social justice, 186
Society for the Christian
    Commonwealth, 144
Sorenson, Theodore C., 3, 44–45, 46,
    53, 60, 61–62
Spain, 138–39
Spalding, Martin John, 22
Spanish-American War, 28
Spanish Civil War, 38
Spellman, Francis Cardinal, 77
Stalin, Joseph, 155
states' rights, 118–19, 128, 136
statism, 125, 166–67

Steinfels, Peter, 218
Stevenson, Adlai, 46, 50, 57
Storck, Thomas, 203, 207
Story, Joseph, 141
Strauss, Leo, 206
Sugrue, Tom, 13
Sullivan, Andrew, 178
Supreme Court, 139–40, 169, 204, 205, 206
Syllabus of Errors, 32, 103, 183, 216, 222

Taft, Robert, 115–16, 128
Taney, Roger B., 18
Taylor, Myron C., 34
Tenth Amendment, 118, 141
Tertullian, 203, 207
theocons, 206–7, 211
theocracy, 145, 202
Thomas, Norman, 126
Thomism, as "un-American," 207
Toolan, David S., 205
Triumph (magazine), 143–45, 146–48, 150, 157, 203
Trump, Donald, 226

ultramontanism, 72, 226
United Nations, 71, 75, 105–6, 119, 127, 214
United States
  Christian origins of, 123–24
  as *novus ordo seclorum*, 194, 206
Universal Declaration of Human Rights (1948), 71, 127
U.S. Ambassador to the Vatican, 34, 47, 54, 90
U.S. Bishops, 167, 168, 190

Valladeres, Armando, 170
Varacalli, Joseph A., 197–98
Vatican
  on Americanism, 5–7
  authoritarianism of, 41
  diplomatic relations with US, 47
  on just-war theory, 168
  on Kennedy's election, 1–2
  suspicions of Americanism, 188

Vermeule, Adrian, 223–24
Vidal, Gore, 158
Vietnam War, 155, 157–58, 163–65
Villeré, Jacques, 18
Virginia Statute of Religious Freedom, 55

Wallace, George, 158
Warren Court, 139–42, 145
Warren, Earl, 139–42
Washington, George, 213
Watergate, 160, 165
Waugh, Evelyn, 99
Weigel, George, 13, 16, 171–73, 176, 177–81
  Americanism of, 197, 200–201, 203
  on Dolan, 186
  on freedom, 180
  on John Paul II, 225
  as theocon, 211
Welch, Robert, 132–33
welfare, 118, 125, 170
Western civilization, 136, 143, 149, 158
White, Edward Douglass, 18
White, Theodore H., 49
Wilhelmsen, Frederick, 139
Wills, Garry, 7, 16, 70, 144, 149–59, 176
  break from Americanism, 138, 159
  on John XXIII, 105–6
  loss of faith, 154–55
  at *National Review*, 100–107
  on Nixon, 152–53
  on papal authority, 120, 147
  on Second Vatican Council, 88–89, 156
  on Vietnam, 155
Wilson, Woodrow, 126, 154
Winters, Michael Sean, 203, 222
Winthrop, John, 59–61
World Council of Churches, 86, 170
World War I, 28–29, 126–27
World War II, 34, 127

Yale, 8–9, 11, 91–95, 97, 172, 182
Young Americans for Freedom, 130–32, 134, 144, 152